The Colleges and the Courts

THE DEVELOPING LAW OF THE
STUDENT AND THE COLLEGE

The Colleges and the Courts

THE DEVELOPING LAW OF THE STUDENT AND THE COLLEGE

Department of Education Administration
Illinois State University

THE INTERSTATE
Printers & Publishers, Inc.

Danville, Illinois

Library of Congress
Catalog Card Number: 76-182243

Printed and Published by

THE INTERSTATE PRINTERS & PUBLISHERS, INC.

Danville, Illinois

Printed in U.S.A.

THE DEVELOPING LAW OF THE STUDENT AND THE COLLEGE

Seventh Volume in the Series on
The Colleges and the Courts

"Every person who, under color of any statute, ordinance, regulation, custom, or usage, of any State or Territory, subjects, or causes to be subjected, any citizen of the United States or other person within the jurisdiction thereof to the deprivation of any rights, privileges, or immunities secured by the Constitution and laws, shall be liable to the party injured in an action at law, suit in equity, or other proper proceeding for redress."—*United States* Code, Title 42, Section 1983.

"We cannot, because of modest estimates of our competence in such specialties as public education, withhold the judgment that history authenticates as the function of this Court when liberty is infringed."—Mr. Justice Robert H. Jackson, in the opinion of the court in *West Virginia State Board of Education* v. *Barnette*, 319 U.S. 624, 63 S.Ct. 1178 (1943).

PREFACE

Seventh in the series of volumes on *The Colleges and the Courts,* which were published respectively in 1936, 1941, 1946, 1952, 1964, 1967, and now, 1972, this book is limited to the law of the relationships between the student and the college in recent years. In that area a beneficent revolution in the stance of the courts, especially of the federal courts, has taken place within approximately a decade.

Though focused largely on the years since 1965, this discourse includes nearly 150 federal decisions and a roughly equal number of judgments of state courts in this one segment of college law. Hence, it seemed imperative to classify and discuss them and to publish this volume now.

Apparently changes of equal significance in the law of the relations between the college and its faculty and staff members, as well as its administrators and governing board members, are also in the making. Accordingly it is planned that the eighth volume in this series, tentatively bearing the subtitle *Faculty and Staff Before the Bench,* will appear early in 1973.

Current and prospective developments in the law of private colleges, particularly relating to their eligibility for federal and state tax support in various forms, are also of keen interest. In the public sector, the state and other public institutions will probably somehow be protected from being swallowed up in overcentralized state bureaucracies and subjected to the control of politicians who are less than statesmen, to the detriment of the real public interest. Federal and state judicial decisions concerning the fiscal relationships of colleges to governmental units since 1966, as well as developments in the law of charitable trusts for higher education, tort responsibility, and numerous other pertinent facets of jurisprudence in which trends are moving slowly or swiftly, are now planned to be pulled together in a volume to be published early in 1974, which may again bear the simple title of *The Colleges and the Courts.*

That would be the ninth volume of the total series, and the third in the current cycle, of which this present volume is the first. Briefly, then, the contemplated three volumes of this cycle will deal successively with (1) students, (2) faculty and staff, and (3) finance and property. Each of the volumes, though limited to a major portion of the broad scope of college law, can carry minor parts for the purpose of updating its predecessor in the cycle. Thus, with the expected completion of the cycle in 1974, the 40-year series will again be "caught up."[1]

The purpose of this work is to provide for interested persons concise stories of the subjects covered, divested of technical phraseology as far as practicable, yet stated with accuracy. This series is thus for students, parents, teachers, administrators, and members of governing boards of colleges and universities—and indeed for all citizens, few of whom are uninterested in the subjects or untouched by them in some way.

The legal practitioner or law student will want to pursue the cases further in the full official reports of the judicial decisions and in learned commentaries found in bar journals and law reviews. The succinct stories found here will supply a convenient classification and index, an over-all survey of the particular field, and a solid basis from which to go on with further research.

The purpose is emphatically not to offer a substitute for professional legal counsel or advice in any particular case nor to encourage the layman to be his own lawyer. Rather it is to assist all readers in reflecting in a broad philosophical and comparative way upon the questions of right and wrong involved here so they may gain the satisfaction of knowing something of the trends and changes occurring in an important area of knowledge, with which every citizen may wish some familiarity. Neither the publisher nor the author is engaged in rendering professional legal services.

ACKNOWLEDGMENTS

Illinois State University has been my congenial academic base since 1969, and it would be ungracious indeed to fail to mention that many of the

---

1. The first five volumes of the series are out of print, but are accessible in many hundreds of libraries. The sixth, entitled *The Colleges and the Courts, 1962-1966,* is available in limited supply from Danville, Illinois: The Interstate Printers & Publishers, Inc., 1967. xii + 326 pp.

University's people (too many, alas, to name) contribute to an ambience which encourages good work and high morale in study, teaching, research, writing, and related forms of public service.

Let me stress the influence of the scores of advanced graduate students (all above the master's level) and half a dozen post-doctoral students who have filled my courses in general administration of higher education, financing higher education, and legal aspects of higher education, all offered in the graduate department of educational administration.

Contrary to a widespread current misapprehension, teaching and research, properly comprehended, are generally inseparable. Each benefits the other. The professor who does not work constantly to keep abreast and ahead of his field is in danger of forfeiting the respect of his students as well as that of his colleagues, and his teaching is in peril of becoming sterile and boring. The productive professor usually enjoys keenly his opportunity to teach and to associate with students in classroom, library, and laboratory; and at the same time he is busy and happy with research and writing. I find many such colleagues at Illinois State University and am stimulated by their presence.

In the complex community that is a university, students and teachers are not all. The great variety of supportive functions that must be performed generally means that the "non-academic" staff is approximately equal in numbers to the teaching staff. These services are indispensable. For example, completion of this present volume expeditiously, in addition to my concurrent duties, would have not been possible without the faithful and competent work of Joan Marie (Mrs. Peter F.) Schuetz, an employee of the department of educational administration assigned as my secretary and general assistant. I name her for conspicuous fidelity to duty. As already acknowledged in part, I owe debts of gratitude to many other persons not named.

M. M. CHAMBERS

Illinois State University
Normal, Illinois

January 4, 1972

ANALYTICAL TABLE OF CONTENTS

4. EXCLUSION FOR ACADEMIC REASONS; CONFERRING
OF DEGREES 31

5. TUITION FEES AND OTHER CHARGES TO STUDENTS 45

6. DIFFERENTIAL FEES FOR OUT-OF-STATE STUDENTS 57

7. ASPECTS OF STUDENT FINANCIAL AIDS 69

INTRODUCTION: CURRENT TRENDS

The benign tendencies mentioned in the brief Introduction to the volume which immediately preceded this one (*The Colleges and the Courts, 1962-1966*) were grouped under the rubric "Toward a Humane Law of Higher Education." Those trends have continued and need not be rewritten here. Some of them have been accelerated.

Most prominent of all has been judicial recognition, in federal and state courts, that the freedoms accorded to, and the restraints imposed upon, college and university students are to be measured by the Bill of Rights in the United States Constitution.

Freedom of speech and assembly; freedom of the press; the right to petition for redress of grievances; the right to *due process* when accused of infractions of discipline of sufficient gravity to lead to the penalty of expulsion or suspension for a substantial period of time—these have held the center of the stage in recent litigation.

Scores of decisions of federal courts have dealt with these matters during the last five years, whereas prior to that time the presence in federal tribunals of issues involving students *vis-à-vis* colleges and universities was extremely rare, except for those related to racial discrimination, which have a history of a third of a century.

Even the desegregation cases are now taking a new turn. Racial discrimination in public college admissions is legally a lost cause; but in a few states there appears a tendency to plan, finance, and construct necessary new and additional facilities for higher education in such places and in such manner as to seem to favor the perpetuation of *de facto* racial segregation. Federal courts respond to this allegation by declaring that the states have an affirmative duty to dismantle their dual discriminatory statewide systems of higher education and to make long-range plans in accord with that principle. Recent federal decisions regarding this issue appear in Chapter 3, pages 21-30.

Some decisions illustrating the place occupied by religion in student life and activities in different types of colleges and universities are discussed in Chapter 8, at pages 83-88.

Most of the decisions demonstrating the recent revolution in the attitude of the federal courts toward the rights and responsibilities of college students are concentrated in Chapters 13 through 18, pages 141-256 in this volume. They deal successively with freedom of speech and assembly, including invitation of off-campus speakers; student organizations; freedom of the student press; and due process in disciplinary proceedings, including the necessary specificity of college or university rules and regulations.

More than one court has recently declared that "the student need not leave his civil rights at the campus gate." This does not mean, of course, that violence against persons or property, or disruption of the operation of an educational institution, is protected by the Constitution. Nor does it abrogate the inherent right and duty of college authorities to adopt and enforce reasonable rules and maintain a degree of tranquility befitting a place of study and learning.

It does seem to mean unmistakably, however, that henceforth this duty will have to be exercised with a good deal more solicitude for the rights of students as citizens than was generally exhibited during the first century and a half after the Constitution was adopted. Moreover, fairness and justice are emphasized by the federal courts, and these courts now appear to be somewhat more receptive to allegations of unreasonableness, arbitrariness, malice, or caprice than at times in the past.

Frightened or disturbed by these changes, a few educators and administrators have cried "Wolf!" and warned that "The courts are taking over the universities." This is a false alarm. Again and again the judges repeat their reluctance to substitute their judgment for that of persons who are supposed to possess superior expertise in matters educational; but they reassert their obligation to safeguard civil rights.

One example out of many is in the words of U.S. Circuit Judge Donald P. Lay of the Eighth Circuit Court of Appeals. After stating that federal courts do not possess the competency in the field of public education to moralize or lecture on educational questions, he says: "And conversely, but of greater significance, a federal Judge should not yield his jurisdiction or competency to protect fundamental liberties of individual citizens to a school administrator." (This quotation at somewhat greater length appears on page 253 herein.)

We appear simply to have moved into a new era in which federal judges are giving comprehensive and careful attention to the constitutional rights of students, in contrast with a long earlier period during which these rights were rather largely ignored or minimized. This, it may be hoped, will help to inject into the relations between students and colleges a new spirit of candor, forthrightness, and integrity.

The idea of serious concern for the civil rights of students is not new, but there is now certainly a great fresh surge of stress on its practice. The principle was expressed with clarity by Mr. Justice Robert H. Jackson of the U.S. Supreme Court in 1943 in *West Virginia State Board of Education* v. *Barnette* (319 U.S. 624):

"The Fourteenth Amendment, as now applied to the States, protects the citizen against the State itself and all its creatures—Boards of Education not excepted. These have, of course, important, delicate, and highly discretionary functions, but none that they may not perform within the limits of the Bill of Rights. That they are educating the young for citizenship is reason for scrupulous protection of Constitutional freedoms of the individual, if we are not to strangle the free mind at its source and teach youth to discount important principles of our government as mere platitudes."

Justifying judicial assumption in some instances of what some critics call functions of educational governing boards, Mr. Justice Jackson added: "We can not, because of modest estimates of our competence in such specialties as public education, withhold the judgment that history authenticates as the function of this Court when liberty is infringed." (Justices Hugo L. Black, William O. Douglas, and Frank Murphy wrote concurring opinions.)

What might thus perhaps be called the Jackson doctrine has had widespread acceptance in the federal courts at the lower echelons since 1960, and especially since 1966, as is evidenced by the fact that approximately half of the nearly 300 decisions discussed in this volume are judgments of federal courts regarding aspects of the rights and responsibilities of students. The story is a fresh wind blowing.

In each of the 21 groupings which have been developed into chapters in this discourse, the cases of the recent decade show important progress—accelerating with each year—toward more enlightened and humane concepts of the place of the student in college and the role of colleges and universities in the total society. The trend is no less than an orderly revolution in law and social progress. It points toward closer partnership between justice and education.

CHAPTER 1

OBLIGATION OF DIVORCED
PARENTS TO PAY
COLLEGE EXPENSES

COURTS will not require parents to finance the schooling of their children beyond the level specified in the compulsory education statutes, except in cases where there is a divorce or separation. This makes the children, in a sense, "wards of the court," and gives the court jurisdiction to issue appropriate orders regarding their education.

For half a century, since the *Esteb* case in Washington,[1] there has been considerable progress in the building of judge-made law to the effect that divorced parents, if their own individual financial resources enable them to do so without serious hardships, will be ordered to pay all or part of the expense of a four-year college course for each minor child. In other words, a college career leading to a bachelor's degree comes more and more to be regarded as a "necessary" for which a parent can be made financially responsible.[2]

---

1. *Esteb* v. *Esteb*, 1138 Wash. 174, 244 P. 264, 246 P. 27, 47 A.L.R. 110 (1923), discussed at pages 4-6 in Elliott and Chambers, *The Colleges and the Courts*, (1936).

2. This was convincingly stated in *Pass* v. *Pass*, 238 Miss. 449, 118 So. 2d 769 (1960), discussed at pages 6-7 in M. M. Chambers, *The Colleges and the Courts, 1962-1966* (1967).

In that respect, the current condition of the judge-made law continues to vary widely in different states.

Progress in Some States

For example, Judge Frederick J. Singley, Jr., of the Maryland Court of Appeals, in a complex divorce case adjudicated in 1970, spoke for the whole court and said unequivocally:

"That a college education is a necessity if the station in life of the child justifies it and the divorced father is financially able to pay or contribute to the payment for such education is no longer an open question in Maryland."[3]

This rule had been previously enunciated and applied by the same court in another case wherein Judge Wilson K. Barnes wrote the unanimous opinion.[4]

The Iowa supreme court, dealing with a case in which there was no divorce or decree of separate maintenance, but only a *de facto* separation of long duration between the irreconcilable parents, held that this did not relieve the father of his obligation to provide education beyond high school for his son. Justice F. H. Becker, discussing the main question, said:

"The facts of each case are important. Factors governing a proper decision include the financial condition of the parent, the ability of the minor for college work, the age of the minor, whether the child is self-sustaining or not, the father's willingness to provide an education and other factors."

In this case the father was a farmer owning land worth $100,000 and having at least $50,000 worth of personal property and an annual income of $8,000 to $10,000. The court affirmed a decree ordering him to pay $60 per month and retaining jurisdiction for further consideration of the needs of a son who had recently been graduated from high school and was earning further education by working in a hospital. The estranged wife and mother worked and was able to support herself, but was not able to pay college expenses of her son.[5]

In a more recent Iowa decision, Justice C. Edwin Moore, for the full court, declared:

---

3. *Wooddy* v. *Wooddy*, (Md.), 265 A, 2d 467 (1970).
4. *Rhoderick* v. *Rhoderick*, 257 Md. 354, 263 A. 2d 512 (1970).
5. *Gerk* v. *Gerk*, (Ia.), 144 N.W. 2d 104 (1966).

"A college education is valuable and desirable for every child. It is the duty and responsibility of both parents to furnish financial assistance for higher education in such an amount as their financial condition will permit."

The court affirmed an order to the divorced father, currently under order to pay $47 per month for each of the six children of the marriage, to increase the payment for the oldest son to $75 per month because he was attending college. Both parents apparently had lower-middle level annual incomes.[6]

In New Jersey, a divorced wife had custody of the four children, and the former husband was under court order to pay $15 per week for the support of each child, plus medical and dental expenses; this order dating from 1966. In 1968, Edward, the eldest son, was aged 18 and a college freshman at Rensselaer Polytechnic Institute in New York. He had shown particular aptitude in science and had received an Allied Chemical Corporation grant. He intended, after completion of his freshman year, to apply for admission to Drexel Institute of Technology in Philadelphia.

When the mother asked that the order for support money be raised to $20 per week for each child, including Edward, the father resisted, arguing that he was financially unable to pay that much, and especially that he should be relieved of paying anything for Edward after his eighteenth birthday. He also complained that the cost of board and tuition at Rensselaer was $3,200 a year, whereas it would be much less at Rutgers, the State University of New Jersey, which was nearer at hand.

Judge Polow of the Juvenile and Domestic Relations Court ordered the requested increase in weekly payments for each of the four children, and noted that since the mother had requested only a weekly contribution and made no special mention of tuition and board, the father's objection to Edward's choice of college need not be considered. The father was earning $10,500 a year.[7]

The foregoing decision cited a slightly earlier and somewhat similar case. A dentist, with an established practice and a net income of $11,500 after taxes in 1966, also owned $13,000 worth of stock in a realty corporation and had recently purchased a $45,000 home (mortgaged for $31,500). The divorce decree of 1967 ordered him

6. *Sandler* v. *Sandler*, (Ia.), 165 N.W. 2d 799 (1969).
7. *Hoover* v. *Voigtman*, 103 N.J. Super. 535, 248 A. 2d 136 (1968).

to pay $25 a week for the support of each minor child—Jeffrey, aged 18, who entered Lafayette College in Pennsylvania in the fall, and Anne, aged 11—and $50 a week for support of their mother, who had their custody. A third child, John, was 21, emancipated, and about to be graduated from Princeton University. In November the mother asked for an order to the father to pay for Jeffrey's tuition, or to pay increased support for her and the two children so that she herself would be able to pay the tuition. (Tuition, room and board at Lafayette College then cost $2,880 a year.)

The court took judicial notice that "a high quality education is available at Rutgers, the State University of New Jersey. There is nothing in the record to indicate that Jeffrey could not gain admission there, or that the courses available there are not adequate for his needs." Noting that the annual cost at Rutgers would be about half that at Lafayette, the court ordered the father to "contribute no more than $1,500 a year toward the expense of Jeffrey's college education as long as the cost at Rutgers remains at its present level."

In the course of his opinion Judge William Fillmore Wood said:

"Higher education is no longer a luxury for the affluent few. It is almost an economic necessity. Opportunities for earning an adequate livelihood without college, professional or technical training are already very scarce and they are becoming scarcer."[8]

High Fee Private College or Low Fee State University

Judge Wood, in support of his position regarding the choice between private and public colleges in cases of this kind, referred to a Pennsylvania decision touching the same question. In that case, a practicing physician, aged 67 and earning $25,000 to $29,000 a year, had mutual fund investments of $105,000 and owned a house on 100 acres of land. He had been divorced since 1947, and made court-ordered payments for the support of his only son, James (born one month after the divorce). Since 1957 these payments had been at the rate of $2,600 a year, and the total of all payments since 1947 was more than $51,000.

The divorced wife was a physical therapist who earned a gross

---

8. *Nebel* v. *Nebel,* 99 N.J. Super. 256, 239 A. 2d 266 (1968); affirmed in memorandum opinion by three-judge Appellate Division of the Superior Court, 103 N.J. Super. 217, 247 A. 2d 28 (1968).

annual income of $6,000. Her two other children by a former marriage were attending college with their expenses amply covered by a trust fund.

Her son, James, became a premedical student at Washington and Jefferson College, where the cost of tuition and other expenses was about $3,600 a year. Noting the gap between his father's support payments and his college expenses, he and his mother asked for an order to increase the payments. His father counter-pleaded for a decrease, showing that his own earnings were declining somewhat because he was already past retirement age; that he would receive no pension or social security benefits; and that he suffered from diabetes and some loss of hearing. He had never promised a college education for James, and he was especially dubious about James' unilateral choice of an expensive private college when an equivalent education could be had at the Pennsylvania State University, where the student's annual expenses were little more than one-third the cost at Washington and Jefferson.

Considering all these matters, Presiding Judge John A. Cherry of the Quarter Sessions Court reduced the order to $1,275 a year, which was the approximate cost of a year at Pennsylvania State. His conclusion was that in this case the order should be only for "such reasonable sum as would allow for a proper education in a wholly acceptable state university."

This decree was affirmed by the seven-judge Superior Court (with Judge J. Colvin Wright absent), in an opinion by Judge Theodore O. Spaulding. The order for $1,275 a year was modified to $1,335 because of a $60 increase in fees at Pennsylvania State.

Said Judge Spaulding: "We are reluctant to formulate a rule which would in all cases, prevent a child from attending the college of his choice simply because it is more expensive than the state-supported university. On the other hand, we do not believe that the child should have absolute discretion in selecting a college, and thereby unilaterally increasing the father's support obligation. The determination of whether such an additional burden should be imposed on the father is a matter for the trial court."[9]

In 1962 in Missouri a decree of divorce was granted to a wife, and

---

9. *Commonwealth ex rel. Larsen* v. *Larsen*, 211 Pa. Super. 30, 234 A. 2d 18 (1967).

she was awarded custody of the only child of the marriage, Candace Reeve Anderson, then 12 years old. The father was ordered to pay $80 per month for child support and $20 per month alimony. In 1964 the former wife asked the court to increase these allowances, but her petition was denied.

In 1968 she came again to court, alleging that the condition of the parties had materially changed since the original order. Candace was about to be graduated from high school, and about to pass her eighteenth birthday. She wished to attend Washington University in St. Louis, but her mother was unable to pay her expenses for that purpose. (The mother worked as a legal secretary with take-home pay of $372 a month. Her only other income was the $100 a month child support and alimony. She owned no property except an automobile and some household goods.)

On the other hand, although the father's annual income was modest—in the range of $5,000 to $6,000—he had recently inherited from his deceased father real property worth at least $200,000.

Candace had been in the top fifth of her class in high school, and demonstrated a consistent and keen interest and aptitude in fine arts. She had been art editor of the school yearbook. She had done paintings in oils, water colors, and acrylics. She had exhibited her work, won prizes, and sold some of her paintings. Consulting with her mother and her art teacher, she decided that the school of art at Washington University was distinctly her best available choice, after she and her mother had visited and inspected it. They believed it was one of the best schools of art in the country; much superior to the instruction in fine arts offered at either of the state universities in Kansas and at the University of Missouri campuses at Columbia and Kansas City.

The mother's motion for increased support payments was denied by the trial court, but this decision was flatly reversed by the Kansas City Court of Appeals, which thereupon entered an order that the payments of $80 per month be increased to $375 per month for September through May, and $125 per month for June, July, and August. Said Judge Gerald Cross for the unanimous court (Presiding Judge Fred L. Howard and Judge Charles Shangler): "It is our finding that plaintiff has satisfactorily established that defendant is financially able to bear the expense of his daughter's attendance at Washington University without undue burden to himself. . . . Under all the circumstances shown in evidence, it has become defendant's legal duty to provide the funds necessary for his daughter's education . . . even if he has to mortgage or sell a portion of his property, or borrow the loan value of life insurance policies he carries, which, as the evidence shows, have a cash surrender value of $4,800."[10]

This was apparently a case in which the choice of Washington University was thought justified, even though it is a high-fee private institution, and there are several low-fee state universities in the region.

In Wisconsin the divorced father of four minor children, under court order to pay $300 per month for their support, obtained an order reducing his obligation by $75 per month because the eldest daughter had passed the age of 18. The state supreme court, by Justice Nathan S. Heffernan, reversed this order as based on a patent misunderstanding of Wisconsin law. The trial judge had flatly stated, with expressed reluctance and distaste, that he was without jurisdiction to order support payments for a child above the age of 18 and that he had no choice. This was an error.

Justice Heffernan readily cited Wisconsin decisions of the middle 1950's, one of which we quote here:

"In a case where a child under 21 years of age who has completed high school is desirous of attending college and whose high school record has demonstrated that he has the capacity to do college work, a court should not relieve the father from at least being required to pay the monthly support money provided in the divorce judgment."[11]

Hence Wisconsin is another among the states whose statutes and decisions are generally favorable toward support of education beyond high school, at least up to the age of 21, by divorced parents in suitable circumstances.[12]

In Pennsylvania a divorced father, under order to pay $600 a month for support of his four minor children, wished to have this reduced to $400 for the remaining three after the eldest son passed the age of 18, saying he wished to finance that son's college education himself, directly, rather than under court order. The trial court judgment was favorable to this plea, but was remanded by the Superior Court with instruction to set an amount which the father must pay toward his son's college education.[13]

---

10. *Anderson* v. *Anderson*, (Mo. App.), 437 S.W. 2d 704 (1969).
11. *Peck* v. *Peck*, 272 Wis. 466, 76 N.W. 2d 316, 56 A.L.R. 2d 1202 (1956).
12. *Beberfall* v. *Beberfall*, (Wis.), 171 N.W. 2d 390 (1969).
13. *Commonwealth ex rel. Flick* v. *Flick*, (Pa. Super.), 257 A. 2d 360 (1969).

Separation Agreement May Be Binding
on Estate After Death

Parents contemplating separation or divorce sometimes draw up in advance a formal separation agreement concerning the disposition of property and provisions for the welfare of the children, including their education. If a divorce subsequently occurs, such an agreement, if deemed appropriate in all respects, is sometimes, but not always, adopted by the court and made a part of the divorce decree. Such an agreement, if it embodies the requisites of a contract, may be made binding against the estates of the signers after death.

Thus, when in New York a father of two sons made a separation agreement with their mother in 1961 stipulating that he would pay the four-year college expenses for each son, and died in 1965 bequeathing his entire estate to his subsequent wife (widow), the agreement was binding upon his estate. At that time the elder son had already completed a four-year course at Princeton University, but the younger son, Robert, was 18 years old and a freshman at Rutgers, the State University of New Jersey.

Up to the date of his death the father had paid the college expenses of both sons, in accord with the terms of the separation agreement, which provided that his obligation would not exceed $4,000 a year nor exceed four academic years for each son. In the interest of Robert's education his mother asked for an order to the executrix of her former husband's estate to provide for the expenses of the remaining years of Robert's undergraduate course, as stipulated in the agreement.

The case was simple. The written agreement, by its own terms, specified that it applied "to the parties, their heirs, distributees, executors, representatives, and assigns." It is well established that a husband may voluntarily contract to bind himself and his estate for maintenance and support after death. Accordingly the order was granted by Surrogate Arthur A. Davis, Jr., and unanimously affirmed by the five-judge Appellate Division, in an opinion by Justice Felix J. Aulisi.[14]

A 1971 decision in North Carolina is to the same effect. The divorced parents were parties to a "consent judgment" under which the father obligated himself unconditionally to provide a four-year college education for each of the children, Walter and Sarah. This was

---

14. *In re Chilson's Estate*, 54 Misc. 2d 51, 282 N.Y.S. 2d 53 (1966); affirmed in 28 A.D. 2d 766, 282 N.Y.S. 2d 80 (1967).

binding on his estate after his death; and as to the daughter, it was unaffected by the fact that she married and then resumed her studies in college.[15]

A Maryland case was concerned with a separation agreement between divorced parents. Under the stipulation that the father would make specified payments, and that the mother would not incur any indebtedness of any kind chargeable to him, she could not afterward recover from him sums she alleged she had paid for a son's college expenses.[16]

Some Negative Decisions Continue to Appear

The foregoing judgments have been grouped to exhibit the directions in which the law is apparently moving. There are other states in which no advancement in these directions is perceptible; and there are circumstances, as must have already become visible to the observant reader, in which any court in any state might hesitate to issue orders of the type here discussed.

For example, as recently as 1970 the Kentucky Court of Appeals reaffirmed its own decision of three years earlier to the effect that:

"In the absence of a contract the legal obligation of a father to support his children terminates upon their reaching their eighteenth birthday. There may exist a moral obligation for a father to assist his children in acquiring a college education but this is not legally enforceable."[17]

Trial court judgments that favor support for children above the age of 18 seem to have been consistently reversed in Kentucky.[18]

However, when a divorce decree incorporates an agreement between the parties as to custody, alimony, and child maintenance, such agreement will be enforced. Thus a divorced father was held to the terms of his agreement that "payment of $50 per month for each child is to continue until such child becomes self-supporting, attains the age of 21 years, or is emancipated."[19]

In one New York case the judgment was unfavorable to the 20-

---

15. *Mullen* v. *Sawyer*, (N.C.), 178 S.E. 2d 425 (1971).
16. *Groner* v. *Davis*, (Md.), 272 A. 2d 621 (1971).
17. *Young* v. *Young*, (Ky.), 413 S.W. 2d 887 (1967).
18. *Miller* v. *Miller*, (Ky.), 459 S.W. 2d 81 (1970).
19. *Turner* v. *Turner*, (Ky.), 441 S.W. 2d 105 (1969).

year-old "child" because he was a "peripatetic student" who had been in and out of several colleges in rapid succession, at substantial expense to his father, and had a record of numerous types of misbehavior.[20]

In another case, in the same state, the court thought the circumstances did not warrant compulsion against the father where his pay was $9,900 a year, and that of his divorced wife was $12,670. The son had left a tuition-free college and enrolled in Long Island University, where tuition fees were over $800 per semester. His own earnings for a recent summer had been $1,900.[21]

Another Pennsylvania decision was adverse to a requested increase of support payments from $25 to $50 a week for a daughter because she was of college age and wished to attend college. The father's income was small and his health was not good. The divorced mother's income was also small, but it appeared that the daughter was the beneficiary of a trust fund. The trial court had excluded testimony as to the nature and extent of this fund, and it did not become a part of the record. The opinion of the seven-judge Superior Court was by President Judge Harold L. Ervin, with Judges Robert Lee Jacobs and J. Sydney Hoffman dissenting.[22]

This chapter does not purport to be a comprehensive traverse of the law in 50 states, but only of recent decisions in a few states. Each of the six prior volumes in this series discusses and cites several earlier cases in states not mentioned here. In some of the western states, particularly Washington and Oregon,[23] and in some states of the South,[24] an advanced stage had been reached a quarter of a century ago; while in some other states the law of this subject has not progressed beyond nineteenth-century concepts.

---

20. *Bates* v. *Bates,* (N.Y. Fam. Ct.), 310 N.Y.S. 2d 26 (1970).
21. *Dicker* v. *Dicker,* 54 Misc. 2d 1089, 283 N.Y.S. 2d 941 (1967).
22. *Commonwealth ex rel. Schearer* v. *Schearer.*
23. *Jackman* v. *Short,* 165 Ore. 626, 109 P. 2d 860, 133 A.L.R. 887, (1941).
24. *Atchley* v. *Atchley,* (Tenn. App.), 194 S.W. 2d 252 (1946).

CHAPTER 2

ADMISSION AS A STUDENT

IN EARLIER DAYS, when most colleges were private and the idea of state-supported higher education as a public service was not fully developed, the custom that each college had full discretion to select its own students from among those who applied was firmly fixed. A college could be regarded as a more or less precarious small oasis in the desert of ignorance; it was responsible for its own protection and perpetuation, and hence could admit only those whom it selected, and on its own terms. This is the original basis of the theory that attending an institution of education above high school is a *privilege*—the gift of a grantor presumably having the right and power to bestow its favors upon whom it will.

During the nineteenth century the concept of the state university, free and open to all qualified citizens of the state on equal terms, became current, as is evidenced by the wording anent the state university in many state constitutions. Its spread was accelerated by the coming of the land-grant colleges stimulated by the Morrill Act of 1862 and its subsequent train of supplementary acts. But until the decisions of the 1960's holding that a student can not be excluded for disciplinary reasons from a state university or college without substantive and procedural due process guaranteed under the First, Fifth, and Fourteenth Amendments to the United States Constitution, no court held that attendance at college had any color of a *right* appertaining to federal

11

citizenship, nor even to state citizenship. Always admission and retention in college was a "benefaction of the law"—a gift of the state to
those fortunate enough to be offered it—which must be accepted on the
state's terms, if at all.

Thus a student could be excluded for refusing military instruction, or immunization against a communicable disease, or compulsory
medical examination for tuberculosis. He could also be excluded for
refusing to promise not to join a secret society, and chapters of the
national college fraternities could be banished from the campus. Statutes
and university regulations and federal and state judicial decisions regarding these matters continue currently in force; but possibly some
of them begin to appear to have a somewhat anomalous relationship
with the numerous decisions of the 1960's holding that admission and
continuance in an institution of higher education partakes of the nature of a *right* to the extent that it is under the protection of the guarantees of freedom of expression, assembly, and association under the
Constitution of the United States.

Increasingly in recent decades state and federal courts have spoken
eloquently of the importance and value of education beyond high
school. There is a great current wave of feeling that this opportunity
must not be denied to any worthy person because of race, religion,
sex, political beliefs, or economic deprivation. Nor should it be denied
to anyone whomsoever for any reason coming within the protection
of the great guarantees of civil rights in the federal and state constitutions and statutes. It is thrilling to observe the changes that are now
occurring in all these respects.

Institutions Segregated by Sex

The idea of keeping certain important universities or colleges open
solely and exclusively to students of either the male or female sex (excluding one or the other sex) seems to be suffering rapid decline.

In 1970 two cases were decided by special three-judge federal
courts in Virginia and South Carolina respectively. In each case the
plea for admission was grounded on the "equal protection of the law"
clause of the Fourteenth Amendment.

In Virginia it was decided that it was a denial of equal protection
for the University of Virginia to deny admission to women as freshmen and sophomores. (Apparently women were already being ad-

mitted to the upper classes.) The opinion carefully refrained from holding that maintaining any single-sex institution was *ipso facto* unconstitutional, and confined its purview to the facts of the case at hand. The *ratio decidendi* was that without question the women applicants were being refused opportunity to take "courses of instruction that are not available elsewhere" in the Virginia public institutions of higher education.[1]

In South Carolina, when young men sought admission to Winthrop College, an all-female state college, the court declared that the Fourteenth Amendment does not require identity of treatment of all citizens where a rational justification for the discrimination is present; and remarked that there was merit in the contention that a single-sex institution can advance the quality and effectiveness of instruction by concentrating upon areas of primary interest to only one sex. The old statute creating Winthrop College as a school for women only established it for instruction in teaching and in "such other subjects as may be suitable to their sex and conducive to their support and usefulness," including designing, engraving, sewing, dressmaking, millinery, art, needlework, and housekeeping.[2]

District Judge Donald Russell said in his opinion (in which Chief Circuit Judge Clement F. Haynsworth, Jr., and District Judge Robert W. Hemphill concurred):

"It is no doubt true, as plaintiffs suggest, that the trend in this country is away from the operation of separate institutions for the sexes, but there is still a number of private and public institutions which limit their enrollment to one sex and do so because they feel it offers better educational advantages. While history and tradition alone may not support discrimination, the Constitution does not require that a classification 'keep abreast of the latest' in educational opinion, especially when there remains a respectable opinion to the contrary; it only demands that the discrimination not be wholly wanting in reason."[3] This decision was affirmed in March 1971 by the United States Supreme Court, with Mr. Justice Harlan dissenting for a procedural reason.

---

1. *Kirstein* v. *Rector and Visitors of the University of Virginia,* (U.S.D.C., Va.), 309 F. Supp. 184 (1970).

2. *Code of South Carolina, 1962,* Title 22, section 408.

3. *Williams* v. *McNair,* (U.S.D.C., S.C.), 316 F. Supp. 134 (1970). Affirmed by U.S.S.Ct., *U.S. Law Week* 3388 (March 8, 1971).

Apparently there was no contention that attendance at Winthrop would be for any reason more advantageous for men than would attendance at any of the other state institutions in South Carolina. The issue of geographic propinquity did not seem to be raised or considered. The decision evidences a rather astringently conservative approach; and one may hazard a guess that single-sex state universities and colleges will not continue in that condition for any great length of time. One recalls that a Texas state court declined to order women applicants to be granted admission to the Texas Agricultural and Mechanical University a dozen years ago, though the proximity of their homes to the campus would have made it advantageous for them.[4] The board of trustees of the institution soon thereafter began to admit women without any further court action.

Professional Schools Such as of Law or Medicine

Graduate-professional schools, such as those of medicine or law, customarily limit admissions because the number of applicants usually exceeds the number of places available, and because "the standing of the institution is thereby enhanced in the view of the educational and professional communities." The prestige factor is somewhat short of being wholly admirable. Though there has as yet been little or no litigation on the subject, these schools are openly and widely accused of exercising prejudice against women, as well as against men and women who are above the usual age of graduate students who have recently completed their undergraduate studies.

A 1970 Arizona case appears to have faint overtones of discrimination on the basis of sex and age, though neither of these factors seems to have entered the arguments. The issue was that of the jurisdiction of the courts to review actions of the Arizona Board of Regents of State Universities. The board had sustained a decision of the Law Faculty Admissions Committee at Arizona State University rejecting the application of a 37-year old woman who had had extensive experience as a legal secretary, as chief clerk to a U.S. referee in bankruptcy, as a securities examiner with the Arizona Corporation Commission, and as an employee of the AFL-CIO. She was recommended

---

4. *Heaton* v. *Bristol*, (Tex. Civ. App.), 317 S.W. 2d 86 (1958), discussed at page 18 in *The Colleges and the Courts Since 1950*.

to the law school by several professors in the university who had been her undergraduate teachers in such subjects as statistics, real estate, finance and business policies, and industrial relations and collective bargaining.

Judge Howard V. Anderson of the Maricopa County superior court held a hearing *de novo*. He was impressed by the significance of the matter: "The issues pointed up by this confrontation are of eminently great importance to all the people of this state. They draw into focus the whole agonizing process of deciding which of our citizens should be granted opportunity for higher learning in our state colleges and universities." It was his opinion that the superior court, under Arizona statutes, had authority to determine issues of both fact and law in such a case: "The wisdom of *de novo* Court review of decisions on admissions to our state colleges and universities is not in question here. The legislature has seen fit to make the Courts the final arbiters on this score and the Court is bound by such declaration of public policy."

Judge Anderson refrained from declaring unreasonable the admissions committee's mathematical formula for deriving a "law school admission index number" from the undergraduate grade average and the score on the law school admissions test. But: "From the evidence it appears that these factors were given much greater weight in determining the prospect of success than were other relevant factors. . . . The situation of the plaintiff appears to be somewhat unique as compared to the usual law school applicant. In addition to being a woman somewhat older, we assume, than the average woman applicant, she has had a wealth of experience in law-related employment. . . . She excelled in her under-graduate work in law-related subjects."

Expressly saying his judgment did not imply that the decision of the admissions committee was arbitrary, capricious, or involved any abuse of discretion, Judge Anderson ordered the board of regents to admit the plaintiff (Barbara Caldwell) to the College of Law at Arizona State University in September 1970.[5]

The regents appealed immediately to the Arizona supreme court

---

5. *Barbara Caldwell* v. *Arizona Board of Regents of State Universities*, Superior Court of County of Maricopa, No. C-225842 (September 3, 1970); effectively *reversed* by peremptory writ of prohibition, *Arizona Board of Regents* v. *Maricopa County Superior Court*, (Ariz.), No. 10280 (1970).

for a peremptory writ of prohibition against the enforcement of Judge Anderson's order in this case, and the writ was summarily granted. The court declared flatly: "On review from an administrative determination the Superior Court can only decide whether the administrative action was illegal in that it was arbitrary, capricious, or involved an abuse of discretion. . . . It was therefore without jurisdiction to supplant the independent judgment of the Admissions Committee."

The issue may not really be as simple as it appears on the surface. The only citation used by the supreme court in support of its opinion was a Connecticut decision (*Jaffee* v. *State Department of Health*), 135 Conn. 339, 64 A. 2d 330 (1949); and although Arizona State University had hoped the board of regents might be held to be outside the coverage of the Arizona Administrative Procedures Act (Arizona Revised Statutes, Section 12-901 *et seq.*), the court expressly declined to reach that question. Conceivably a determination of that issue might have important consequences for the future integrity and autonomy of the board of regents.

Myra Lee Glassman applied for admission to the New York Medical College in the fall of 1969, being one of 2,800 aspirants to 138 available places. She was a Phi Beta Kappa graduate of City College of The City University of New York holding many scholastic honors. In the medical college admissions test she scored in the top percentile in science and quantitative ability. She was among 800 selected for interviews with members of the admissions committee, and was interviewed by two members on different days, and thereafter received a letter of rejection. It appeared that she had once spent 14 months as a voluntary patient in a mental hospital, and that she had twice attempted suicide, thus raising some question as to her mental stability and stamina.

She contested the rejection in court, believing it was a violation of section 70 (5) of the New York Mental Hygiene Law:

"Notwithstanding any other provision of law to the contrary no person admitted to a hospital by voluntary or informal admission shall be deprived of any civil right solely by reason of such admission nor shall such admission modify or vary any civil right of any such person, including but not limited to civil service ranking and appointment, or rights relating to the granting, forfeiture or denial of a license, permit, privilege or benefit pursuant to any law."

Justice Bernard Nadel of the New York County supreme court

held that there was no violation of the quoted section. There was, he said, a constitutional right to apply for admission; but there was no right to be automatically admitted. The admissions committee had considered her entire record, including her grades, recommendations, tests, and personal interviews. He saw no evidence that the criteria were unreasonable or arbitrary or unfairly applied. Her past mental history was given weight only insofar as it was relevant to her being able to cope successfully with the rigors of the medical school curriculum and the ultimate practice of medicine. There was, he thought, no denial of due process or of equal protection of the law under the federal or state constitutions.[6]

Aside from the legal issues as decided, could it have been that the applicant was not ambitious to become a practitioner, but wished to become highly competent in medical research, and that she was apparently equipped in a superior manner for that pursuit? Is medical education exclusively for the training of practitioners? One is reminded of the famous sentiment of Karl Jaspers: "Every selection is an injustice." Fortunately, studies leading to medical discoveries can be pursued in graduate science departments as well as in medical colleges.

When a Highly Qualified White Student Is Rejected, While Minority-Race Applicants Having Lower Qualifications Are Admitted

A 22-year-old honors graduate of the University of Washington, a resident of the state, was refused admission to the university's law school, while 30 applicants having qualifications lower than his were accepted, he alleged. Judge Lloyd Shorett of the state superior court orally declared on September 22, 1971, after hearing the case, that this was a denial of the equal protection guaranteed by the Fourteenth Amendment, and ordered the university to admit the complainant to the law school. An appeal will be taken to the state supreme court.

The case poses a difficult problem accompanying the laudable effort to increase the enrollment of deprived persons. Judge Shorett was quoted as saying, "In doing this the Admission Committee assumed

---

6. *Glassman* v. *New York Medical College,* 64 Misc. 2d 466, 315 N.Y.S. 2d 1 (1970).

that all members of minority races, except Asians, were deprived persons. . . . Excluding the Asians, only one minority student out of the 31 admitted had a predicted first-year average above the plaintiff's. Since no more than 150 applicants were to be admitted, the admission of the less qualified resulted in a denial of places to those otherwise qualified."

It is gravely questionable that the practice of limiting enrollments to rigid quotas can be continued unmodified. Despite whatever predictive value the various tests, records, and interviews may have, decisions based exclusively on them inevitably carry some odor of arbitrariness, and may work severe injustices in individual cases. Ways must be found to provide opportunity for reasonable numbers of deprived persons of minority races, without rejecting other applicants having high qualifications. The final outcome of the University of Washington law school case will be of crucial interest.

Retake of Standard College Entrance Examination When Doubt Exists

Colleges make widespread use of the standard tests of the College Entrance Examination Board, or of the American College Testing Program, or of other makers of tests, and use the scores as one type of criterion in determining the admission of students.

On March 2, 1968, Ronald De Pina, a senior in high school, took the CEEB tests. The CEEB scored his papers and reported his scores to the U.S. Merchant Marine Academy, to which he was applying for admission; and soon he was notified of his acceptance as an alternate candidate.

Meantime the CEEB observed circumstances which led to the belief that De Pina had "cheated" in the examinations (mainly the fact that his papers closely resembled those of another student who had taken the examination at the same time). The CEEB did not directly charge him with cheating; instead it requested that he be re-examined, and stated that if his new marks approximated those achieved on the first examination, the original scores would be confirmed, but if not, the new scores would be substituted for those first reported.

De Pina asked the trial court of Nassau County, New York, for an injunction to restrain the CEEB from any contemplated action in the matter. The injunction was granted; but the five-judge Appellate Division decided this was an "improvident exercise of discretion," and declared the CEEB "acted within its rights and indeed within its obligations and duties to the Academy and to the public in requesting (De Pina) to take a re-examination."[7]

---

7. De Pina v. Educational Testing Service, 31 A.D. 2d 744, 297 N.Y.S. 2d 472 (1969).

CHAPTER 3

PROGRESS IN RACIAL
DESEGREGATION

SCORES OF DECISIONS have been made in federal courts since the 1930's including several by the Supreme Court, upholding the constitutional right of qualified persons of the Negro race not to be denied admission to public universities or colleges solely or primarily on the ground of race or color. Many of those decisions have been discussed in each of the six volumes in the series on *The Colleges and the Courts*, which have preceded this present volume.

A new type of case has arisen, apart from and different from the well-known individual or class action to enjoin racial discrimination in admissions.

Affirmative Duty to Dismantle Dual
Systems of Higher Education

The first of this new type of litigation appears to have arisen in Alabama, and was concerned with the development and expansion of public higher educational facilities at the state capital, Montgomery. That city is the seat of Alabama State College, a predominantly black institution, and prior to 1968, of a predominantly white two-year branch of the University of Alabama, whose main campus is at Tuscaloosa. About 1965 the Montgomery Chamber of Commerce began actively to urge that this branch campus of junior college level be developed to become a four-year degree-granting institution; but the University of Alabama was negative on this proposition, so the proposal was made that Auburn University, whose main campus is at Auburn, should take over the University branch in Montgomery and make it a four-year institution.

Both universities agreed to this solution, and the 1967 legislature enacted a measure authorizing the Alabama Public School and College Authority to issue and sell bonds for $5 million, in addition to all other bonds theretofore authorized, and to allocate the net proceeds to Auburn University . . . "for construction and equipment of physical facilities for conducting a four-year college or branch in the city of Montgomery and for the support and maintenance of such college for each of the fiscal years ending September 30, 1968 and September 30, 1969."

Looking askance upon this act was the Alabama Teachers Association, composed of about 10,000 persons, mostly black and largely alumni of Alabama State College, and other black teachers throughout the state. The view of these persons was that the act looked toward a condition in which Montgomery would have two public colleges—Alabama State College (black) and the Auburn University branch (white); that it would tend to perpetuate racial segregation rather than to decrease it, and should therefore be declared unconstitutional.

The opinion of the three-judge federal court to decide this issue was written by Chief District Judge Frank M. Johnson, Jr., with Circuit Judge Walter Pettus Gewin and District Judge Virgil Pittman concurring without opinion. First, a second issue needed to be disposed of. The legislative act authorized the bond proceeds to be used not only for capital construction but also for "support and maintenance" usually construed as current operating expenses. It was alleged that this was in violation of the state constitutional provision prohibiting borrowing for current operating expenses.[1] Judge Johnson correctly perceived this as a question of state law for adjudication by state courts, and declined to assume jurisdiction as to it. He dismissed it without prejudice to the plaintiffs' proceeding on it in an appropriate state court.

---

1. *Constitution of Alabama of 1901*, Article 11, section 213.

As to the primary issue, the court also rejected the arguments that the 1967 act should be declared in violation of the United States Constitution because it would allegedly tend to perpetuate racial segregation.[2] Judge Johnson indicated that Auburn University had for some years been under judicial order to admit all qualified Negroes on terms consistent with the equal protection clause of the Fourteenth Amendment.[3] He believed that "Auburn has abided and will continue to abide by that order in good faith. Testimony indicates that it has recruited and will continue to recruit more Negro faculty members." He saw no reason to believe Auburn University would practice unconstitutional racial discrimination in admissions to its Montgomery branch, which legally and in practice would not be an "all-white" institution, but would admit qualified Negroes without discrimination, just as Alabama State College is not an "all-black" institution, but admits qualified white students who apply.

Arguments had been advanced that the scheme had been developed simply because Auburn University was a much larger and better-financed institution than Alabama State College, and could be expected to provide more diversified offerings of somewhat higher quality than could be expected from Alabama State. "Some evidence that the preference for Auburn's offerings over those of Alabama State was based on educational grounds is the fact that defendants rejected an offer to operate the branch from Troy State University, an institution not unlike Alabama State except that it is larger and is traditionally predominately white."

The court concluded: "As long as the State and a particular institution are dealing with admissions, faculty and staff in good faith, the basic requirement of the affirmative duty to dismantle the dual school system on the college level, to the extent that the system may be based upon racial considerations, is satisfied." Earlier in the opinion, Judge Johnson had said: "Freedom to choose where one will attend college, unlike choosing one's elementary or secondary public school, has a long tradition and helps to perform an important function, viz., fitting

---

2. *Alabama State Teachers Association* v. *Alabama Public School and College Authority*, (U.S.D.C., Ala.), 289 F. Supp. 784 (1968); affirmed by the United States Supreme Court, January 20, 1969: 393 U.S. 400 (1969); Justice William O. Douglas and Justice John M. Harlan dissenting separately for different reasons.

3. *Franklin* v. *Parker*, (U.S.D.C., Ala.), 223 F. Supp. 724 (1963); affirmed in (U.S.C.A., Ala.), 331 F. 2d 841 (1964). Discussed at pages 43 and 44 in *The Colleges and the Courts, 1962-1966*.

the right school to the right student." And, "If the Auburn branch at Montgomery is administered as 'just a school,' (meaning without racial discrimination), as we are assured it will be and as we are confident it will be, our conclusions as herein outlined will receive significant confirmation." Only the lapse of time will produce results tending to confirm or deny the wisdom of the court in this case.

Approximately contemporaneous with the foregoing case, a similar controversy occurred in Tennessee, where Nashville has, in addition to some seven private colleges, two state institutions—Tennessee State University (formerly named Tennessee Agricultural and Industrial College), predominantly black, and the extension center of the University of Tennessee (whose main campus is at Knoxville), predominantly white. This center had been established some 20 years earlier primarily to provide evening courses for employed persons, and had continued to be chiefly an evening college, though the number of its offerings had increased to the point where students could complete their studies for a bachelor's degree there. In addition, the center operated the Graduate School of Social Work for the University of Tennessee, and offered a two-year day program leading to the degree of Associate of Arts in nursing.

When the University of Tennessee disclosed plans to erect a large new building for its Nashville Center to house the foregoing activities, and a new program designed to provide continuous in-service training and career development for state and local government employees, it was opposed by representatives of Tennessee State University who brought suit in the federal district court to prevent it. The U.S. Government was permitted to enter as an intervener, and asked the court to order the State of Tennessee to submit a plan for the "desegregation of the higher educational institutions of Tennessee, with particular attention to Tennessee State University, such as to indicate the dismantling of the dual system now existing."

District Judge Frank Gray, Jr., said in the course of his opinion: "There is nothing in the record to indicate that the University of Tennessee has any intention to make the Nashville Center a degree-granting day institution. On the contrary, the record clearly indicates and the court finds that, in its expansion program for the Nashville Center, the University of Tennessee seeks only to provide a quality continuing education and public service center for Nashville and Middle Tennessee with overwhelming emphasis being placed upon the provision of educational opportunity for employed persons of all races who must seek their education at night."

He therefore refused to grant an injunction to prevent or delay the contemplated expansion, but ordered the defendants in this case (the higher educational authorities in the state of Tennessee) to prepare and submit to the court a plan for the eventual dismantling of the dual racially segregated systems of higher education in the state.[4]

Junior Colleges in Alabama

Alabama fared differently in an action decided by a three-judge federal court in 1967, chiefly involved with desegregation of elementary and secondary schools, but also concerned with the 17 state junior colleges and the 27 public trade schools (21 white, 6 black), as well as the four-year state colleges then governed by the state board of education.

This was a step in a long course of litigation.[5] The special court was headed by Senior Circuit Judge Richard T. Rives, and included District Judge Harlan Hobart Grooms and Chief District Judge Frank M. Johnson, Jr.

As to the trade schools, junior colleges, and state colleges governed by the state board of education, the 1967 decree was that "No person shall be denied admission upon the ground of race, nor shall he be subjected to racial discrimination in connection with his application for enrollment or in his attendance. Dual attendance zones based on race shall be abolished. Teachers shall be recruited, hired, and assigned so as to accomplish some faculty desegregation by September 1967."

Early in 1969 the same court ordered that the defendant school districts and trade schools and junior colleges prepare plans for complete compliance with the order of 1967, and set forth further steps for the disestablishment of the dual systems of trade schools and junior colleges based on race. On May 27, 1969, the court advised that the plans for desegregating the trade schools and junior colleges were deficient. On September 17, 1969, the court directed the U.S. Office of Education to prepare a plan for this purpose. This plan was submitted March 3, 1970,

---

4. *Sanders* v. *Ellington*, (U.S.D.C., Tenn.), 288 F. Supp. 937 (1968).

5. *Lee* v. *Macon County Board of Education*, (U.S.D.C., Ala.), 267 F. Supp. 458 (1967). Preceded by 221 F. Supp. 297 (1963); 222 F. Supp. 485 (1963); 231 F. Supp. 772 (1964); and 231 F. Supp. 743 (1964).

and on July 16, 1970, a proposed alternative plan was submitted by the defendants. On August 4, 1970, the court, after describing the situation in part, issued a decree with an order to submit two progress reports—one within 60 days thereafter, and the second on September 15, 1971.

As to the junior colleges, 2 of the 17 had been established as black colleges—Mobile State and Wenonah State. In each case there was a somewhat larger and better-supported all-white junior college only a moderate distance from the black college—the pairs being Mobile State (black) and Faulkner (white); and Wenonah (black) and Jefferson State (white), both of the latter being in Jefferson County.

Regarding the first-named two of these junior colleges, the decree was that facilities will be constructed and curriculum developed that will expand the program at Mobile State so that it is comparable to that offered by Faulkner. Facilities and curriculum will be so developed as to attract a large proportion of white students as well as Negro students.

Further capital outlays for projects to be undertaken at any of the junior colleges are enjoined until Mobile State has been transformed into a fully desegregated two-year institution, and is equal in physical facilities and curriculum to Faulkner Junior College. "Immediate curriculum enlargement is to be undertaken at Mobile State, including acquisition of a computer needed to develop a computer science and data processing program, teacher aide and library programs, and associate degree programs in nursing, medical technology, and other health-related areas."

This was the spear-point of the multiple decree, which embodied many other detailed mandates regarding the desegregation of the state-wide system of junior colleges and trade schools. For example, "Effective immediately the officials responsible for the recruiting of students at each of the junior colleges and trade schools will make special efforts to recruit students who are of the race different from that of the students whom the institution was originally designed to serve. Any recruiting team which visits high schools to discuss its institution will be composed of members of both races. All promotional literature and catalogs sent to high schools and to prospective students will state clearly that students are accepted without regard to race or color."[6]

Thus comes a new phase in the 35-year course of litigation in federal courts to effectuate the law of the land as to racial desegregation in

---

6. *Lee* v. *Macon County Board of Education*, (U.S.D.C., Ala.), 317 F. Supp. **103 (1970)**.

education above high school. An affirmative duty of the states to move toward the dismantling of dual segregated systems of public higher education has been recognized and declared. Some federal courts have required a state to submit detailed plans for the accomplishment of this purpose over a period of years, beginning at once.

One three-judge federal court has ordered Alabama's agencies to develop and desegregate one black junior college (Mobile) until its facilities and offerings are at least equal to those of a neighboring white junior college (Faulkner), even specifying certain additions to its curriculum; and further ordered that there be no further expenditure of state funds for capital outlays at any of the other 16 state junior colleges until the plant and equipment at Mobile are brought up to standard.

Federal Judges Richard T. Rives, H. H. Grooms, and Frank M. Johnson, whose names are already famed for their decisions in earlier desegregation cases, are earning additional laurels. True, they cast aside conventional judicial restraint, substitute their own judgment for that of state legislative and administrative bodies when these are in contravention of the law of the land, and issue injunctive orders accordingly. To a limited extent, the federal courts in Alabama have temporarily taken over the duties of state and local boards of education in an emergency such as occurs hardly once in a century. That both the ends of justice and the purposes of higher education will be well served thereby, few will doubt.

The Case of Richard Bland College in Virginia

The College of William and Mary at Williamsburg has for several years operated a two-year branch campus known as Richard Bland College at Petersburg, predominantly for white students. Also located at Petersburg is Virginia State College, a senior institution predominantly for blacks. The situation in some respects resembles those described earlier in this chapter as prevailing at Montgomery, Alabama, and Nashville, Tennessee. An incipient plan to escalate Richard Bland College to four-year status has recently been enjoined by the federal District Court, on petition of complainants who alleged that the plan would frustrate the efforts of Virginia State College to desegregate, and would perpetuate the racially identifiable dual system. Item 600 of the current Appropriations Act, providing for the escalation of Richard Bland, was declared in violation of the Fourteenth Amendment.

Other parts of the petition, seeking to require ultimate merging of Richard Bland with Virginia State, and to order the state to prepare a plan looking toward the desegregation of all state colleges and universities, were denied. The court referred, however, to "the affirmative duty to take whatever steps might be necessary to convert to a unitary system in which racial discrimination would be eliminated root and branch," and noted that, although all Virginia colleges now admit students of both races, this fact has not abolished the racial identity of the colleges. The caption of the case is *Norris* v. *State Council of Higher Education* (U.S.D.C., Eastern District of Virginia, Richmond Division, Civ. Action No. 365-70-R (1971).

State-Sponsored In-Service Training Activities for Teachers

During the 1960's there was protracted litigation between Negro pupils and parents and the city of Jackson, Tennessee, concerning various details of desegregation, including the integration of faculties, faculty organizations, and faculty in-service training. While this latter appears not to have required any enrollment in any institution of higher education, but only occasional one- or two-day regional or county-wide "teachers' meetings," it was financed by public funds and conducted under state law.

In a case which reached the Sixth Circuit Court of Appeals in 1967, it was held, *inter alia*, that the Negro pupils had standing to assert that the existence of racially separated teachers' organizations and the school authorities' cooperation with their segregated activities such as the in-service training program "impaired the students' right to an education free from any consideration of race"; and in remanding this issue to the district court for consideration of the facts, the Court of Appeals made clear that if the language of a prior district court opinion "could be read as a contrary holding, it was error." The Circuit Judges in this case were Clifford O'Sullivan, Harry Phillips, and John W. Peck, with the opinion delivered by Judge O'Sullivan.[7]

---

7. *Monroe* v. *Board of Commissioners, City of Jackson, Tennessee,* (U.S.C.A., Tenn.), 380 F. 2d 955 (1967). Preceded by (U.S.D.C., Tenn.), 269 F. Supp. 758 (1965); and (U.S.D.C., Tenn.), 244 F. Supp. 353 (1965), Chief District Judge Bailey Brown.

Desegregation of Private Colleges

There are three important cases in which private institutions, founded many years ago on testamentary trusts containing words which restricted admissions to *white* applicants, have been directed or authorized by courts to deviate from that term of the trust because any state action toward enforcing racial discrimination is now unlawful under the Fourteenth Amendment and the civil rights acts of Congress.

The case of Rice University in Houston was settled in state courts after a tortuous course in which it was once before the state supreme court and twice before the court of civil appeals. All but the final step is discussed in some detail at page 238 in *The Colleges and the Courts, 1962-1966.*[8] Thereafter the court of civil appeals authorized Rice University to deviate from *two* features of the will of the founder: the word limiting the service of the trust to *white* beneficiaries, and the words prescribing that the institution should be tuition-free. Justice Tom F. Coleman, in a lengthy opinion, held that the evidence to the effect that it is now difficult, if not impossible, to operate a high-quality university on a racially segregated basis, and that also it is impracticable to operate a private university tuition-free, justified the trial court in exercising its equitable power to authorize the deviations. Rice University is now free to accept qualified applicants without regard to color, and to charge tuition fees to those able to pay.[9]

Sweet Briar College in Virginia was founded at the turn of the century as a testamentary trust which limited its admissions to "white girls and young women." More than half a century later, after futile efforts to have the racial restriction nullified in Virginia courts, the college brought the issue before a three-judge federal district court. The first result was an order of abstention, retaining jurisdiction until all possibility of a remedy in state courts should be exhausted. (The then District Judge John D. Butzner entered a lengthy and cogent dissent.) This order was reversed by the U.S. Supreme Court, remanding the case for consideration on the merits.[10] (Mr. Justice Potter Stewart and Mr. Justice John M. Harlan would have affirmed.)

---

8. Danville, Ill.: The Interstate Printers & Publishers, Inc., 1967. 326 pp.

9. *Coffee* v. *William Marsh Rice University*, (Tex. Civ. App.), 408 S.W. 2d 269 (1966). Preceded by (Tex.), 402 S.W. 2d 340 (1966), reversing (Tex. Civ. App.), 387 S.W. 2d 132 (1965).

10. *Sweet Briar Institute* v. *Button*, 387 U.S. 423, 87 S.Ct. 1710, 18 L.Ed. 2d 865 (1967).

Going straight to the point, Circuit Judge Albert V. Bryan, joined by District Judges Thomas J. Michie and John D. Butzner, said as to whether Virginia may enforce the racial restriction in the will: "We conclude it can not. The state can not require compliance with the testamentary restrictions because that would constitute state action barred by the Fourteenth Amendment.[11] The opinion includes a long appendix on the history of the litigation. A permanent injunction was ordered, restraining the attorney general of Virginia and the county attorney of Amherst County from enforcing the restrictive clause. At last Sweet Briar College was liberated from compulsory racial discrimination under the terms of the trust on which it was founded.

Litigation regarding the admission of non-white orphan boys to Girard College, a home and school for white orphan boys established in Philadelphia by the will of Stephen Girard nearly a century and a half ago, came to rest after a dozen years of simmering, during which it was the subject of at least two decisions of the Philadelphia orphans' court, two of the supreme court of Pennsylvania, one of the United States Supreme Court, and several of inferior federal courts.[12]

After the U.S. Supreme Court had decided that the school, under the Board of Directors of City Trusts, an agency of the commonwealth of Pennsylvania, could no longer discriminate racially, the orphans' court substituted a private board of trustees for the public agency. It could then be maintained that the Fourteenth Amendment would not apply. The fact that the wealthy institution ($100 million endowment) had never received a cent of tax money added some color to this view. At long last, however, in 1968 the Third Circuit Court of Appeals held that the decree of the orphans' court was itself unconstitutional state action; and the U.S. Supreme Court declined to review.[13]

The mandate of the Fourteenth Amendment is not yet held to apply directly and generally to private colleges, where "state action" is not involved. Many such colleges have desegregated without coercion.

---

11. *Sweet Briar Institute* v. *Button*, (U.S.D.C., Va.), 280 F. Supp. 312 (1967).

12. For some of the history of the litigation, see pages 172-173 in *The Colleges and the Courts Since 1950;* and pages 167-169 in *The Colleges and the Courts, 1962-1966.*

13. *Commonwealth of Pennsylvania* v. *Brown*, (U.S.C.A., Pa.), 392 F. 2d 120 (1968). *Certiorari* denied, 88 S.Ct. 1811 (1968). Preceded by 260 F. Supp. 358 (1966), 373 F. 2d 771 (1967), and 270 F. Supp. 782 (1967).

CHAPTER 4

EXCLUSION FOR ACADEMIC
REASONS; CONFERRING
OF DEGREES

EVERYWHERE it is the prerogative of colleges and universities to require the withdrawal of any student for failure to meet academic standards set by the faculty. In such cases, the controlling factor is the discretion of the faculty, exercised fairly and free of malice, caprice, or bad faith.

A court will not substitute its judgment for that of the faculty in academic matters, and will not hear a student's complaint unless he alleges that his academic work has been appraised unfairly, arbitrarily, or with malice or caprice. If he is heard on these allegations, he undertakes a heavy burden of proof.

The institution may dismiss the student on grounds of academic failure without the necessity of the "due process" that must precede suspension or expulsion for disciplinary reasons, and which is discussed in other chapters herein.

Disputes over the marking of student papers and other appraisals of the quality of academic work sometimes involve litigation regarding readmission to a program of study after having been dropped for academic deficiency; and sometimes suits to compel the conferring of a degree or other credential upon completion of a specified course of instruction.

Academic Failure in All Courses Prejudices
Plea for Readmission

In the spring of 1967, after serious campus disorders at Texas Southern University, a number of students were suspended at the end of the academic year, without notice or hearing, for what they described as "participation in several peaceable assemblies on the campus."

On September 8, 1967, eight of these students sued in the federal district court for an injunction to restrain the university from excluding them, alleging that they were being denied readmission in violation of their constitutional rights under the First and Fourteenth Amendments. District Judge John V. Singleton, Jr., issued a temporary restraining order commanding the university to admit these students pending a hearing on the merits. Within two days the hearing was held, after which the university moved to dismiss the case and dissolve the injunction. These motions were granted, denying relief.

On appeal, the U.S. Court of Appeals (Circuit Judges James P. Coleman, Robert A. Ainsworth, Jr., and David W. Dyer), in an opinion by Circuit Judge Coleman, affirmed. Insofar as the case involves university disciplinary action for breaches of *discipline*, as distinguished from failure to meet *academic* standards, it would appear to be a classic case governed by the decision in *Dixon* v. *Alabama* (1961), and this explains the temporary injunction and the hearing on the merits by District Judge Singleton. This aspect of the case would place it in another chapter herein on "Due Process in Disciplinary Cases"; but as to five of the students complaining, it was found that they were scholastically ineligible for admission to the fall term. One had failed 12 of the 13 hours for which he had been enrolled. Four had failed all their courses. Under the rules of the university, all five were thus ineligible for readmission until January 1968 for academic deficiencies alone, and without regard to any disciplinary infractions.

Commenting, Judge Coleman said: "We know of no case which holds that colleges and universities are subject to the supervision or review of the courts in the uniform application of their academic standards."[1]

As to the other three students, two had changed their mailing ad-

---

1. *Wright* v. *Texas Southern University*, (U.S.C.A., Tex.), 392 F. 2d 728 (1968); affirming (U.S.D.C., Tex.), 277 F. Supp. 110 (1967).

dresses without notifying the university, thus frustrating the process of notice and hearing; and the third had been given personal interviews with both the dean and the president, and these interviews were adjudged to have constituted sufficient "due process" as preliminary to disciplinary action in his particular case. In all these matters the university had exercised due diligence.

District Judge Singleton had said: "In a day when the population of some of our state colleges and universities now approaches that of small cities, where there is a decided increase in off-campus residency, and where there are in many instances no attendance rules imposed on the students, to require more of university officials than was done here, would in many cases render university officials 'powerless to command or rebuke the fanatic, the irritant, the malingerer, the rabble-rouser.' " He had concluded: "The constitutional umbrella should afford no protection to those who choose to go out in the rain bareheaded."

In a somewhat similar case, two students at Eastern Michigan University, who were denied readmission for academic reasons, obtained no recourse in a federal district court when they pleaded lack of due process.

One student, Galia, after one semester's attendance, either withdrew or received incomplete in all courses taken. The other, Mazmanian, during two semesters completed only two courses, and withdrew or received incompletes in all other courses taken.

Distinguishing between disciplinary and academic matters, the court said: "Suffice it to say that there may be a very important distinction between expulsion and refusal to readmit, as far as the burden of proof and other procedural considerations are concerned."[2]

The court admonished the administration of Eastern Michigan University for certain apparent uncertainties in its own rules and ambiguities in its procedures in the internal disposition of this case. In many institutions there has sometimes been a tendency to confuse matters of disciplinary infractions with matters of academic deficiencies. That the two should be kept distinct was acerbly attested by a Florida court of appeal in 1966, where, on a rather confused state of facts, the court made clear its belief that a professional faculty should not exclude

---

2. *Mazmanian and Galia* v. *Board of Regents of Eastern Michigan University,* (U.S.D.C., Mich.), Case No. 35344 (September 22, 1970).

a student in good academic standing merely because he had been accused and acquitted of a serious infraction of discipline.[3]

Medical School Cases

In the state courts of Florida and Alabama, students in medical colleges, whose faculties dropped them for failure to complete certain courses in accord with the standards maintained by the college, vainly sought legal recourse.

Robert J. Militana was admitted to the school of medicine of the University of Miami in 1959. A year later he was admitted to the second year on probation. His second year's work having been unsatisfactory, he was allowed to repeat it, after which he was promoted to the third year. He was promoted to the fourth year on probation, conditioned upon additional satisfactory work in pediatrics and obstetrics-gynecology. During the summer of 1963 he completed the first of these with satisfactory marks, but not the second; and at the end of the summer the executive committee of the school of medicine dismissed him for academic failure.

Twice the local trial court ordered him readmitted, and twice the court of appeal nullified this judgment.[4] Pending the outcome of these proceedings he had attended the 1965-66 academic year as a fourth-year student. On June 10, 1966, the medical school notified him by official letter that he was dropped for academic failure of the fourth-year's work. He then asked the court for a mandatory injunction to compel the university to confer on him the degree of doctor of medicine. This time the judgment was adverse to him.

His allegations were (1) that he had successfully passed the academic requirements prescribed by the school, but had been denied credits by arbitrary action of the faculty; and (2) that he had been denied due process because of not having had notice of the proposed action of the executive committee and an opportunity to appear before the committee and defend against the charge of academic failure.

The three-judge court of appeal (Judges Charles A. Carroll,

3. *Woody* v. *Burns*, (Fla. App.), 188 So. 2d 56 (1966); discussed at pages 34-39 in *The Colleges and the Courts, 1962-1966*.

4. *University of Miami* v. *Militana*, (Fla. App.), 168 So. 2d 88 (1964) and 184 So. 2d. 781 (1966); discussed at pages 24 and 25 in *The Colleges and the Courts, 1962-1966*.

Thomas H. Barkdull, and Richard H. M. Swann), affirming the adverse judgment of the trial court, decided that the record showed no evidence of arbitrary or capricious action by the faculty; and quoted with approval the words of the trial court:

"Notice of charges and an opportunity to be heard are certainly essential to due process and required when a student is dropped from school for disciplinary reasons; however, such is not required when the dismissal is for academic failure."[5]

The College of Medicine of the University of Alabama in March 1964 notified three third-year students that they were being dropped for scholastic deficiencies. One of these, Frederick P. Mustell, asked the trial court for a mandatory injunction to require the university to reinstate him, to promote him to the senior class, and to change his grades in specified courses in medicine and surgery from failure to passing.

In a pre-trial held by the court in March 1966 it was determined and agreed by both parties that the sole issue was:

"Whether or not the Junior Promotion Committee, arbitrarily and capriciously conspired to effect the dismissal," and altered the grades earned by Mustell in his junior year, without just cause and in bad faith. The trial court immediately ordered that "as many of the regularly constituted members of the Junior Promotions Committee who were in that status on May 28, 1964, as are presently alive and connected with the Medical College of Alabama shall hold a meeting forthwith and review the record of complainant . . . and deliver its recommendations immediately thereafter to this court."

The surviving members of the committee performed as ordered; and from much detailed testimony and documentary evidence, including the published rules of the medical college and the departmental and other records of the student in question, the court decided that: "The attitude of the heads of the departments and the dean of the Medical School and those who had the responsibility of final decision regarding the scholastic destiny of the student was uniformly beneficent and manifested a desire on the part of these persons to aid this student in his scholastic endeavors.

"It further appears that there was no conspiracy of any kind against this complainant. . . . The ultimate decisions regarding his scholastic progress came as a composite calculation of all the elements of his

---

5. *Militana* v. *University of Miami*, (Fla. App.), 236 So. 2d 162 (1970).

performance and knowledge. The use and purpose of grades was to afford general information regarding some, but not all, of the factors involved in the student's performance."

The court then asked a question: "Do the scholastic heads, in charge of the course of study of a medical student . . . have the power to determine, from an overall consideration of a student's knowledge and performance (including his grades), his ultimate fitness to practice medicine, and to dismiss him as a student if, in their professional opinion, in fairness and without bias, the overall knowledge and performance of the student warrants dismissal?" And concluded: "This Court must answer this question in the affirmative."

The judgment was affirmed by the Alabama supreme court in an opinion by Justice Pelham J. Merrill, with Chief Justice J. Ed Livingston and Justices Robert B. Harwood and John P. Kohn concurring. The opinion includes some 2,500 words of detailed examination of the evidence in the record.[6]

In each of the two medical school cases just outlined, the respective courts quoted from a federal district court decision of 1965 in Vermont, on a somewhat similar state of facts:

"Where a medical student has been dismissed for a failure to attain a proper standard of scholarship, two questions may be involved; the first is, was the student in fact delinquent in his studies or unfit for the practice of medicine? The second question is, were the school authorities motivated by malice or bad faith in dismissing the student, or did they act arbitrarily or capriciously? In general, the first question is not a matter for judicial review. However, a student dismissal motivated by bad faith, arbitrariness or capriciousness may be actionable."[7]

Apparently an expelled medical student in California has succeeded in obtaining a trial on the facts of his case. Wong had repeated the third year, but was then dropped. A rule of the University of California (Section 900, *Academic Manual*) stipulates: "Students in Dentistry, Medicine, Nursing and Pharmacy may be placed on probation or made subject to dismissal not only for scholastic deficiencies but also for deficiencies in other qualifications for these professions."

Wong's complaint was that the regents had abused their discretion

---

6. *Mustell* v. *Rose*, (Ala.), 211 So. 2d 489 (1968).
7. *Connelly* v. *University of Vermont and State Agricultural College*, (U.S.D.C., Vt.), 244 F. Supp. 156 (1965); discussed at pages 23 and 24 in *The Colleges and the Courts, 1962-1966*.

because this rule is too vague, ambiguous, and overbroad. In the trial court the university's answer was a demurrer (no cause of action) which was sustained by that court; but this judgment was reversed by the Court of Appeal. Justice Ellington, with Presiding Justice Molinari and Justice Sims concurring, interpreted the complaint as alleging that the regents had acted arbitrarily and capriciously. Therefore, it stated a cause of action. The judgment was remanded with instructions to overrule the demurrer and conduct a trial of the disputed facts.[8]

School of Social Welfare

A 1971 trial court judgment in Albany County, New York, held that Warren Bower, a student who had been dropped from the two-year program leading to the Master of Social Work at the State University of New York at Albany, was not entitled to an order compelling his reinstatement.

During the first year he had maintained a "B" average in academic studies and an "S," or satisfactory, in the field work portion of the course. At the end of the next semester he had maintained his "B" in academic work, but was marked "U" (unsatisfactory) in field work, whereupon he was suspended. He alleged that his "U" in field instruction was due to the fact that the dean and other officers and faculty members had, by their own actions, prevented him from completing the work.

Justice Harold E. Koreman concluded that "the only issue before the court is whether under the facts and circumstances here there was a clear abuse of statutory authority or a practice of discrimination or gross error." Under its rules, he said, the university reserves the right to terminate the registration of any student who does not meet the standards acceptable to the university.

In evidence were affidavits by faculty members, advisers, instructors, the director of field instruction, and the dean of the School of Social Welfare, all attesting that Bower's performance in the prescribed field work was unsatisfactory and that he should not be continued in the program. There had not been, said the Justice, "any showing of abuse of discretion."[9]

---

8. *Wong* v. *Regents of University of California,* (Cal. App.), 93 Cal Rptr. 502 (1971).

9. *Bower* v. *O'Reilly,* (Supreme Court of Albany County), 318 N.Y.S. 2d 242 (1971).

Student Persona Non Grata for Practice Teaching

Bluefield State College in West Virginia has working agreements with two county school systems in West Virginia and one in Virginia for the practice teaching periods of students who are required to have this experience as prerequisite to being licensed as teachers.

During 1968-69 Bluefield was troubled with exacerbated student unrest, demonstrated in various ways, including the bombing of the physical education building, with damage of $82,000, in November 1968. A student, then engaged in practice teaching in Tazewell County, Virginia, was arrested, along with others, and charged with felonious conspiracy to bomb the building. He was also suspended from the college. He was never brought to trial on the criminal charge and the indictment against him was dismissed in August 1969.

Lacking only 34 days of practice teaching to be graduated and licensed as a teacher, he demanded that he be placed as a practice teacher in Mercer County, West Virginia. The college found that neither the Mercer County nor Logan County boards of education would accept him because of the wide publicity he had received as a militant and as a participant in various disorders and turbulent occurrences on the campus and in the vicinity. The college, after much effort, was able to find a school in Tazewell County, Virginia, about 50 miles distant, willing to accept him as a practice teacher. At this he was enraged and threatened to kill the director of student teachers if he did not get the assignment changed. He sued in federal district court to vindicate his alleged rights to do practice teaching in Mercer County, and for compensatory and punitive damages for being deprived thereof, allegedly under the Civil Rights Act and the First and Fourteenth Amendments.

District Judge Sidney L. Christie held an evidentiary hearing from February 5 through 9, 1970; and, after completion of the transcripts and the submission of briefs, found, as a matter of fact, and concluded, as a matter of law, that there was nothing in the record to show entitlement to any of the relief sought.[10] A school district can not be forced to accept a practice teacher who is *persona non grata*.[11] For an-

---

10. *James* v. *West Virginia Board of Regents*, (U.S.D.C., W.Va.), 322 F Supp 217 (1971).

11. For a somewhat similar earlier case involving a practice teacher in Florida, see *Robinson* v. *University of Miami*, (Fla. App.), 100 So. 2d 442 (1958). Discussed at pages 22-23 in *The Colleges and the Courts Since 1950.*

other case growing out of troubles at Bluefield State College, see *Barker* v. *Hardway*, *infra* Chapter 17.

Conferring of Degrees

Closely related to the right to continue as a student is the right to receive suitable credentials upon satisfactory completion of the prescribed courses of study. The power to issue diplomas and confer degrees is commonly vested in the institutional governing board, to be exercised only upon the recommendation of the faculty.

As will certainly have been deduced from earlier portions of this chapter, the courts will not interfere in these processes, except upon evidence that an aggrieved student has passed all examinations and fulfilled all other requirements, so that nothing remains to be done but the mere ministerial duty of signing and delivering the diploma, which the faculty arbitrarily or unreasonably refuses to do. Such cases are not entirely unknown.

There is a classic case in which a student, who had met every academic requirement, engaged in a contumacious altercation with his dean just prior to commencement day, and the court sustained the faculty denial of his degree, though it directed that he be given a document certifying that he had completed the course successfully.[12] It is scarcely likely that such a commingling of academic and disciplinary matters would take place today.

Yet, there is at least one recent case in which a court actually ordered a college to confer a degree on a student who alleged that it had been unjustly withheld from him. He had taken the arts-law option at Brooklyn College of The City University of New York, which allowed him, after spending three years at Brooklyn, to spend his fourth year at law school in Syracuse, and then receive a bachelor's degree from Brooklyn, if all requirements were met. When he transferred he was lacking two courses to complete his undergraduate major in psychology. He sought advice from his dean, who referred him to the office of guidance and counseling, whence he was sent to the chairman of the psychology department, who advised him that he could take these courses by examination only and without attending class, pro-

---

12. *People ex rel. O'Sullivan* v. *New York Law School*, 68 Hun 118, 22 N.Y.S. 633 (1893).

vided the instructors involved consented. Both consented and informed him of the necessary reading materials, whereupon he registered, did the reading, took the examinations, and passed the courses. When he came down from Syracuse to the commencement at Brooklyn, accompanied by his parents and friends, to receive his degree, he was told he would receive no degree because there was a college policy prohibiting the earning of credits without attending class.

The dean of the faculty insisted on this; but it seemed no one in the psychology department had known of this policy—it was apparently a textbook case of failure of internal communication. The court gave it short shrift, in these words: "The dean of faculty may not escape the binding effect of the acts of his agents performed within the scope of their apparent authority, and the consequences that must equitably flow therefrom. Having given permission to take the subject courses in the manner prescribed, through his agents, . . . he can not in the circumstances later assert that the courses should have been taken in some other manner."[13]

There is a line between broad academic discretion and unreasonable or inequitable academic decision.

Retroactive Changes in Academic Requirements

Four young men, who were students at Franklin University in Columbus, Ohio, during the years 1961-1963, were confronted in September 1964 with a change in the academic regulations establishing new standards of scholarship. These new rules, they alleged, were applied to them retroactively, resulting in their dismissal from classes. The trial court sustained a demurrer to their plea, and dismissed their petition for an injunction to compel their reinstatement; but the court of appeals reversed and remanded the judgment for further proceedings, believing that they had presented a plausible claim of arbitrary and discriminatory treatment which must be heard in court on the facts and the law.[14]

Efforts to compel a college to confer a degree do not often succeed.

Having attended the Brooklyn Law School during a time when the rules of the Board of Regents of the University of the State of New

---

13. *Errol Blank* v. *Board of Higher Education of the City of New York*, 51 Misc. 2d 724, 273 N.Y.S. 2d 796 (1966).

14. *Schoppelrei* v. *Franklin University*, 11 Ohio App. 2d 60, 228 N.E. 2d 334 (1967).

York and State Board of Education, under authority of Section 207 of the Education Law, provided that the degree of J.D. could be granted to those persons who, before beginning the study of law, had successfully completed at least three years of acceptable college work, Emanuel Finkel sought an order to compel the law school to confer on him the J.D.

It was found that some of the college studies on which he relied had been completed subsequent to his admission to the law school and did not meet the requirements. Therefore, he had no clear legal right to the degree of J.D., and there was no basis for a mandatory order to the law school to perform a duty imposed on it by law, concluded Justice Joseph Liff of the Nassau County supreme court.[15]

From 1949 to 1964 Elmer Kaelin was enrolled from time to time in numerous courses at the graduate level at the University of Pittsburgh, and accumulated a total in excess of 48 credit hours, allegedly including the requirements for the 48 hour master's degree in business administration.

He was denied credit, however, for some of the courses completed during the early part of that period, because they were outside the maximum time-limit prescribed for completing the degree program from the time of beginning it. In 1963 he had a conference with the appropriate officers, at which he thought it was agreed that he would receive his degree if he completed nine additional credits prior to December 31, 1964. This he did. His complaint was that the university then repudiated that agreement and insisted upon a comprehensive written examination before granting the degree. This, he said, put him at a great financial disadvantage, and he had no adequate recourse at law except the extraordinary remedy of a writ of *mandamus*.

The state supreme court became entangled in its hang-up (not new), as to what the Pennsylvania statutes say about the permissible remedies in such a case, and did not touch the merits. It concluded that *mandamus* is not the proper remedy, and dismissed the case.[16]

The opinion was by Justice Henry X. O'Brien, with Justice Samuel J. Roberts concurring in the result without opinion, and Justice Herbert B. Cohen concurring in the result "only because *Strank* v. *Mercy Hospital of Johnstown*, 376 Pa. 305, 102 A. 2d 170 (1954)

---

15. *Finkel* v. *Brooklyn Law School*, 61 Misc. 2d 198, 305 N.Y.S. 2d 61 (1969).
16. *Kaelin* v. *University of Pittsburgh*, 421 Pa. 220, 218 A. 2d 798 (1966). *Certiorari* denied, 385 U.S. 837 (1966).

indicates that the jurisdiction of the Court of Common Pleas in such cases as this is exercisable in equity."[17] (In other words, the court would have jurisdiction to right the wrong, if any, by an equitable order of specific performance.) Whether Kaelin applied for an order in equity does not appear; but it is known that the U.S. Supreme Court declined to review the case at this stage.

Litigation Regarding Doctoral Degree

Every candidate for a degree, and especially every aspirant for a doctoral degree in any field of study, knows there is a certain hazard, right up to the last minute, that he may not be awarded the degree. This is because the power residing in the faculty is traditionally almost absolute. Balanced against this is the principle of fairness—the school will give the student a fair opportunity to complete the prescribed course of study, and after he has met all requirements will confer on him the appropriate credential.

The requirements for doctoral degrees in most fields have conventionally been flexible in the sense that there is no exactly prescribed number of years or of credit hours; though for the vast majority of candidates the necessary time is the equivalent of three academic years or 90 semester hours beyond the baccalaureate, or two academic years or 60 semester hours beyond the master's degree. Conferring of the degree is conditioned on the submission of an acceptable dissertation and the passing of a final oral examination traditionally known as "the defense of the dissertation" before a committee of the graduate faculty. There are variations as to these and other requirements in different graduate schools.

Comes now a case in which an aspirant completed all the specific requirements of his school, but found the faculty refused to read his dissertation or give him a final examination; but instead made heavy additional prescriptions for him as prerequisite to his being considered for the degree.

Frank John Cieboter was admitted as a candidate for the degree of Ph.D. in education at the University of Florida on May 7, 1963. He then worked as a teacher in the Palm Beach Junior College from 1963

---

17. The *Strank* case is discussed more fully at page 30 in *The Colleges and the Courts Since 1950*. 1964. 415 pp.

through February 1965, when he resigned rather than undergo an investigation regarding rumored misconduct. He returned to the university and resumed his studies. Both the chairman of his doctoral committee and the head of his department had heard of the incident, but told him no charges had been substantiated and the matter would be dropped. He submitted his completed dissertation to his committee in January 1967.

The dissertation was neither read nor considered by the committee. Instead, a special committee was appointed by the university to confer with the applicant to determine what additional work, if any, would have to be performed by him to meet the degree requirements for his particular case. He met with this committee and submitted to questioning, *inter alia*, concerning the cause for his resignation from the junior college in 1965. The committee decided he must have a full year of once-a-week sessions with a qualified counselor, psychologist or psychiatrist "to increase his openness," and after that he would have to complete three full quarters (equivalent of one academic year) of additional study at the university before the conferring of his degree would be considered.

His view was that he was being penalized for rumored past misconduct with which he had never been formally charged, much less had any opportunity for a fair hearing; and he asked the local trial court for a writ of *mandamus* to direct the university to appraise his dissertation and give him the final doctoral examination. The writ was denied, and the denial affirmed by the three-judge Court of Appeal. Judge John T. Wigginton, joined by Chief Judge Dewey M. Johnson and Judge Sam Spector, noted that there was no allegation, in so many words, that the university's determination was arbitrary or capricious or in bad faith; and in the absence of such a complaint the educational discretion of the faculty can not be judicially questioned.[18]

The court was impressed by the university's statement that the junior college incident was only one of several factors in the total picture of the plaintiff's relations with students, faculty, and others which motivated its prescription for him; and since his major was in student personnel services, the university withheld its highest credential in that field from him for the time being because it had the impression that

---

18. *Cieboter* v. *O'Connell, President of University of Florida*, (Fla. **App.**), 236 So. 2d 470 (1970).

he himself needed counseling. For legal precedent, the court relied heavily on *Connelly* v. *University of Vermont* (1965), cited earlier in this chapter. (Footnote 7.) The case in its present status seems to leave some unanswered questions regarding policies and practices of a graduate school of education.

CHAPTER 5

TUITION FEES AND OTHER
CHARGES TO STUDENTS

FROM TIME IMMEMORIAL the education of children has involved some financial outlay by the parents, unless they do all the teaching themselves. Recall the Roman patricians who purchased and maintained one or more Greek slaves to act as tutors. Hence there is tradition behind the view that the relation of the student to his college is largely a contract to pay fees, very much like a commercial contract. Even today, something like 70 per cent of the annual operating income of all the more than 1,200 private nonprofit colleges and universities in the United States comes from student fees, not including charges for room and board, which are classified as charges for auxiliary services operating on a break-even or modestly profitable basis.

Student fees are largely for tuition, but in smaller part they are for the support of other student services such as health and medical service, and "student activities" such as athletics, student newspapers, and other types of campus enterprises not entirely within the compass of classroom and laboratory instruction. Charges for room and board are in another and separate category, not properly classifiable as "fees," though it is a custom of some private institutions to lump them with tuition and other fees.

The Contract to Pay Fees

At least until recently, student fees were expected to be paid in advance at the beginning of the academic year; and this gives rise to perplexing questions as to whether the student is entitled to any refund, and if so, how much, in case he withdraws from the college early in the period. Often the college prints in its catalog a precise statement on this point, usually weighted heavily against anything resembling *pro rata* or proportionate refunds.

A lower court case in New York was a suit for refund of fees paid by a dental student who resigned his place six days before classes began, after having paid $200 and $910 for the balance of charges for the first semester, at New York University. Moving away from the literal black-letter view of the matter, the court decided that the student was not rigidly bound by every word in the somewhat Shylock-like provision in the catalog, because this would "place an unfair burden upon student applicants," and ordered a refund of the $910.[1]

There are many older cases in several states to illustrate that generally the courts have been much more hard-nosed in matters of this kind. The oft repeated rule, quoted many times in earlier cases involving private schools, is: "A contract for schooling for a specified term is entire, and when a student withdraws for reasons of his own, without fault on the part of the school, the school is entitled to the fees for the entire period."

Two decisions as recent as 1967 and 1968 afford examples. The operators of a private preparatory school in Berlin, Connecticut, known as St. James School, had a student during the academic year 1959-60, and his father paid the usual $50 registration fee for the next academic year. The written contract provided for a charge of $1350, due September 15. A few days after the term began in September the boy left the school because he was dissatisfied with the living accommodations furnished him, and his father stopped payment of a check he had written for the charges for the first half of the year.

The sufficiency of the living accommodations was a question of fact for the jury, and a verdict for the school was reached. The trial court set aside the verdict. The appellate court reversed and remanded the case with instruction to render judgment in accord with the verdict.

---

1. *Drucker v. New York University*, 57 Misc. 2d 937 (1968), in civil court of Queens City, N.Y.

"The agreement was a valid contract for the year 1960-61."[2] The three judges sitting as the appellate division concurred in this judgment.

In New Jersey, a girl had attended a private nonprofit school styled St. Mary's Hall for six years prior to the spring of 1967, when her father sent in a signed re-enrollment contract and $50 deposit to reserve a place for her for the following year. In September 1967 he notified the school that he was withdrawing her and requested a release from the contract. The school refused to cancel the contract because it had reserved a place for the daughter, and it had become too late to obtain a replacement for her. Its policy was not to allow for withdrawals except prior to July 1. The school withheld a transcript of the girl's record of past school work. Her parents sued to compel issuance of the transcript. The school counterclaimed for $425, the amount of the tuition fee for the first half of the year. (Only half because it had enrolled a replacement student in the middle of the year.)

Judgment was for the school. Judge Wick of the superior court decided that the school should not be compelled to issue the transcript covering prior years until all financial obligations for the latest year had been paid; and held the school entitled to a judgment for $425.[3]

This, of course, should not be interpreted to mean the transcript could be withheld after the financial obligation was liquidated; nor that a student's transcript can be permanently withheld for disciplinary reasons. In 1955, the supreme court of Pennsylvania, in an emphatic opinion by Chief Justice Horace Stern, held that a student nurse who had completed two years in a private hospital nursing school and had then been expelled for an alleged infraction of discipline was entitled to obtain her transcript in equity proceedings. "It would be a reproach to our system of jurisprudence," he said, "if plaintiff is entitled to the transfer credits which she seeks, but nevertheless neither law nor equity could furnish her any adequate means of redress."[4]

Martin Silver, a graduate student, registered for three courses in chemistry at Queen's College in The City University of New York, to begin in the fall of 1969. In May 1969 he paid the required fees and was given a receipt. (The City University is tuition-free for regular

2. *Leo Foundation, Inc.* v. *Kiernan*, 5 Conn. Cir. 11, 240 A. 218 (1967).
3. *Fayman* v. *Trustees of Burlington College*, 103 N.J. Super. 476, 247 A. 2d 688 (1968).
4. *Strank* v. *Mercy Hospital of Johnstown*, 383 Pa. 54, 117 A. 2d 697 (1955).

full-time undergraduates but charges tuition fees to graduates and all part-time students.)

No conditions or reservations were mentioned in Silver's bill or in his receipt. On June 23 the board of higher education increased fees in all units of The City University, and Silver soon received an "adjusted bill" for an additional $110, which he paid under protest and sued to recover. The board pleaded that long delays in the making of the appropriations of state and city funds had finally compelled it to increase fees unexpectedly.

Judge Anthony F. Zagame of Queens County Small Claims Court awarded Silver a judgment for $110, and spoke sharply: "The court has neither the intuition nor the power to correct any legislative or administrative shortcomings or delays, if there be any, in budgetary allotments, and the existence of such a condition can not be implied in the contract which is complete in all its other terms."[5]

At New York University classes were suspended May 6, 1970, on account of believed danger to life and property because of campus disorders, and then cancelled for the remainder of the semester, which ended on May 30. Faculty members continued on duty for consultation. Nineteen days of instruction time were lost. A parent, who had paid tuition fees for his son, sued for a *pro rata* refund of $277.40 and won a judgment in the small claims court of New York County. Judge Patrick J. Picariello saw the matter as a contract rigid in its terms: "The defendant breached its contract during its lifetime. It matters not at what point in its duration."[6] He also indulged in a rather lengthy and somewhat opaque reprimand to the university authorities in the circumstances.

The judgment was reversed on appeal. The higher court was more inclined to give suitable weight to the university's plea that its board of trustees is authorized and directed to use its property "as they shall deem for the best interests of the institution," and disinclined to take the *bourgeois* view that a university is solely a dispenser of instructional days and hours after the manner of a delicatessen dispensing slices of salami at so much per slice.

---

5. *Silver* v. *Queen's College of The City University*, 63 Misc. 2d 186, 311 N.Y.S. 2d 313 (1970).

6. *Paynter* v. *New York University*, Civil Court of New York County, 314 N.Y.S. 2d 676 (1970). Reversed in (App. Div.) No. 594, February Term (April 2, 1971).

The reasoning of the Appellate Division:

"In the light of the events on the defendant's campus and in college communities throughout the country on May 4 to 5, 1970, the court erred in substituting its judgment for that of the university administrators and in concluding that the university was unjustified in suspending classes for the time remaining in the school year prior to the examination period. Moreover, while in a strict sense, a student contracts with a college or university for a number of courses to be given during the academic year, the services rendered by the university can not be measured by the time spent in the classroom. The circumstances of the relationship permit the implication that the professor or the college may make minor changes in this regard. The insubstantial change made in the schedule of classes does not permit a recovery of tuition."

Accessibility of Institutional Financial Records

In 1971 certain students at Temple University in Philadelphia began an action to obtain access to current budget and financial records and the minutes of the governing board and its committees, which, they alleged, had been repeatedly denied when requested by the student senate. They averred that these are "public records" as defined in the Pennsylvania Right to Know Act (65 Pa. Stats., Section 66.1), wrongfully withheld from their inspection. Moreover, they pointed to the charter of the university, which makes it a nonprofit corporation expressly to operate an educational institution "intended primarily for the benefit of working men"; and they argued that the enrollment of working men had decreased because of tuition fee increases, and that it cannot be determined whether these increases are due to mismanagement of funds unless the records are opened to public inspection.[7]

Summer Session Fees in Junior Colleges of
The City University of New York

The City University of New York has a long and stoutly-defended tradition of free tuition for regular full-time undergraduate students; but for some years fees have been charged for summer session instruc-

---

7. *Mooney* v. *Board of Trustees of Temple University*, Civ. Action No. 199-CD1971, in Commonwealth Court of Pa.

tion at least in some components of the university. In 1970 the board of higher education imposed a fee of $10 per credit hour on "matriculated students" in the junior colleges of The City University. The fee was not assessed against "matriculated students" in the several senior colleges (mostly five-year colleges) that are components of the same university.

In early June, practically simultaneous with the opening of the summer session, 31 students and prospective students brought a class action against the university under Rule 65, Federal Rules of Civil Procedure, asking for a preliminary injunction restraining the charging of fees to students who would be unable to attend summer session if these fees were assessed. Federal District Judge Irving Ben Cooper first noted that a preliminary injunction has for its purpose to preserve the *status quo* and prevent irreparable injury until the case can be ultimately resolved; and cited the doctrine that a "clear showing of probable ultimate success *and* possible irreparable injury" is necessary.

In this case he denied the injunction, primarily on the ground that he perceived no strong probability of ultimate success in the suit. His view was: "Involved in this litigation is not the opportunity to pursue elementary education but the taking of courses at college level during the summer to enable a student to complete a college career at a faster pace. This limited interest, as we see it, has not been fastened within the ambit of the concept of fundamental right."

He was influenced by testimony that abolition of the summer session fee would necessitate a sharp cutback in junior college summer session programs; and by the fact that the junior colleges and the senior colleges of The City University are financed under quite different statutes (the state and the city share the operating costs of the senior colleges, less their income from fees, about equally; the junior colleges receive 40 per cent of their operating funds from the state, and the city must supply the remainder, less income from fees). Said he:

"We can not require the City to allocate more of its budget to education than it already does. The Constitution requires only that in using the funds made available the lines drawn be rationally based and not individually discriminatory."[8]

His concluding remark was to the effect that any injury suffered by the plaintiffs was chargeable in good part to "the lateness of the hour

---

8. *Grier* v. *Bowker*, (U.S.D.C., N.Y.), 314 F. Supp. 624 (1970).

at which they brought their suit," this by implication leaving the door ajar for further argument of the constitutional issues in subsequent litigation.

Fees for "Student Activities"

Public colleges and high schools have often charged comparatively small fees, not for tuition, but for "registration," "incidentals," or "student activities." Wherever the school operates under a state constitutional or statutory provision requiring it to be a "free school," "tuition-free," or "free of fees," a delicate question is latent as to what items all students can lawfully be required to accept and pay for, as a condition of admission or retention. Can students be uniformly compelled to purchase tickets to athletic contests or musical or dramatic performances? Subscriptions to student newspapers or yearbooks? Student health services? Membership in student organizations? Or must they be allowed the option of voluntarily paying for only such of these things as they choose to accept and make use of?

Students at Colorado State University in 1969 challenged the power of the State Board of Agriculture (the governing board of the institution) to charge "activity fees" aggregating $156 a year. Payment of the fee was a condition of admission to the next term, as well as a condition of the release of grades and transcripts. Part of the money was applied to financing a $2.8 million football stadium, some to the annual support of intercollegiate football, and some to various other extracurricular enterprises. Each student received tickets to four home football games, which in many instances they did not want or could not use; and the cost to them was said to be more than if they purchased all four tickets at the general admissions gate.

The challenge was unsuccessful in the local district court of the county of Larimer. Studying the legislative history of the powers of the State Board of Agriculture as governing board, the judge concluded that the board operates under a general grant of power delegated by the legislature, which embraces the authority to impose these fees, and it is not necessary to find any specific statutory grant of such authority. Instead, an express legislative limitation would have to be found, and none existed. Swept aside were the students' arguments that non-payment of the fee resulted, in effect, in summary suspension without due process, that equal protection of the law was denied them because some other Colorado state universities and colleges had no such fee policies, and that the money was disbursed for some projects having no relation to the educational process.[9]

The decision is on sound ground when it speaks of a broad general grant of authority to the governing board, which can be narrowed only by express legislative limitations; but there is perhaps some legitimate question as to whether students in a state institution, in the historic tradition of open admission to all qualified citizens of the state, should be compelled to pay for a multiplicity of "incidental" services, some of which are not wanted or used by some students. As early as 1912 this question was litigated in Oklahoma in the case of *Connell* v. *Gray*, wherein the state supreme court held that the regents of the Oklahoma A & M College (now Oklahoma State University) could not charge fees for the YMCA, the YWCA, the athletic associations, or the college news publication as a condition precedent to the admission of any student.[10] The institution was required by law to admit and instruct all properly qualified citizens of the state between the ages of 12 and 30. The court upheld the right of the regents to collect incidental fees for expenses "necessary and convenient to accomplish the object for which the institution was founded," and saw no objection to the collection of the disputed fees in this case from students who voluntarily participated in the respective activities.

It seems however, that the practice of charging an omnibus "activity and service fee" compulsory for all students has become very widespread among state universities and colleges. By the beginning of 1971 the practice was beginning to be questioned in some places.

Early in that year bills were introduced in the legislatures of Indiana and Illinois designed to stop the practice. The Indiana bill would prohibit the Indiana tax-supported universities and colleges from collecting student assessments for "activities unrelated to their instructional courses in which they do not wish to participate and which they do not wish to support financially." The "student government" organization was specifically pointed out as an activity that should be voluntary, not compulsory.

The Illinois bill took fees for the support of athletics as its principal

9. *Randall* v. *Colorado State Board of Agriculture*, (Dist. Ct., County of Larimer, Civ. Action No. 19032, December 23, 1969).

10. *Connell* v. *Gray*, 33 Okla. 591, 127 P. 417, Ann. Cas. 1914 B 399, 42 L.R.A. (N.S.) 336 (1912).

target. Its sponsors asserted that most of the tax-supported universities in Illinois were charging compulsory fees of something approaching $10 per semester chiefly to support the recruiting of athletes by paying their room and board and providing them with some $15 a month as spending money. These fees were said to be part of an "activity and service fee" of about $15 to $17.50 per semester, charged to all students. State Representative Gerald Bradley was reported as saying, "I think it's all right if the state will pay—but not the student." He continued, "I don't think it's right for a boy to work on a construction job all summer long or a girl to get a job waiting tables and then be forced to help pay for athletes."

The board of trustees of the State University of New York adopted a resolution May 9, 1968, authorizing the student body at each component campus to fix an annual fee for the support of programs of "an educational, cultural, recreational, and social nature" as approved by the campus-wide representative organization of the students. The fee is mandatory for each student at the time of his registration; and in cases where it is deferred, the administration of the component campus is empowered to withhold grades and transcripts of credits until it is paid.

This led to a suit in which the argument was that since the fees are mandatory, the funds derived from them are subject to the statutory requirements for the disbursement of state funds, set out in paragraphs (3) and (4) of Section 355 of the Education Law. Justice Harold E. Koreman of Albany County decided that this is the case. This means that the student bodies and their representative councils were prohibited and enjoined, as of September 17, 1970, from expending any funds already allocated by them, and from making any further allocations of the funds derived from student activity fees, without first obtaining the approval of the board of trustees.[11]

A notable feature of the opinion is in the words, "It is not within the province of the courts to determine in each instance whether a student-sponsored program or activity is educational, cultural, recreational, or social in nature. Interference in matters involving the internal affairs of the State University would have the anomalous result of usurpation by the courts of the powers and duties vested in the trustees by the legislature."

---

11. *Stringer* v. *Gould*, 64 Misc. 2d 8a, 314 N.Y.S. 2d 309 (1970).

From other sources it is reported that under the prior system of voluntary payment of student activity fees, the activities were not supported on a scale satisfactory to a majority of the students; and that more recently, when the students were given opportunity to vote their choice between (1) a voluntary fee with full student control of its allocation, and (2) a mandatory fee with required approval of the board of trustees for allocations of the funds, they chose the latter by a heavy majority.

The trustees, during the period from 1968 to 1970, delegated the function of allocating student activity funds to representative student councils. Justice Koreman says this can not be done with a mandatory student fee under current state statutes. A broader construction of the statutory powers of the trustees might be possible.

Special Fees to Finance Stadium at State University

In a number of states the courts have sustained the imposition of special student fees to amortize the cost, or part of the cost, of constructing or enlarging academic facilities, or of student union buildings.[12] A 1970 decision of the state supreme court upholds a statute authorizing this method of repaying in part a bond issue of $5 million to enlarge and improve the football stadium at the University of South Carolina.

The court concluded: "We find no constitutional proscription against the allocation of a student fee toward a permanent improvement."[13]

The *per curiam* opinion includes long quotations from the decision of Common Pleas Judge John Grimball of Richland County, which it affirms. One of the quoted paragraphs is illustrative of the spirit of the opinion and also provides an appealing definition of a state university:

"A university, by its very nature, is a highly diversified institution whose aim is the highest development, mentally, morally, and physically, of those who repair there to pursue excellence in their chosen fields. Indeed, one of the widely recognized criteria for judging the quality of a university is the breadth of activities, academic, social and athletic,

---

12. For example: *Iowa Hotel Association* v. *State Board of Regents,* 253 Ia. 870, 114 N.W. 2d 539 (1962).

13. *Moye* v. *Board of Trustees of University of South Carolina,* (S.C.), 177 S.E. 2d 137 (1970).

which it is able to offer both its students and the state of which it is an integral and vital part. The modern university is a monument to the idea that the greatest benefit will be derived when men are free to choose among a variety of possible pursuits, to follow those which they find appealing, and to test themselves and their ideas in an atmosphere of tolerance and cooperation."

Charges to Pupils in Free Public High Schools

The Michigan Constitution of 1963 (Art. 8, Section 2) directs: "The legislature shall maintain and support a system of free public elementary and secondary schools as defined by law." The Ann Arbor public school district required all pupils to purchase textbooks and school supplies, and also required "general fees" for high school pupils ($5 per semester, later $7 per pupil for the entire year) to be used for the support of various school activities, including interscholastic athletics. In 1969 the Michigan court of appeals held that requiring pupils to purchase textbooks and various school supplies for individual use did not conflict with the constitution; but that the "general fees" were unlawful, as contrary to the constitutional mandate for free public schools. The court did not order refunds of fees previously paid, because the only source of funds for the purpose would be the current budget, and such payment would diminish the funds currently available for the education of all pupils, and thus work a hardship upon all.[14]

Sensitive administrators and teachers in public schools have long been confronted in many places with demands from some of the more affluent and snobbish pupils and parents for a multiplicity of more or less expensive "school activities," to be paid for by assessments upon all pupils. The practice is generally in contravention of constitutional or statutory mandates of "free public schools."

A 1970 suit, brought by graduates of elementary and secondary schools in Illinois, all in families receiving assistance under the Aid to Families with Dependent Children title of the Social Security Act, complained of a total of $33 charged for full participation in all the activities of a typical high school graduation (Du Sable High School) in 1969, and denial of constitutional rights because of their inability to

---

14. *Bond* v. *Public Schools of Ann Arbor*, (Mich. App.), 171 N.W. 2d 557 (1969).

pay for the following: graduation exercise fee, dinner dance ($18), yearbook ($7.50), cap and gown ($3.75), announcements ($1.40), class gift, class ribbon, and contingency fund. The implication was that these fees should be paid by the public school system or by the Illinois Department of Public Aid.

Federal District Judge Alexander J. Napoli decided no constitutional question was at issue and dismissed the case as failing to state a claim on which relief could be granted. He noted that the Department of Public Aid provided up to $8.25 for rental of cap and gown; and that all the complainants had been graduated and had received their diplomas. He said: "It is possible that a child, from a family whose subsistence depends on public aid, may not be able to attend the school-sponsored graduation dinner dance because of his or her poverty. This situation must evoke genuine sadness and concern in every socially conscious citizen, but every social malady is not remedied by attempting to invoke the finite guarantees of the federal constitution."[15]

Article 9, Section 1 of the Constitution of Idaho declares:

"The stability of a republican form of government depending mainly upon the intelligence of the people, it shall be the duty of the legislature of Idaho to establish and maintain a general, uniform and thorough system of public free common schools."

When an Idaho public school district assumed to charge all high school pupils a mandatory fee of $25 a year, and to withhold transcripts of academic credit until the fee was paid, the state supreme court affirmed a decision holding the constitution precludes the charging of the fee. Justice Henry F. McQuade delivered the opinion joined by Chief Justice Joseph J. McFadden and Justices Charles R. Donaldson and Clay V. Spear.

The fee was itemized as $12.50 for extracurricular activities and $12.50 for books. The former can be collected only from such pupils as opt to participate in the activities; and the latter (books), is held to be an indispensable essential of a free school, for which no charge can be made to any pupil, other than perhaps a refundable deposit of reasonable size to cover possible loss or damage.[16]

---

15. *Williams* v. *Page*, (U.S.D.C., Ill.), 309 F. Supp. 814 (1970).
16. *Paulson* v. *Minidoka County School District*, 93 Ida. 469, 463 P. 2d 935 (1970).

CHAPTER 6

DIFFERENTIAL FEES FOR
OUT-OF-STATE
STUDENTS

THE INCREASING MOBILITY OF THE POPULATION, the augmented diversity of educational institutions, the great growth in total numbers of students, and other factors have made the charging of dispropor-tionately high fees by state institutions to "non-residents" of the state an issue bearing increasing investigation.

In the constitutions and statutes of many of the states there is wordage unmistakably indicating an intent that the state university should be tuition-free. Several of the state universities, even to this day, charge no *tuition fees*. Instead, they style the fees as "registration fees," "general fees," "incidental fees," or by some other fuzzy and innocuous name, so that it has long been the custom for all state universities to charge student fees on a roughly similar scale; though there is always a rather wide range between the highest and the lowest.

During the early decades of these institutions, fees were always negligible by today's standards. There was often a differential against nonresidents of the state, but it was usually small, and was often "honored in the breach." Since 1960, fees have gone up by leaps and bounds, due to the parsimony of state legislatures under the urging of representatives of the private sector, and over the seemingly rather feeble resistance of the state university governing boards. The boards usually possess the power to fix fees; but, faced with legislative appropriations they regard as insufficient, time and again they have raised fees "to make up the difference" and avoid cutting back programs on account of sheer lack of money. They know very well that raising fees will exclude at least some students who cannot meet the additional expense; but they regard this as the lesser of two evils. Placing a governing board in this dilemma has been a common form of legislative arm-twisting.

Along with the foregoing recent development has come increased emphasis on differentials against out-of-staters, so that by 1970 the fees for non-residents of the state were commonly at least twice as large as those for residents, and in some instances the ratio was about three to one. During the late 1960's came the notion, advocated in a few states and actually enacted by the New Hampshire legislature, that non-residents should be required to pay the full actual cost to the institution of its provision for their education. This idea is unconscionable. It means, for non-residents of the state, that the cost of attending a state institution of higher learning is as high or higher than it is in most private institutions.

Private institutions as a whole, nationwide, collect about 70 per cent of their annual operating income in the form of student fees. No reputable non-profit private college charges full cost. A few weak and struggling private colleges do that because they can command virtually no other source of income. Proprietary schools (rare in the higher education field) do it because this practice is theirs by definition. To put public institutions on this basis points toward the total destruction of tax supported higher education. Howard R. Bowen, distinguished economist and university president, has written words to the effect that charging differential fees against non-residents "is as improper as tariffs on the interstate movements of commodities, which are forbidden by the United States Constitution."

Considering the amounts of money that are coming to be involved, the interstate movement of students from one state university or college to another does indeed appear to have important commercial aspects, and could conceivably be within the exclusive power of Congress to "regulate commerce among the several states"; but at this writing no court has yet so held. But litigation in federal courts, on this and related points, has recently increased.

The Definition of Residence for Fee-Paying Purposes

A rule maintained by most state courts and by many state universities for a long time is that one who leaves his parental roof or his own home and goes to another state for the purpose of attending its state university will be presumed to intend to leave that state when he completes his college course; and hence he ordinarily does not become a resident as long as he is in uninterrupted attendance at the regular terms of the university, even if that be for several years; and he may be required to pay non-resident fees during the full duration of his stay.

It is to be noted carefully that the rule only creates a presumption which may be susceptible of being overthrown by suitable evidence; and, like all rules, it may be subject to some exception. Obviously the case against the student is weaker if he is of adult age, married, has his family with him, and has no permanent place of residence in any other state. Most important is *intent* (the French say *cherchez le motif*); the student should be afforded opportunity, if he requests it, to declare formally his intent to reside permanently in the state, and to support it with such evidence as he can muster.

Thus the Idaho supreme court in 1960 invalidated a rule of the state board of education which stipulated that: "Any person who is properly classified as a non-resident student retains that status throughout continuous regular term attendance at any institution of higher learning in Idaho." The plaintiff was a man aged 25, fully self-supporting, whose former home had been in Vermont prior to his spending four years in the armed services. He registered at Idaho State University at Pocatello in 1957 and paid the non-resident fee. (The rule permitted anyone to become a resident for this purpose after residing only six months in Idaho, but not as a student.) He continued during subsequent years, but, under a rigid interpretation of the rule above quoted, was not granted reclassification nor an opportunity to be heard on the matter. The state supreme court unanimously held the rule was arbitrary and unreasonable, and that it denied equality of opportunity to persons of the same class who were similarly situated, and was therefore invalid.[1]

Later a taxpayer's suit was brought in an Idaho county court,

---

1. *Newman* v. *Graham et al., State Board of Education,* 82 Ida. 90, 349 P. 2d 716, 83 A.L.R. 2d 492 (1960).

vainly seeking an order to compel the Idaho state institutions of higher education to charge each non-resident student the full cost of the facilities and instruction furnished him. Judge Merlin S. Young of the Ada County court decided that it was within the lawful discretion of the board of regents to pay part of the cost of educating students from outside the state; that this was a public benefit to the university and to the state.[2]

Another case in the U.S. district court in Iowa, somewhat similar to the *Newman* v. *Graham* case in Idaho, resulted not in a holding that the university rule on residency was invalid, but only that it had been too harshly interpreted in the case of George Clarke, originally a resident of Illinois, who had attended the University of Iowa for six years, had married an Iowa resident and declared his intent to reside and practice law in Iowa after his graduation from the University of Iowa Law School, and offered various other evidences of this intent. He did not ask for any refund of non-resident fees paid during his six years, but only to be classified as a resident during his seventh and final year. The federal district court expressly refrained from deviating from the customary legal doctrine and from invalidating any rule of the University of Iowa, but declared the application of the rule in the George Clarke case had been erroneous and directed the university residency review board to reconsider and reverse its determination in this case only. It gave scant notice to Clarke's contentions that discriminative charges against non-residents are in violation of provisions of the U.S. Constitution regarding the federal system and the relations among the several states.[3]

Challenges to Non-resident Fees
on Constitutional Grounds

Later, Charles Twist, a resident of California and a student at the University of Iowa Law School, challenged the university's maintenance of separate and higher tuition fees for non-resident students. Both the federal district court and the United States Court of Appeals held that

---

2. *Cobbs* v. *State Board of Education (as Regents of the University of Idaho)*, Third Judicial District of Ida., Civ. Action No. 36600, January 16, 1967. Discussed at pages 18-19 in *The Colleges and the Courts, 1962-1966.* Danville, Ill.: The Interstate Printers & Publishers, Inc., 1967. 326 pp.

3. *Clarke* v. *Redeker*, (U.S.D.C., Ia.), 406 F. 2d 883 (1966).

the case presented no substantial federal question; and the United States Supreme Court declined to review the decision.[4] The inferior courts had said equal protection of the law is not denied by imposing differential fees against non-resident students; and that this kind of classification of students is a reasonable one, permissible under the Constitution.

In another instance, the United States Supreme Court recently declined to review a decision upholding the non-resident fee by a California court of appeal, after the California supreme court had denied an appeal for a hearing. In this case, a young woman teacher resident in Cleveland, Ohio, married a California resident in 1967, joined him in that state, and enrolled as a graduate student at the University of California. A section of the California Education Code required her to pay non-resident fees because she had not been a resident of California for one year prior to her enrollment.

She alleged that this provision denied her equal protection of the laws, and that it impaired a fundamental right to move across state lines. She placed considerable reliance on the 1969 decision of the U.S. Supreme Court declaring state laws that prescribed periods of residence in the state prior to application for relief payments to destitute persons, unconstitutional and invalid.[5] The California court of appeal brushed this aside by saying: "*Shapiro* (the relief decision) involved the immediate and pressing need for preservation of life and health of persons unable to live without public assistance. . . . The durational residence requirements for attendance at publicly financed institutions of higher learning do not involve similar risks."

Attorneys for the university pressed three arguments, all of which seem, at best, somewhat circular. They contended that Mrs. Kirk lacked standing to raise the constitutional issues because it could be argued that her primary motive for moving from Ohio to California was not to continue her education at the university, but to live with her husband. They maintained that the statistics of student migration demonstrated that non-resident fees do not constitute a bar to interstate travel. They argued that there was no evidence that Mrs. Kirk sought financial as-

---

4. *Twist* v. *Redeker*, (U.S.C.A., Ia.), 406 F. 2d 878 (1969), and *Clarke* v. *Redeker*, (U.S.C.A., Ia.), 406 F. 2d 883; *certiorari* denied, 396 U.S. 853 (1969).
5. *Shapiro* v. *Thompson*, 394 U.S. 618, 89 S.Ct. 1322, L.Ed. 2d (1969). This conclusion had already been reached in at least two U.S. district courts. See *Harrell* v. *Tobriner*, (U.S.D.C., D.C.), 275 F. Supp. 22 (1967); and *Denny* v. *Health and Social Services*, (U.S.D.C., Wis.), 285 F. Supp. 526 (1968).

sistance under a program the university administers to help "needy students meet the expenses of their education, including the non-resident fee where applicable." They concluded that nothing in Mrs. Kirk's averments "suggests that graduate education in the liberal arts is so essential as to bar public universities from imposing a reasonable charge for non-residents and new residents."[6]

Mrs. Kirk's appeal to the United States Supreme Court was dismissed in a summary action on February 3, 1970: "California Education Code and Regents' Standing Order requiring nonresident students to pay higher tuition fees than resident students and classifying as nonresident any student who has not been state resident for 12 months succeeding enrollment does not unconstitutionally infringe fundamental right to travel; classification is reasonable and reasonably related to legitimate state objective. (Appeal dismissed)."

Among other recent litigation is a suit filed December 11, 1969, in the U.S. District Court for the Western District of Wisconsin, by a second-year law student at the University of Wisconsin challenging the constitutionality of the Wisconsin law which requires generally, that to be eligible for classification as a resident for tuition fee purposes, a person must have been a resident of Wisconsin for at least one year preceding his registration as a student at the University. (Wisconsin Statutes, Section 36.16.) As already indicated for some other states, it is impossible to become a resident for fee purposes without having resided in the state for one year as a non-student.

In this case the student, Walters, was 21 years of age and had resided in Wisconsin more than one year (though not for one year prior to his registration at the university). He was a registered voter, held valid Wisconsin driver's and chauffeur's licenses, and had worked for remuneration and paid income taxes in Wisconsin. His arguments were that the statute denied equal protection of the law, due process, freedom of travel among the states, and freedom of association. A hearing was held February 25, 1970.

The case was dismissed, not on the merits, but because Walters had failed to place in evidence before the Non-Resident Appeals Committee of the university the fact that he was emancipated prior to reach-

---

6. *Deborah Dickey Kirk* v. *Board of Regents of University of California*, (Cal. App.), 78 Cal. Rptr. 260 (1969). Hearing denied by Cal. supreme court, Civ. Action No. 25734 (1969).

ing the age of 21. Subsequently he did so and was reclassified as a resident.[7]

A federal district court has sustained a rule of the regents of the University of Minnesota:

"No student is eligible for resident classification in the University ... unless he has been a *bona fide* domiciliary of the state for at least a year immediately prior thereto. This requirement does not prejudice the right of a student admitted on a nonresident basis to be placed thereafter on a resident basis provided he has acquired a *bona fide* domicile of a year's duration within the state. Attendance at the University neither constitutes nor necessarily precludes the acquisition of such a domicile. For University purposes, a student does not acquire a domicile in Minnesota until he has been here for at least a year primarily as a permanent resident and not merely as a student; this involves the probability of his remaining in Minnesota beyond his completion of school."

Lynn G. Starns and Lynda J. Mack were married women who moved to Minnesota and entered as students at the university when their husbands obtained employment in Minnesota. They challenged the one-year residence rule as unreasonable and arbitrary, and contrary to the equal protection clause of the Fourteenth Amendment because it establishes a class of residents for less than one year who, until the year expires, are absolutely precluded from escaping from that class. In other words, the presumption that they are not residents until the year expires is not rebuttable by any declaration of intent or any evidence whatever, however persuasive. (Note the contrast with the theory advanced in *Harper* v. *Arizona, infra,* that it is possible, with sufficient evidence of intent, to acquire residency in one day.)

The Minnesota regents' rule was upheld by a special three-judge federal court composed of Circuit Judge Myron H. Bright, Senior District Judge Gunnar H. Nordbye, and District Judge Miles W. Lord, with the opinion delivered by Judge Lord. He defended the one-year residence prerequisite as a "reasonable attempt to achieve a partial cost equalization between those who have and those who have not recently contributed to the state's economy through employment, tax payments, and expenditures therein." As such, it was said to bear a rational relation to a legitimate interest of the state. However, the court refrained from

---

7. *Walters* v. *Hoover,* (U.S.D.C., Wis.), No. 69-C-304 (1970).

placing it in the same category as the waiting period for welfare payments, which can only be saved from unconstitutionality by showing an overriding or "compelling" state interest to the contrary, as expounded in *Shapiro* v. *Thompson, supra.*

The plaintiffs argued that the only possible purpose and effect of the rule is to deter students or potential students from becoming residents of Minnesota, and to punish them severely for at least one year if they do so. The court asserts that, since of 50,000 students in the university in the fall of 1968, over 6,000 were non-residents, "we believe that the one-year waiting period does not deter any appreciable number of persons from moving into the state," and denies any "chilling effect" upon the constitutional right of interstate travel. These assertions could be a *non sequitur* of large proportions. A 12 per cent ratio of out-of-state students to total enrollment in a great cosmopolitan state university such as the University of Minnesota is a markedly low ratio.

The United States Supreme Court disposed of this case in a summary action of March 30, 1971: "Regulation requiring one year domicile within Minnesota to acquire resident classification for tuition purposes at University of Minnesota is constitutional." (Judgment affirmed.)[8]

Early in 1970 a suit was filed in a Nebraska county court to challenge the constitutionality of *Nebraska Statutes,* Section 85-502, which precludes establishment of residency for tuition fee-paying purposes while a person is attending the university. The student, Thompson, matriculated at the University of Nebraska in 1967. He was 30 years of age, married, and declared his intent to remain in Nebraska where he owned a home, was registered to vote, paid income and sales taxes, and had registered his automobile.

He had been born in Nebraska, but his parents took him out of the state in 1959. He had obtained his undergraduate education outside Nebraska, had spent a tour of duty in the armed forces, and had lived and worked in two other states before returning to Nebraska in 1967.

He alleged that the statute contravened the equal protection and due process clauses of the Fourteenth Amendment, and violated the Nebraska Constitution's prohibition of discrimination between classes of citizens in the acquisition and enjoyment of property. The local

---

8. *Starns* v. *Malkerson,* (U.S.D.C., Minn.), 326 F. Supp. 234 (1971). Summarily affirmed by U.S.S.Ct., 39 *U.S. Law Week* 3420 (March 30, 1970).

court gave a judgment in favor of Thompson, but this has been reversed by the Nebraska supreme court. [9]

There may be a cloud on the horizon, no larger than a man's hand, but possibly capable of swift expansion. Late in 1970, a report in the daily press indicated that an Arizona superior court judge had declared unconstitutional the one-year residency requirement, under which about one-fourth of the University of Arizona's 6,200 non-resident students paid out-of-state fees; and ordered refunds of such excess fees paid by seven students who challenged the discriminatory fees in a suit. He was careful to say his order "shall not be interpreted to imply that any person can gain a residency status merely by coming here as a pleasure-seeker or for the sole purpose of attending the University."

He noted the similarity between the one-year residency requirement adopted by the board of regents and the welfare and medical indigency rules already declared unconstitutional in federal courts; and held that the rule hampers freedom of movement and violates the equal protection and due process provisions of the United States Constitution, as well as other state and federal constitutional guarantees. He reprimanded the regents for failing to publish their standards used by the residency committee, and ordered "objective" application of residency rules.

The key of the decision is that legal status as a resident may be achieved either before or after enrolling at a university by anyone who demonstrates his *intent* to stay in the state. Residency might be established, thought the judge, in as short a time as one day if the newcomer proclaims his intent to remain in the state and supports his declaration by such acts as buying a home or registering to vote. The students in this case had registered to vote, bought property, got Arizona drivers' licenses and automobile titles, held jobs, opened bank accounts, married, and paid taxes.[10] In September 1971 this case was on appeal, pending before Division 2 of the Arizona Court of Appeals.

Efforts To Upgrade the Statutes Piecemeal

Short of a sweeping remedy such as a Supreme Court decision

---

9. *Thompson* v. *Board of Regents of University of Nebraska,* 187 Nebr. 252, 188 N.W. 2d 840 (1971).

10. *Harper* v. *Arizona Board of Regents,* Ariz. Superior Court, Pima County, Cases Nos. 111,657, 116,642, and 116,643 (May 29, 1970).

holding discriminatory fees against non-residents of the state contrary to the federal Constitution, or such as an act of Congress underwriting payment out of federal funds (within specified limits) of the difference between resident and non-resident fees in all public institutions of higher education, there are some on-going attempts to improve the generally rigid and archaic state statutes and university regulations on the subject.

Robert F. Carbone, special assistant to the president of the University of Wisconsin, prepared a 58-page report entitled *Resident or Non-Resident? Tuition Classification in Higher Education in the States*, which was published in March 1970 by the Education Commission of the States.[11] It includes thumbnail sketches of the pertinent statutes and university regulations in all the states; digests of a few germane court decisions; twelve recommendations by the author as to detailing the rules in such manner as to cover many "hardship cases" and other instances which are currently largely ignored or often resolved inequitably; emphasis on interstate and interinstitutional reciprocity across state lines; and the 14 "general principles" adopted in 1968 by the Advisory Committee on Higher Education of the Midwest Conference of the Council of State Governments.

It also appears that efforts are under way to accomplish the drafting of a model state statute to be made available for consideration and adoption or adaptation by all the states.[12]

Meantime, the legislature of Idaho, having in mind the case of *Newman* v. *Graham* discussed earlier herein, and alerted by augmented dissatisfaction with the existing state of affairs, enacted in 1970 a statute embodying some of Carbone's recommendations, and making at least seven types of students eligible for classification as residents:

1. Those under voting age whose parents or guardians live in the state.

2. Those of voting age who have lived in the state for at least six months.

3. Those under voting age who graduate from high school in the state and enroll at a state college or university the following term, regardless of where their parents live.

---

11. Robert F. Carbone, *Resident or Non-Resident?* Denver: Education Commission of the States, 1970. 58 pp.

12. Under auspices of the Council of State Governments, Iron Works Pike, Lexington, Ky.

4. Spouses of those classified as residents.

5. Members of the armed forces based in the state, and children of armed force members based in the state.

6. Married students under voting age who have lived in the state with their spouses for at least six months.

7. Those who designated Idaho as their home of record when they are separated from the armed services under honorable conditions after two years' service.

No doubt many inconsistencies and injustices can be avoided or mitigated by this type of foray into the morass; but in the long view (perhaps 20 years or more) it seems probable that eyes may be raised above the thicket of detail to encompass the broader succor that is likely eventually to come from decisions of the Supreme Court or from acts of Congress, or both.

CHAPTER 7

ASPECTS OF STUDENT FINANCIAL AIDS

COLLEGE SCHOLARSHIPS have been a favorite object of charity for centuries. Philanthropically inclined individuals continue to provide for them by deeds of gift or wills. This is accomplished with the aid of that branch of law (or, more accurately in most cases, branch of equity jurisprudence) known as the law of charities.

Not only private individuals, but also business corporations often provide gifts or agreements whereby the children of their employees may receive scholarships, or agreements whereby their adult employees themselves may receive fellowships or leaves of absence for the purpose of completing studies for advanced graduate or professional degrees.

The federal and state governments provide limited but increasing numbers of paid leaves or fellowships and scholarships for their own employees or prospective employees; and the vast social security system includes operative provisions for aid to college students up to specified ages, such as under the aid to families with dependent children (up to 21 years), and under the old age, survivors and disabled insurance system (up to 22 years). Some 25 states operate state scholarship systems of differing kinds.

The vexing question of whether payments received in the guise of scholarships, fellowships, or stipends under agreements for some kind of *quid pro quo* are taxable against the student recipient under the federal income tax law or state personal income tax laws is another aspect of student aids.

To the foregoing categories must be added the considerable numbers of fellowships available under the National Defense Education Act, the Higher Education Act of 1965 and its amendments, and companion acts which provide aids for students of medicine and other health-related occupations; as well as the research assistantships often included in the research grants and contracts which link many universities and colleges with half a dozen great federal agencies and, in some instances, with industrial firms. A mere catalog of the types of student aids requires much space; but despite their number and variety they have never been sufficient to the need.

This chapter deals with only a few recent decisions concerning a few of the categories.

Charitable Trusts for Student Aids

The will of a testatrix in Pennsylvania, Lena B. McClain, directed the residue of her estate to be sold, and "the proceeds to be used for Scholarships, to be directed by Fred D. Lamberson." No other descriptive words or instructions appeared. The Pennsylvania supreme court, through Chief Justice John C. Bell, Jr., held that this instrument created a charitable trust, even though it did not contain either the word "trust" or "trustee"; and affirmed a lower court order assigning the residue to Fred D. Lamberson, to be administered under a plan of distribution to be approved by the court.[1]

The University of Vermont Trust, established by James B. Wilbur in 1928, is a charitable trust to assist in financing the education, in any school at any level in Vermont, including the university, of selected boys or girls, residents in the state, who are certified by their school principals as of good character, extraordinary ability, and otherwise financially unable to obtain the desired schooling. It is administered at the discretion of the trustees of the University of Vermont, except that "no person shall suffer disadvantage by reason of race or creed."[2]

The trust instrument embodies an important condition: the trust

---

1. *In re McClain's Estate*, (Pa.), 435 Pa. 408, 257 A. 2d 245 (1969).

2. *Wilbur* v. *University of Vermont*, (Vt.), 27 A. 2d 889 (1970). Earlier suit (Vt.), 127 Vt. 284, 247 A. 2d 897 (1968).

was not to come into existence unless the state legislature or the university board of trustees mandated that the number of students attending the College of Arts and Sciences of the University of Vermont in any one year should not exceed 1,000 (but it allowed this number to be increased by 250 for each 100,000 persons added to the population of Vermont after 1920); and no students from outside the state were to be admitted until after all native Vermonters who apply and qualify. If at any time there is any failure of these conditions, then the entire corpus of the fund is to be paid to the U.S. Library of Congress Trust Fund Board.

In 1960, the enrollment in the College of Liberal Arts exceeded 1,000, and in that year the Congress of the United States enacted a law authorizing the U.S. Attorney General to consent to a modification of the trust instrument only as it related to maximum permissible enrollment, and because the limitation was in conflict with national policy as expressed in the National Defense Education Act of 1958. In 1961 the Court of Chancery of Washington County, Vermont, having jurisdiction, modified its decree of 1932 which had directed the then principal of the trust to be paid to the trustees of the University of Vermont. The modification order of 1961 authorized the university to admit qualified applicants without numerical limitation.

Later came heirs-at-law of the deceased founder of the trust claiming it was not now being executed in accord with its terms, and therefore the entire fund should revert to the residuary estate of the founder and thus pass to them under his will. Their suit failed, because, in the words of Chief Justice James S. Holden who wrote the unanimous opinion of the supreme court of Vermont:

"The changing circumstances and policy considerations which have developed since the trust was created, justified the trustees of the University of Vermont to petition the court of chancery for a modification of the terms upon which they held and administered the Wilbur gift. . . . It was within the jurisdiction of the equity court to grant a deviation from the limitation to allow the trust estate to remain in the trustees of the university. It is apparent that this arrangement was well suited to serve the donor's dominant purpose of aiding the students in Vermont who qualified for his gift."

Also: "It was Mr. Wilbur's primary intention to apply the yield of the trust property for the benefit of deserving Vermont students"; and other considerations are secondary to that purpose; and, "The fact that the trustees of a charitable trust violate its terms does not cause the trust to fail nor entitle the settlor or his successor to enforce a resulting trust." Finally, "unless it is impossible or impractical to execute the donor's purpose, the remedy for a breach of trust is by suit at the instance of the attorney general of the state to compel compliance. It creates no right in the donor's heirs to enforce a resulting trust."

A Mississippi testatrix provided that a remainder of her estate should be used "for Christian education of poor boys and girls" in sectarian schools of any denomination, but she expressed her preference for Methodist colleges. Taking note that "there are large numbers of poor boys and girls desirous of a college education, both in Bolivar County and elsewhere throughout this state and nation," the chancery court decreed that the court itself would administer the trust to provide college education for suitable applicants in Bolivar County, Mississippi, in a Methodist college in Mississippi; and this decision was affirmed by the state supreme court.[3]

The will of Miriam E. Owsley, dated 1944, established a trust, the income thereof to pay or assist in the payment of tuition fees at Carthage College, Carthage, Illinois, "of worthy men and women who desire to obtain an education and who do not have sufficient funds therefor."

In 1964 Carthage College moved to Kenosha, Wisconsin. It had been for 90 years a 4-year liberal arts college affiliated with the Lutheran Church, and continued as such in its new location. In 1965, a two-year institution, known as Robert Morris College, started classes at Carthage, Illinois. It was neither a four-year liberal arts college nor church-related. When the trustee of the Owsley trust asked for instructions, the Hancock County district court advised him to shift the benefits to students at Robert Morris College, under the doctrine of cy pres; but the Appellate Court of Illinois reversed and remanded this decision with instruction that the income must be used as provided in the will, for the benefit of students at Carthage College, now in Kenosha, Wisconsin. The trust was in no way conditioned on any perpetual location of Carthage College in Illinois; and in the view of Presiding Justice Jay J. Alloy, joined by Justices Scheineman and Allan L. Stouder, the facts afforded no reason for application of the cy pres doctrine.[4]

---

3. *In re Estate of Hall*, (Miss.), 193 So. 2d 587 (1967); opinion clarified in 195 So. 2d 94 (1967).

4. *Bell* v. *Carthage College*, (Ill. App.), 243 N.E. 2d 23 (1968).

Another case illustrates how demographic changes and changes in the law of the land may cause the terms of a trust to be judicially modified in accord with the general broad charitable intent of its founder. Dr. Joseph P. Pyle of Wilmington, Delaware, who died in 1917, established a trust "to provide each year for the maintenance and education of one (white) young man of Wilmington at one of the leading colleges or universities of this country, to the end that they may become men of character and capability, useful members of society and creditable citizens." The awards were to be made by a committee composed of the principal of the Wilmington high school, the Chief Justice of the State of Delaware, and the president of the Equitable Guarantee and Trust Company.

In 1917 Wilmington's population was 10 per cent non-white. In 1969 it was 40 per cent; and 61 per cent of all pupils in grades 10 through 12 were non-white. In these circumstances the trustee bank asked for instructions as to whether it should accept applications from non-whites. Chancellor William Duffy decided that the provision for a high state officer and an officer of the public school system constituting the majority of the selection committee gave the operation a sufficient color of "state action" to bring it within the sweep of the Fourteenth Amendment, and ordered that applications be accepted and considered without regard to race.[5]

Aids Under Federal and State Statutes

Antoinette M. Money, the mother of five minor children, with sole support from welfare payments under the Aid to Families with Dependent Children Program (AFDC), enrolled as a junior college student with the goal of becoming an elementary school teacher. Her educational expenses were about $70 per month. She applied for an educational allowance from the Cook County (Chicago) Department of Public Aid (under an Illinois statute of 1967), so she could continue college without depriving her family of the funds necessary for food, clothing, and shelter.

The department refused her request because a regulation of the Illinois Department of Public Aid (Section 1000, paragraph 1032) provided that such allowances would be given only to recipients (1) at-

---

5. *Bank of Delaware* v. *Buckson*, (Del. Ch.), 255 A. 2d 710 (1969).

tending a vocational school, or (2) attending a college with not more than one year to complete before receiving a bachelor's degree. The intention was to provide such allowances for not more than one year to any recipient; and while this amount of vocational training might produce substantial increase in earning-power, because the manual skills thus taught were in short supply, a year in a college not leading immediately to a degree would likely result in only limited increase in employment opportunities.

Hence the U.S. Court of Appeals for the Seventh Circuit, in an opinion by Circuit Judge Wilbur F. Pell, Jr., joined by Circuit Judge Walter J. Cummings and District Judge Jesse E. Eschbach, affirmed a District Court judgment upholding the rule and denying that it infringed any constitutional right of Antoinette Money.[6] Judge Pell indicated that the Social Security Act Amendments of 1965 provided elbow-room for flexibility by the state authorities in matters of this kind.

He referred to another U.S. District Court decision of 1970 in Illinois where the issue was that of extending AFDC benefits to children above the age of 18; and there it was held that federal law allows benefits to be paid up to age 21 if the child is regularly attending a school, college, or university, but does not mandate it. This was a special three-judge court composed of Chief Circuit Judge Luther M. Swygert and District Judges Joseph Samuel Perry and Abraham L. Marovitz.[7]

Judge Pell also relied heavily on the recent U.S. Supreme Court decision in which Mr. Justice Potter Stewart, for the divided court, concluded that "The Constitution does not empower this Court to second-guess state officials charged with the difficult responsibility of allocating limited public welfare funds among the myriads of potential recipients." From this decision, Justices William O. Douglas, Thurgood Marshall, and William J. Brennan dissented.[8]

It would appear that all the judges named (except the three illustrious dissenters in *Dandridge* v. *Williams*) were of the opinion that the Illinois statute and regulations denying AFDC benefits to junior

---

6. *Money* v. *Swank*, (U.S.C.A., Ill.), 432 F. 2d 1140 (1970).
7. *Alexander* v. *Swank*, (U.S.D.C., Ill.), 314 F. Supp. 1082 (1970).
8. *Dandridge* v. *Williams*, 397 U.S. 471, 90 S.Ct. 1153, 25 L.Ed. 2d 491 (1970); Justices Douglas, Marshall and Brennan dissenting.

college students and to college students except in rare cases when they are within one year of receiving a degree, do not violate the equal protection clause of the Fourteenth Amendment, though all refrained from any expression as to the wisdom of that result.

Marion Adele Kaplan was awarded a Regents' Graduate Teaching Fellowship for the academic year 1969-70. It was withdrawn on the ground that she had not been a resident of New York for one year prior to the award, as required by Section 602, subdivision 3 of the Education Law. It was shown that she had married in New Jersey in August 1967 and immediately moved to Bologna, Italy. In June 1968 she registered to vote in New Jersey, and voted in New Jersey in the November 1968 election. She filed no New York State income tax return for 1968, and renewed her New Jersey automobile driver's license in March 1969. Practically her sole basis for claiming residence in New York, as of September 1, 1968, was a lease for an apartment in New York City dated August 12, 1968, and covering the two-year period from October 11, 1968, through September 30, 1970.

Her petition for an Article 78 writ to compel the commissioner of education to confer the fellowship as originally granted was dismissed by Justice A. Franklin Mahoney of the Albany County supreme court.[9]

Tuition Grants for Students in Denominational Colleges Are Unconstitutional in South Carolina

"The property or credit of the State of South Carolina, . . . or any public money, from whatever source derived, shall not, by gift, donation, loan, contract, appropriation, or otherwise, be used, directly or indirectly, in aid or maintenance of any college, school, hospital, orphan house, or other institution, society or organization of whatever kind, which is wholly or in part under the direction or control of any church or of any religious or sectarian denomination, society or organization." This section of the state constitution has been held to prohibit "tuition grants" out of state tax funds made directly to students in sectarian colleges in South Carolina.[10]

---

9. *Kaplan* v. *Allen, Commissioner of Education,* (Misc.), 311 N.Y.S. 2d 788 (1970).

10. *Hartness* v. *Patterson,* Supreme Court of S.C., 1971. Not yet reported as of this writing.

The South Carolina supreme court rejected the argument that such grants are primarily for the benefit of the students as individuals, to enable them to attend the college of their choice, and that any resultant benefit to the colleges is no more than incidental or negligible, or of such minor consequence as not to contravene the state constitution.

There may be subsequent litigation to resolve such questions as precisely what constitutes denominational or sectarian control. Some other states (notably Michigan) have relatively new legislation providing for "tuition grants" exclusively for students in private colleges. Whether the constitutionality of these statutes may be litigated in the respective states depends in part on the exact wording of different prohibitory clauses that are found in more than 40 state constitutions.

Pennsylvania's 1969 Act to Cut Off Aids to Disruptive Students Is in Part Unconstitutional

Pennsylvania has large scholarship and loan programs for which residents of the state attending accredited colleges inside or outside the state are eligible for selection. In 1969, the legislature, in a hysterical interlude, enacted measures purporting to require every college, in every state having Pennsylvania students enrolled, to report to the Pennsylvania Higher Education Assistance Agency the names of any Pennsylvania students who had been (1) convicted of a felony, or a "misdemeanor involving moral turpitude"; (2) expelled or denied enrollment for refusing to obey a lawful regulation or order; or (3) convicted in a court for disturbing or attempting to disrupt the orderly activities of an institution of higher education.

Haverford College was a leader among colleges questioning the constitutionality of these measures. Goddard College was among 26 institutions which refused outright to make such reports. Both, as well as several students, were among the joint plaintiffs who asked a special three-judge federal court to declare the measures unconstitutional and void. District Judge Joseph S. Lord III wrote the opinion for the court, which was delivered July 19, 1971. Circuit Judge John Biggs, Jr., concurred. District Judge J. William Ditter, Jr., dissented, maintaining that the legislation should not be regarded as a punitive statute, but rather as "part of a legislative plan to provide financial assistance to college students."

The decision left standing the provision regarding felonies, because conviction of a felony is always a matter of public record. It struck down the clause about "moral turpitude," saying:

"The term 'moral turpitude' tells us very little about what misdemeanors trigger the loss of financial aid eligibility. . . . In essence . . . the legislature is saying that any immoral misdemeanor will subject the student to the extra sanction of loss of financial aid. If the state insists on legislating morality, we will insist at least that it spell out its moral code, particularly where those affected by the statute are of a different generation from the lawmakers and generally share a somewhat different outlook on what is and what is not moral. The phrase 'misdemeanor involving moral turpitude' is so vague it is unconstitutional . . ."

Regarding other phrasing: "It is impossible for a student to know what an institution may consider to be a disruption, or whether a given course of conduct contributed to a disruption. No objective standards have been set forth to guide what is basically a subjective determination as to when an activity has been disrupted, or whether the student's conduct contributed to it . . . The subsection can not constitutionally stand in the face of such manifest indefiniteness. . . ."

Also: "Since the hazy terms 'disturb' and 'interfere' may naturally be construed to include various sorts of student activities which are constitutionally protected. . . . The cautious student . . . thus will be deterred from First Amendment activities which might fall within those descriptions. . . . This is precisely the result against which the principle of overbreadth attempts to guard. . . . Since this wording sweeps so broadly as to invade the area of protected First Amendment freedoms, it is unconstitutionally overbroad. . . ."

The decision of a special three-judge court on a question of constitutionality is appealable directly to the Supreme Court of the United States. This does not necessarily mean that the Supreme Court will accept the case for review. At the moment of this writing no one knows whether the Pennsylvania case will be appealed, and if it is appealed or not, whether the decision of the three-judge federal court will stand permanently; but there is a likelihood that it will.

At the moment, various options were open to the Pennsylvania Higher Education Assistance Agency, already a burgeoning bureaucracy with an ego-conscious identity of its own. If it did not choose to appeal the decision, it could hopefully redraft the parts of the statute which the federal court had pointed out as contrary to the Constitution, and ask the legislature to re-enact it in the revised form, in the expectation that it would probably pass muster if again attacked in court.

Then, too, it might possibly simply be allowed to remain in the books as a dead letter, unenforced, inoperative, and eventually forgotten. Whatever its fate, it will probably be remembered as an example of legislative overkill, vintage 1969. For remotely analogous discourses, compare Chapter 19 herein, on "State Statutes as Applied to Campus Disruptions"; and Chapter 20, "Executive, Judicial, and Grand Jury Overkill." The present decision not having been reported officially as yet, no citation or other documentary identification of it is available. One can only cite secondary sources in which it was announced and discussed.[11]

Taxability of Student Aid Payments Against the Student Under the Internal Revenue Code

This field has been called one of "limitless diversity of facts," the income tax law evidences a general intent to exempt the student from taxation of gifts received to aid him in getting an education, but to tax payments received in the nature of salaries or stipends for work.

Section 117 of the Internal Revenue Code, in part:

"(a) General rule.—In the case of an individual, gross income does not include—(1) any amount received—

   (A) as a scholarship at an educational institution. . . .

   (B) as a fellowship grant. . . ."

In regulations promulgated by the Commissioner of Internal Revenue, Section 1.117-3 defines "fellowship grant" and provides that it does not include any amount representing compensation for past, present, or future services, or any services subject to the direction of the grantor; or any amount to enable the recipient to pursue studies primarily for the benefit of the grantor.

Westinghouse Electric Corporation, operating the Bettis Atomic Power Laboratory at Pittsburgh under contract with the Atomic Energy Commission, operated what was known as the Bettis Fellowship and Doctoral Program. It paid stipendiary grants to selected em-

---

11. *Higher Education and National Affairs* 20, No. 28, July 23, 1971; and *The Chronicle of Higher Education* 5, No. 37, August 2, 1971.

ployees and gave them leaves of absence for study at either the University of Pittsburgh or Carnegie-Mellon University, in avenues related to the programs of the laboratory in nuclear engineering.

Each fellow agreed "that after the end of his educational leave he will assume such duties commensurate with his education and experience as may be assigned to him by Westinghouse, and will thereafter continue in the employ of Westinghouse for at least two calendar years at a rate of salary commensurate with the duties assigned."

In the case of three employees who received grants to enable them to "research, write, and defend their Ph.D. theses in engineering," these grants were held taxable against the recipients as ordinary income by the U.S. District Court for Western Pennsylvania; but this judgment was reversed and remanded by the U.S. Court of Appeals for the Third Circuit, in a well-reasoned opinion by District Judge Charles R. Weiner, sitting with Chief Circuit Judge William H. Hastie and Senior Circuit Judge J. Cullen Ganey.

"The concept and content of 'scholarship' are developing ones," said Judge Weiner. "Fundamental in the exclusion afforded such stipends by Section 117 is its encouragement toward graduate study. Without an arrangement of subsidies on a sliding scale based on prior income, employees such as appellants here would probably be hard pressed to leave work for a year to return to school to earn an advanced degree. We think the purpose of the instant fellowship program entirely consistent with the scheme of the exclusion afforded scholarships. . . . To us, the nature of the grants here involved is not such as to deprive them of the normal characteristics associated with scholarships or fellowship grants."[12]

Persuasive though this view of the Third Circuit was, it was subsequently reversed by the United States Supreme Court, with the opinion delivered by Mr. Justice Potter Stewart. There was one dissent, by Mr. Justice William O. Douglas, who simply said he would affirm the judgment for the reasons stated by the Court of Appeals. The majority opinion runs to some 7,000 words, and seems to stress technical canons of statutory interpretation as distinguished from broad philosophical or social considerations. Mr. Justice Stewart noted several recent Court of Appeals decisions from other Circuits were gen-

---

12. *Johnson* v. *Bingler*, (U.S.C.A., Pa.), 396 F. 2d 258 (1968); reversing U.S.D.C.

erally contrary to the judgment under review.[13] Accordingly, the judgment of the District Court was reinstated, holding the stipends taxable against the recipients as ordinary income.[14]

In a nearly contemporaneous case, somewhat different as to facts, the Eighth Circuit Court of Appeals affirmed the decision of the federal district court in Minneapolis in holding that compensation paid to a staff physician by the Veterans' Administration Hospital at Minneapolis under a three-year contract as a "career resident" while he was concurrently pursuing studies in the University of Minnesota Medical School in a graduate program leading to the degree of Master of Science in Physical Medicine and Rehabilitation, was in the nature of salary and not a fellowship grant.

The appeal was before Chief Circuit Judge M. C. Matthes and Circuit Judge Myron H. Bright, with Circuit Judge Harry A. Blackmun not participating. The relations between the university and the veterans' hospital were very close, with some of the hospital work credited toward the degree; and Judge Bright mentioned the possibility of an apportionment of the pay partly as salary and partly as a fellowship grant, but declined to pursue this idea because the pleadings appeared to be on an "all or nothing" basis, and stated no facts on which a jury might base a verdict for such an apportionment.[15]

An inkling of how teachers may fare in seeking exemption of their expenses for a year of graduate education to earn an advanced degree is provided by the case of Mary O. Furner, a junior high school teacher at Crookston, Minnesota, who resigned and devoted the year 1960-61 to graduate study at Northwestern University, where she was awarded a master's degree. Thereafter she accepted a similar teaching position at De Kalb, Illinois. She had no alternative but to resign at Crookston, because the school district there did not grant leaves of absence. Therefore, during her year of graduate study she was neither engaged in teaching nor on leave from any teaching position.

The U.S. Tax Court (47 T.C. 165) decided that her educational expenses for that year were not deductible from gross income because

---

13. Among these: *Betty Jane Stewart* v. *United States*, (U.S.C.A., Tenn.), 363 F. 2d 355 (1966).

14. *Bingler* v. *Johnson*, 394 U.S. 741 (1969), reversing 396 F. 2d 258 and reinstating U.S.D.C.

15. *Quast* v. *United States*, (U.S.C.A., Minn.), 428 F. 2d 750 (1970); affirming 293 F. Supp. 56 (1968), Phillip Neville, District Judge.

during that year she was not engaged in "carrying on the trade or business of teaching." This absurdly astringent judgment was reversed by the Seventh Circuit Court of Appeals in an opinion by Circuit Judge Thomas E. Fairchild, joined by Circuit Judges Elmer J. Schnackenberg and Roger J. Kiley. In brief, the court held:

"The Tax Court's finding, based as it was on the fact that petitioner was not on leave, is clearly erroneous. The present record, moreover, would not support a finding that petitioner did not reasonably expect to return to teaching activity after her year of study, nor a finding on any other basis that her graduate study was not a normal incident of her carrying on the business of teaching."[16]

This section has dealt with only a few decisions at the Circuit Court level. Scores of such cases, with great diversity of basic facts, are more or less constantly receiving attention in rulings of the district directors of internal revenue, rulings of the Commissioner of Internal Revenue, and litigation in the United States Tax Court and the District Courts and the Courts of Appeal. Only rarely does the United States Supreme Court accept a tax case in this category.

Treasury regulations are frequently developed and modified, so that the body of pertinent law and regulations is large, complex, and subject to changing interpretations in detail. Hence the substance of this section is only a fleeting taste of a complicated sector of the law.

---

16. *Furner* v. *Commissioner of Internal Revenue*, (U.S.C.A., Ill.), 393 F. 2d 292 (1968).

CHAPTER 8

VARIOUS FACETS OF
STUDENT LIFE

KEEPING THE STUDENT AS THE FOCAL POINT, this catch-basket includes such rubrics as (1) religion and the student, both as to the familiar matter of compulsory chapel attendance at some institutions, and as to the newer question of what actions by students at a state or other public college or university may constitute such hostility to one religion or to all religions as to be impermissible under the color of "state action" which is applied to such institutions and their agents and activities; (2) student residence for voting; (3) libel against a student by a fellow-student; (4) motor vehicles on campus; and (5) campus regulations on dress and grooming, sometimes known as "the battle of the beards."

Compulsory Chapel Attendance

Incredible as it may seem today, in 1891, a third-year student at the University of Illinois was expelled for refusal to attend nonsectarian religious exercises in the university chapel.[1] Over the course of 80 years the issue has largely disappeared from academic life, but it has not entirely vanished.

---

1. *North* v. *University of Illinois,* 137 Ill. 296, 27 N.E. 54 (1891).

As recently as 1970 certain cadets at the U.S. Military Academy at West Point and certain midshipmen at the U.S. Naval Academy at Annapolis brought a class action seeking a declaratory judgment that the regulations of the academies requiring compulsory Sunday church or chapel attendance at Catholic, Protestant, or Jewish services were in violation of the First Amendment "establishment and free exercise" clauses, and of that part of Article VI of the U.S. Constitution which prohibits any "religious test."

District Judge Howard F. Corcoran of the district court of the District of Columbia denied the petition, but granted a permanent injunction to restrain the academy authorities from punishing the plaintiffs for their involvement in this suit. The point was made, that although attendance is required, participation is not. Cadets or midshipmen must be present, but need only be attentive and observant; no one is compelled to worship. Moreover, in April 1969 the superintendents issued a joint statement: "It is understood that intelligent provisions must be made for *bona fide* cases where attendance would be in conflict with sincerely held convictions of individual cadets or midshipmen."

The principal basis of the decision was authoritative testimony that the purpose of the requirement is solely secular; that is, it is an essential part of the training of leaders in the armed forces because it is necessary for them to observe and understand something of the parts played in the lives of many different individuals by religious impulses and influences. One can not lead men under conditions of stress or crisis, or maintain military morale in quieter circumstances, without some knowledge gained from this observation.

The opinion embodies scholarly sketches of the history of church and state in this country since colonial days, and of the differences between civil and military law. It concludes that the academy regulations are in harmony with the First Amendment and with the Article VI prohibition of test oaths.[2]

Neutrality Toward Religion in Student Activities in Public Institutions

In New York an Article 78 proceeding was brought to compel

---

2. *Anderson v. Laird*, (U.S.D.C., D.C.), 316 F. Supp. 1081 (1970).

Staten Island Community College and Richmond College (each a component of The City University of New York, governed by the Board of Higher Education of the City of New York) to enforce the Board's regulations prohibiting derogatory attacks on religion in student publications.

The Dolphin, student newspaper of S.I. Community College, had carried an article entitled "The Catholic Church—Cancer of Society," a vitriolic diatribe against Catholicism. *The Richmond Times,* student newspaper of Richmond College, had printed a shocking vilification of Jesus Christ.

Each paper had faculty advisers, was funded in part by mandatory student fees, received office space and telephones on campus, and was promoted in the official student handbook of its respective college. Under these circumstances, publication of the offending articles was a use of state and city property for attacks on religion, thus violating the neutrality required of such governments by the First and Fourteenth Amendments, thought Justice Vito J. Titone of the supreme court of Richmond County.[3]

The reasoning is that "State power is no more to be used so as to handicap religions, than it is to favor them." (Quoted from *Everson* v. *Board of Education of Ewing,* 330 U.S. 1, 67 S.Ct. 504, decided in 1946.) Continued Justice Titone: "The students, or anyone else, are perfectly free to hold views against religions, to voice these views and to publish them. They may not, however, use public facilities to do so."

As often happens, the justice was a trifle impatient with the nebulous wording of a 1959 resolution of the board of higher education that "student publications should be reminded by the faculty . . . that affronting a race, or religion in general, or the religion of a particular group, is incompatible with good citizenship, good journalism, and good academic behavior." He deduced: "The respondents have failed to enforce their own rules, assuming such rules do in fact preclude the publication of attacks on religion"; and concluded: "In any event, they are directed to prevent publication of such articles in the future, whether by enforcement of existing regulations, enactment of new ones, or otherwise."

Consider this decision in comparison with *Antonelli* v. *Hammond,*

---

3 *Panarella* v. *Birenbaum,* 60 Misc. 2d 95, 302 N.Y.S. 2d 427 (1969).

Dickey v. *Alabama State Board of Education,* and others in Chapter 16 herein, on "Freedom of the Student Press."

Shortly before a scheduled football game between the teams of Brigham Young University in Utah (a large private university owned and operated by the Church of Jesus Christ of Latter Day Saints) and the University of Wyoming, some 14 black members of the Wyoming squad adopted the idea of wearing black armbands in protest against the alleged racially discriminative practices of that church.

Head Coach Lloyd Eaton advised them of a coaching rule prohibiting members of the football squad from participating in any protests or demonstrations, and when they persisted in wearing the bands both on civilian clothing and on football uniforms, he dismissed them from the football squad. This led immediately to conversations among President William D. Carlson, Coach Eaton, and the players, and ultimately to a hearing of the matter before a special night meeting of the board of trustees, with the governor of Wyoming present, on the eve of the "big game." At this meeting, after all persons concerned had been heard and interrogated, the board deliberated and voted to dismiss the 14 men from the football team, but not to disturb their football scholarships or other student aids.

The 14 thus aggrieved thereupon sued in U.S. district court for a temporary restraining order and for compensatory damages of $75,000 each, aggregating $1,050,000, plus punitive damages of $50,000.

District Judge Ewing T. Kerr dismissed the complaint for several reasons: (1) All but one of the plaintiffs were non-residents of Wyoming, and the Eleventh Amendment prevents a suit against a state by a citizen of another state; and judicial extension produces the same result when a state is sued by one of its own citizens without its consent. (2) The complaint presented no cause on which recovery could be based; the plea for damages was speculative and insubstantial. (3) If Wyoming authorities had allowed the players to perform on the football field (a state-owned facility on which they would be in the capacity of agents of the university and the state), wearing armbands on their football uniforms in protest against the religious beliefs of the Mormon Church and of Brigham Young University, this would have been an overt violation of the constitutional mandate requiring neutrality of the state as to religion and non-religion and of the principle of separation of church and state.

The contention that the right to wear armbands in symbolic and peaceable demonstration was protected by the First, Ninth, and Fourteenth Amendments was put aside as indefensible in these circumstances, outranked by the First Amendment requirement of religious neutrality for states and public institutions.[4]

The Last of the Anti-Evolution Laws
Are Declared Unconstitutional

"It shall be unlawful for any teacher or other instructor in any university, college, normal, public school or other institution of the state which is supported in whole or in part from public funds derived by state or local taxation to teach that mankind ascended or descended from a lower order of animals. . . ." So runs Section 6798 of the *Mississippi* Code; and Section 6799 provides penalties.

On petition of a girl pupil studying biological science and wishing to pursue a scientific career, and alleging that this law deprived her of the right to learn, the Mississippi supreme court, in a unanimous decision delivered by Justice William H. Inzer, held the two sections unconstitutional and void and of no effect, as contrary to the freedom of religion mandate of the First Amendment and in violation of the Fourteenth Amendment.[5]

The Mississippi supreme court followed the doctrine of the United States Supreme Court decision of two years earlier which invalidated a similar anti-evolution statute in Arkansas. In that case the complainant was a teacher who feared that she would be penalized under the statute if she dared to teach up-to-date biological science. Although her emphasis was on academic freedom for teachers, this is, of course, inseparable from the same freedom for pupils; that is, the right to learn.

The opinion of the high court was delivered by Mr. Justice Abe Fortas. Mr. Justice Hugo L. Black and Mr. Justice John M. Harlan concurred in separate opinions, and Mr. Justice Potter Stewart concurred in the result only, preferring to base his opinion on somewhat more diverse reasons than did the other justices. The main thrust of the opinion of the court was that the anti-evolution law oversteps the

---

4. *Williams* v. *Eaton*, (U.S.D.C., Wyo.), 310 F. Supp. 1342 (1970).
5. *Smith* v. *State of Mississippi*, (Miss.), 242 So. 2d 692 (1970).

stance of neutrality between the state and religion which is required by the First Amendment as interpolated into the Fourteenth Amendment.

Mr. Justice Black, while concurring, expressed doubt that the issue really raised a justiciable question, due to the fact that although the act had been in the statute books of Arkansas for 40 years, apparently no attempt had ever been made to enforce it, and the alleged fears of the teacher-complainant were probably unfounded, or at best no more than highly speculative or conjectural. There is perhaps a good deal to be said for "letting sleeping dogs lie"; but there is an opposite theory that no one should rest while any statute posing a threat to constitutional liberties remains unchallenged, no matter if it is a "dead letter."

Mr. Justice Stewart based his opinion not only on the neutrality of the state toward religion, but thought the Arkansas statute also contravened the First Amendment guarantees of "free communication," and was also void for vagueness under the standards now required under the equal protection clause of the Fourteenth Amendment.[6]

Student Residence for Voting

Local election boards in university or college towns or townships frequently exert various pressures to prevent students who are qualified voters from casting ballots in these precincts, on the theory that they are entitled to vote only in the states or local subdivisions where their parental homes are located. Since the adoption of the Twenty-sixth Amendment in 1971, virtually all college students are of voting age, and the issue is perhaps more important than ever before.

One factor seems certain: married students who have their families with them and *have no voting residence elsewhere* and who have met the ordinary local and state waiting-period (varying from six months to a year in different states and usually about one month in the local subdivision) will vote locally. This was the irrefutable reasoning of the New York Court of Appeals in a 1947 decision holding that student veterans of World War II attending Columbia University and living with their wives and children in "Shanks Village," a former

---

6. *Epperson* v. *Arkansas,* 393 U.S. 97, 89 S.Ct. 266, 21 L.Ed. 2d 228 (1968); reversing 242 Ark. 922, 416 S.W. 2d 322 (1968).

military cantonment, for the duration of their periods as students, must be allowed to vote in the local subdivision (along with their wives and other adult relatives living with them) because otherwise they would be totally disenfranchised.[7]

Other courts in other states have often been less generous, as in an Arkansas case of 1949 where some 170 votes of student-veterans attending the University of Arkansas were thought to have swung the balance in a primary election contest in Fayetteville. There the court enunciated such rules as that requiring each such voter to declare, and provide evidence of, his intention to live in the college town after the completion of his studies; and that specifying one removing from a former home does not acquire a new voting domicile until after he has abandoned his old one—that no one can have two domiciles with a right to choose between them. This necessitated a one-by-one examination of the qualifications of each student voter.[8]

Since 1950 the U.S. Census Bureau has counted non-commuting college students as residents of the college town; and probably the tendency will be to reach some *modus vivendi* permitting them to cast their ballots there, though in many college towns, especially the smaller ones, some local elderly residents and real estate interests bitterly oppose letting the so-called "transients" have any substantial voice in deciding local issues. In the Illinois legislature of 1971 a bill was introduced which would have prohibited college and university students from voting locally; and an action is now pending in U.S. District Court in Alabama, brought by students at the University of Alabama, for an order entitling them to vote in the university town of Tuscaloosa.[9]

Many changes may occur in state statutes or in court rulings at different levels prior to the national elections of November 1972. At present (mid-1971) a wide variety exists. The California attorney general rules that unmarried voters under the age of 21 can not establish a voting residence other than at the home of their parents. But the state of Washington permits a student to vote in the college town if his intent is to live there "either permanently or indefinitely for an ap-

---

7. *Robbins* v. *Chamberlain*, 297 N.Y. 108, 75 N.E. 2d 617 (1947).
8. *Ptak* v. *Jameson*, (Ark.), 220 S.W. 2d 592 (1949).
9. *Harris* v. *Samuels*, Civ. Action No. 68-598-W, U.S.D.C., Northern District of Ala.

preciable period of time." In Vermont a student need only file a declaration that the college town is his residence.[10]

In July 1971 the press reported that the attorneys general of five
other states had issued opinions liberalizing the requirements for student voting in the college town, some of them declaring the student
had the option of using either his college residence or his parental
home as his voting domicile.

Libel Suit by One Student Against Another

At the University of Arizona a personal vendetta developed between a student newspaper editor and a third-year law student who
was a member of the student senate. The latter, in recrimination, advocated the cessation of the Associated Students subsidy to the student
newspaper (*The Wildcat*); and this was the inspiration for a scurrilous
editorial in which the student senator was called a campus demagogue,
and in which it was said he was "hissing in another pit" and emulating
Stalin, Hitler, and Mussolini in his efforts to kill the free press, and that
he was a "troublemaker and fanatic."

On the basis of that editorial the student senator brought a libel
action in the state courts against the editor and the faculty adviser of
the newspaper. His case was dismissed by the Pima County Superior
court, and the judgment affirmed by the Arizona court of appeals.
Judge John F. Molloy of the court of appeals thought: "If all actions
of libel similar to this must go to a full jury trial to ascertain whether
criticism by analogy, invective, and satire is believed 'in good faith' to
be 'true,' the light of freedom of speech and press as enunciated in
Sullivan v. *New York Times* will be frustrated. . . . While that decision concerns itself only with misstatements of fact, and holds they
can not be libelous unless uttered with knowledge of their falsity or in
reckless disregard of their truth, we can not read this and its successor
opinions without coming to the conclusion that a new charter for freedom of criticism of 'public officials' has been declared. We believe that
this charter includes the caustic criticism and biting ridicule exemplified by the subject editorial."[11]

---

10. John Elrod, "Student Voting Residence," *College Law Bulletin*, Vol. III,
No. 9 (May 1971), pp. 89-91.

11. *Klahr* v. *Winterle*, 4 Ariz. App. 158, 418 P. 2d 404 (1966). The citation of
Sullivan v. *New York Times* is 376 U.S. 254, 84 S.Ct. 710, 11 L.Ed. 2d 686 (1964).

Motor Vehicles on Campus

Probably everyone has heard that a modern university is "a collection of colleges and departments held together by a common parking problem." A large educational institution resembles a city in many respects, and, as in cities, regulation of traffic on the campus is a perpetual puzzle, unavoidably involving petty frustrations for many persons.

A Mississippi statute (Section 6726.7, *Mississippi Code of 1942*) authorized the board of trustees of state institutions of higher learning to control traffic on all state university and college campuses, and provided for punishment of violations of rules thus promulgated as misdemeanors before the local justices of the peace, with maximum penalty being a fine of $100 or imprisonment for not to exceed 30 days, or both. A student at Mississippi State University, who was a chronic accumulator of petty parking violations, unsuccessfully challenged the constitutionality of the statute before a federal special three-judge district court, principally on the ground that it was allegedly an unconstitutional delegation of legislative power, and that it was insufficiently specific in its terms.

It seems that the then current regulations of the board on this subject dated from 1954 and continued in force. Meantime, in 1958 and later, the administration of Mississippi State University had issued extensive modifications of the 1954 rules for this university only and without the concurrence of the board (which is the governing board for all the institutions). These additions afforded violators the option of being charged before the local justice of the peace as provided in the statute, or of being heard before the university disciplinary authorities. The evident purpose was to speed up the process and obviate funneling all cases through the criminal court of the justice of the peace.

Before trial in the three-judge federal court, however, all parties agreed that the attempted modifications of 1958 and later were of no legal effect, could not affect the constitutionality of the statute or the regulations of 1954, and would not be enforced against the plaintiff in this case, who was charged under them. This washed out most of his

---

It is discussed at pages 49-50 in *The Colleges and the Courts, 1962-1966*. Danville, Ill.: The Interstate Printers & Publishers, Inc., 1967. 326 pp.

grievances and left only the simple question of the constitutionality of the statute.

Circuit Judge John R. Brown, joined by District Judges Claude F. Clayton and Dan M. Russell, Jr., thought the statute appropriate for its purposes and not in contravention of either the United States or Mississippi constitutions.[12]

At West Texas State University, a student, who speeded at 60 miles an hour on a campus street restricted to 20 miles per hour because of much pedestrian crossing, was then placed on disciplinary probation by the university and prohibited temporarily from driving on campus or in the city of Canyon. The next night he drove at excessive speed in the city and was apprehended by a city patrolman. Nine days later he was given a hearing by the university disciplinary committee, which voted unanimously to recommend that he be indefinitely suspended from the university. After his suspension he asked the local trial court to order his reinstatement by writ of *mandamus*, which was granted; but the judgment was soon reversed by the Court of Civil Appeals, saying:

"From all the authorities cited and the facts of the case, we hold the officers of West Texas State University, in the exercise of the discretion vested in them, had the authority to invoke the indefinite suspension and that the trial court exceeded its authority in issuing the writ of *mandamus*."

The rule requiring "high standards of adult behavior," said the court, was reasonable, and in this case was reasonably interpreted and applied.[13]

A young man residing in Lafayette, Louisiana, entered the Louisiana State University at Baton Rouge, paid a 10 dollar fee to register his car and had a windshield sticker attached. Two nights later hurricane winds broke his windshield, and he returned the car to a Lafayette garage to obtain replacement, and drove his father's automobile back to the campus. Within three days he received three tickets because his automobile had no windshield sticker. He drove this car back to Lafayette to pick up his own car. After again arriving on campus he discovered that the sticker had not been placed on the replacement wind-

---

12. *Cohen* v. *Mississippi State University*, (U.S.D.C., Miss.), 256 F. Supp. 954 (1966).

13. *Cornette* v. *Aldridge*, (Tex. Civ. App.), 408 S.W. 2d 935 (1966).

shield, as he had directed the mechanic to do. Before he could drive back to Lafayette to retrieve the sticker he received another ticket on his car. As a result of the four tickets he was fined $18 and banned from using an automobile on the campus for four and a half months. He sought to have this penalty lifted by injunction in the local trial court, but without success.

His attorney then asked the Court of Appeal for a writ of *certiorari*, which the court granted, and ordered the university authorities to show cause why they should not answer certain questions put to them in the trial court (in an effort to develop a factual basis for a class action). Subsequently the same court recalled its own writ and remanded the case for trial on the merits, having decided after further study that there was no basis for a class action.[14]

The New York Education Law (Section 356) provides: "Subject to the general management, supervision, control and approval of, and in accordance with rules established by the state university trustees, the council of each state-operated institution shall . . . exercise the following powers:

c. Make regulations governing the care, custody and management of lands, grounds, buildings and equipment.

g. Make regulations governing the conduct and behavior of students."

Justice D. Ormond Ritchie of the Suffolk County supreme court has decided that the foregoing authorizes control of traffic and parking on campus, in a case brought by a student at the State University at Stony Brook, whose automobile had been impounded by the university and held to force him to pay parking tickets for past violations. Reading the rules then in force on that campus, the court found they did not authorize impounding for that purpose. (The plaintiff's vehicle had been returned to him before trial by agreement of the parties.) An injunction was issued to restrain the university from impounding motor vehicles pending payment of penalties for past violations. However, the decision expressly did not prohibit the university from towing cars parked in violation of regulations and retaining possession until the towing charges are paid.[15]

---

14. *Trice* v. *Barnette, Judge,* (La. App.), 194 So. 2d 452 (1967).
15. *Drysdale* v. *State University of New York at Stony Brook,* 60 Misc. 2d 180, 302 N.Y.S. 2d 882 (1969).

The State University of New York at Stony Brook has been ordered by the local trial court to cease its former practice of charging $4 for "parking permits" and using the money to pay a "traffic coordinator" and two of his four assistants. The three were appointed to their jobs by a faculty-student association, outside the civil service system. A civil service employee sued to enjoin collection of the fee because, he said, this arrangement was in violation of Article 5, Section 6 of the state constitution:

"Appointments and promotions in the civil service of the state and all of the civil divisions thereof, including cities and villages, shall be made according to merit and fitness to be ascertained, as far as practicable, by examination which, as far as practicable, shall be competitive. . . ."

Justice William R. Geiler of the Suffolk County supreme court agreed that "The State University of New York at Stony Brook can not collect fees for the support of employment which is contrary to and in violation of the mandate of the State Constitution," and granted a permanent injunction against the practice.[16]

Dress and Grooming Regulations:
The Battle of the Beards

Possibly the earliest federal decision regarding the hair styles of male college students was that of Ray Zachry, Jr., and Robert Alexander, aged 18 and 19, who were admitted to Jefferson State Junior College in Alabama for the academic year 1966-67. Both were members of a popular band called "The Distortions." All members of the band wore "page-boy" haircuts. On October 19, 1966, Zachry and Alexander were notified by president Leroy Brown of the junior college that they were "administratively withdrawn"—a euphemism for suspended—for failing to conform to rules pertaining to permissable hair styles for male students, having declined to have their hair cut to conform to conventional standards.

Neither had ever been a disciplinary problem at home or at school. Each ranked within the top 10 per cent nationally on the col-

---

16. *Varacchi* v. *State University of New York at Stony Brook*, 62 Misc. 2d 1003, 310 N.Y.S. 2d 751 (1970).

lege entrance examination. Each had a substantial income from the earnings of the band, and attended the college because of its outstanding department of music. There was no testimony that their hair style had any deleterious effects on the good order, health, safety, and decorum of the college. Chief District Judge Seybourn H. Lynne granted an injunction against their suspension.

"The notion that officials of a state-supported college have a right to dismiss students at any time for any reason . . . was emphatically rejected," he said, in *Dixon* v. *Alabama*, 294 F. 2d 150 (1961). "This court is of the firm opinion that the classification of male students . . . by their hair style is unreasonable and fails to pass constitutional muster."[17]

Carlos Calbillo, a student in good standing at the San Jacinto Junior College, was indefinitely suspended solely because he had grown a beard in violation of the college regulation: "Male students at San Jacinto College are required to wear reasonable hair styles and to have no beards or excessively long sideburns."

When he asked for an injunction to accomplish his reinstatement, Federal District Judge John V. Singleton, Jr., concluded:

"From the record before the Court, it can come to no other conclusion than that the regulation in question constitutes an unreasonable classification in violation of the equal protection clause of the Fourteenth Amendment. There was no evidence of any material and substantial disruption of the school functions, and the justifications offered by the school officials do not support the rule. . . . To continue to deny plaintiff an education by the enforcement of this unconstitutional rule would cause him irreparable harm and consequently the injunctive relief he seeks should be granted."[18]

The court could not refrain from referring to the remark of the sage Senior Circuit Judge Elbert Parr Tuttle, who dissented vigorously in an earlier case upholding the regulation of the hair styles of high school pupils by the school authorities of Dallas:

"It does seem as though this issue is something of a tempest in a teapot. However, we are faced with the problem of three teen-age

---

17. *Zachry* v. *Brown*, (U.S.D.C., Ala.), 299 F. Supp. 1360 (1967).
18. *Calbillo* v. *San Jacinto Junior College*, (U.S.D.C., Tex.), 305 F. Supp. 857 (1969). *Remanded* for consideration of mootness, (U.S.C.A., Tex.), 434 F. 2d 609 (1970).

school children being denied a high school education because the length of their hair did not suit the school authorities."[19]

The college appealed the Calbillo case, and before it came to decision in the Eighth Circuit Court of Appeals in 1970, Carlos had shaved his beard and withdrawn from the college, and his record had been changed to delete all reference to his expulsion. Therefore, the court remanded it, with direction to "consider whether the controversy is now moot, whether it continues appropriate to enjoin the college from enforcing, in whole or in part, the regulation against all students, and to provide the college with opportunity to revise its regulations so that they are clearly related to the maintenance of reasonable discipline and decorum."

In January 1970 a revised dress code was adopted at the Chadron State College in Nebraska. The part material here was as follows:

"Male students will wear their hair short enough that eyebrows, ears, and collars are in full view. Sideburns will be no lower than the ear lobe, and mustaches will be trimmed even with the mouth."

Robert E. Reichenberg, Jr., John S. Streep, and Donald Hume, all students in good standing, were rejected as registrants for the second semester for alleged violation of this rule. Senior District Judge Robert Van Pelt held a hearing upon their application for a restraining order, and ordered that the three students be allowed to register.[20] In the course of his opinion, he quoted the words of Circuit Judge Otto Kerner in the 1969 decision of the Seventh Circuit holding that high school students could not be expelled solely because of their hair styles:

"The right to wear one's hair at any length or in any desired manner is an ingredient of personal freedom protected by the United States Constitution."[21] (Judge Kerner's majority opinion had affirmed the judgment of District Judge James E. Doyle.)

These decisions are undoubtedly the wave of the future, at least so far as college students are concerned. There have been many decisions regarding high school pupils, and there is considerable variance of opinion and division of authority among them; but there are signs

19. Dissenting opinion in *Farrell* v. *Dallas Independent School District*, (U.S.C.A., Tex.), 392 F. 2d 697 (1968).

20. *Reichenberg* v. *Nelson*, (U.S.D.C., Nebr.), 310 F. Supp. 248 (1970).

21. Majority opinion in *Breen* v. *Kahl*, (U.S.C.A., Wis.), 419 F. 2d 1034 (1969); affirming (U.S.D.C., Wis.), 296 F. Supp. 702 (1969).

that the doctrine of *Breen* v. *Kahl* will ultimately prevail, at least unless evidence of proximate disruptions appears.

"Three long-haired young men," students at the Tyler Junior College in Texas, sued to enjoin the operation and enforcement against them of a comprehensive "Dress Code" which had been adopted by the college board of trustees shortly before the start of the academic year 1970-71. U. S. District Judge William Wayne Justice granted a temporary injunction and ordered the suit maintained as a class action.

On the merits, he pointed out that the testimony of the college officials consisted largely of hearsay to the effect that long-haired students had been disruptive at various other colleges, and therefore all long-haired students are disruptive. "I am unwilling to accept a syllogism so perverse and jejune as this to justify the humiliating restrictions which this regulation would place on the plaintiffs." One of the three was a Vietnam veteran, aged 22, a "straight A" student whose conduct was never questioned by college authorities. His hair reached his shoulders. All three had long hair, clean and neatly kept. Each said he wore long hair for fashion and personal expression. All disclaimed any religious, political, or moral reasons for the style. Judge Justice cited several federal decisions, including that of Judge Lynne in the case discussed herein, and half a dozen involving regulated hair length in high schools. He stated: "The right of students to free choice of hair styles granted other citizens has been upheld in cases involving the First, Ninth, and Fourteenth Amendments," and concluded, "This regulation, designed to eliminate all male students with long hair as a deterrent to disruption, is unreasonable, discriminatory, and void."[22]

Lindahl King, Mark Carlson, and Michael Martin were refused registration for a forthcoming term at Saddleback Junior College until they complied with a regulation which proscribed "hair which falls below the eyebrows, or covers all or part of the ear, or hangs entirely over the collar of a dress shirt." U.S. District Judge Harry Pregerson granted a preliminary injunction restraining the college from refusing to register them and from refusing to allow them to enter classes.

The Ninth Circuit Court of Appeals vacated the injunction and remanded the case for further proceedings. Said Circuit Judge Ozell M. Trask, sitting with Circuit Judges Frederick G. Hamley and

---

22. *Lansdale* v. *Tyler Junior College*, (U.S.D.C., Tex.), 318 F. Supp. 529 (1970).

Eugene A. Wright: "It is the function of a preliminary injunction to preserve the *status quo* pending a determination of the action on the merits. Here the students had not yet begun the forthcoming term. The preliminary injunction went beyond the preservation of the then existing *status quo* and decreed that they should be permitted to register in violation of the regulation and prior to a determination of its validity. On this the court abused its discretion."[23]

The opinion introduced a novel suggestion: presumably the rule could be complied with by the use of headbands without cutting the hair, and thus would not prevent the boys from registering; and the court thought ultimate success on the merits of the complaint was doubtful—another factor inhibiting a preliminary injunction.

At the Southern Maine Vocational-Technical School in South Portland (a two-year post-high-school institution), three male students were expelled for wearing beards in contravention of a school rule. U.S. District Judge Edward Thaxter Gignoux denied them any relief, because the argument for the rule was that it was very influential in maintaining a good "image" of the school in the eyes of prospective employers of its graduates. Three-fourths of the graduates went immediately into remunerative work, and this was the main purpose of the school. Judge Gignoux believed that because of the school's interest in advancing the economic welfare of its students and because the hair and beard rules were reasonably calculated to further that interest, the vocational-technical school had sustained its "substantial burden of justification" which is required to save a rule of this kind from unconstitutionality.[24]

The foregoing six cases exhibit a considerable variety of thought. Among the jurists participating have been, among others, Circuit Judges Kerner, Tuttle, Trask, Hamley, and Wright; and District Judges Lynne, Singleton, Doyle, Van Pelt, Justice, Pregerson, and Gignoux. One would say the preponderance of judicial authority favors the invalidity of hair and beard rules in college.

---

23. *King* v. *Saddleback Junior College District*, (U.S.C.A., Cal.), 425 F. 2d 426 (1970).

24. *Farrell* v. *Smith*, (U.S.D.C., Me.), 310 F. Supp. 732 (1970).

CHAPTER 9

COLLEGE DORMITORY RESIDENTS

A MULTIPLICITY OF QUESTIONS may arise as to the rights and obligations of students as dwellers in college or university dormitories. Among these are: (1) Under what circumstances and for what reasons may a student or a designated class of students be required to live in college-operated housing? (2) Precisely what are the rights of a college dormitory resident guaranteed under the Fourth Amendment protection against unreasonable searches and seizures? (3) Will a court, on the petition of a parent of a dormitory resident, nullify changes in college rules which relax the former strictness of parietal regulations and permit bisexual "intervisitation" in dormitory rooms?

Over the decades, as almost everyone knows, the freedom of dormitory residents tends to be broadened. In one of the earlier cases, in which a student who refused to sign an agreement not to be a participant in any continuation of prolonged disorder in a dormitory was summarily evicted from the building (but not expelled or suspended from college), he had no recourse for "damages for unjustifiable humiliation"; and the Missouri supreme court went on to say a college dormitory resident has not the legal rights of a tenant, nor even those of an ordinary lodger.[1] More than 40 years later, in 1970, a Pennsylvania superior court judge said: "A dormitory room is analogous to an

---

1. *Engelhardt* v. *Serena*, 318 Mo. 263, 300 S.W. 268 (1927).

apartment or a hotel room," in setting aside a criminal conviction based on evidence obtained by an unlawful entry into the room by state police officers.

When May Dormitory Residence Be
Required in Public Colleges?

The general practice of requiring designated classes of students to reside in college-operated dormitories has sometimes been challenged by private restaurateurs and rooming-house keepers in the past, always unsuccessfully, whether in state or federal courts.[2] One such case was decided by a United States district court in Oklahoma and affirmed by the United States Supreme Court in 1952. The District Court declared:

"The state has a decided interest in the education, well-being, morals, health, safety, and convenience of its youth. When a situation arises where it becomes necessary to expend great sums for buildings to house students, it is within the power of the state acting through an administrative agency to provide such facilities, and when it is necessary for rules to be passed to provide payment for such buildings in further-ance of the object to be accomplished, such rules will be valid as a means accompanying the over-all policy of furnishing the needed facilities."[3]

The court concluded that there was no deprivation of rights, and no unlawful discrimination involved.

Something of a shock to the established doctrine was a federal dis-trict court decision in 1969 which held that unmarried girl students in the upper three classes at Southeastern Louisiana College, a coeduca-tional state institution, could not lawfully be required to live in campus residence halls while others were allowed to live off campus, where the only reason given was to fill dormitory vacancies and thereby raise sufficient revenue to keep solvent the self-liquidating plan under which construction of the dormitories was financed.

This would be a denial of equal protection of the laws under the Fourteenth Amendment, concluded District Judge Cassibry. The de-cision was based entirely upon pecuniary considerations. The pleadings

---

2. For example: *Hoyt* v. *Trustees of State Normal School,* 96 Colo. 442, 44 P. 2d 513 (1935).

3. *Pyeatte* v. *Board of Regents of University of Oklahoma,* (U.S.D.C., Okla.), 102 F. Supp. 407 (1952); affirmed in 342 U.S. 936, 72 S.Ct. 567, 96 L.Ed. 696 (1952).

of the college, and the testimony of college officials (ineptly, one must believe) contained no hint of any reason for the rule other than the financial one. The judge took brief notice of the usual educational and welfare reasons for dormitory living, even though they were not pleaded; but, confining himself to the pleadings, said:

"The sole issue in this case, on the other hand, is whether the college may require a certain group of students to live on-campus, not for the welfare of the students themselves but simply to increase the revenue of the housing system." Holding to the monetary aspect, he continued: "In effect, it is a requirement that some students must pay while others need not. Why should the particular students who are the plaintiffs in this case bear any more of the financial obligation of the college housing system than any of their fellow-students?"[4]

District Judge Cassibry added: "To select a group less-than-all, to fulfill an obligation which should fall equally on all, is a violation of equal protection no matter how the group is selected. Since the obligation is essentially *monetary*, then all must pay or none." Apparently, in an effort to prevent his opinion from being interpreted overbroadly, he appended a final footnote: "This case neither raises nor decides the issue of whether, apart from the equal protection issue, it is a valid exercise of a state university's power to dictate to a student where he shall live, not for reasons having anything to do with the student's welfare or the educational appropriateness of the place chosen, but simply for the purpose of increasing revenue to support the university housing system. This question has neither been briefed nor argued by the parties." The total effect of the decision is thus circumscribed.

Two Decisions of 1970 Reach Different Results

One of these was by a special three-judge federal court in another district of Louisiana, and involved Louisiana Polytechnic Institute, another of the several institutions governed by the State Board of Education. The board rule was that "all unmarried full-time undergraduate students, regardless of age or whether or not emancipated," must live in on-campus residence halls as long as space is available. Provisions were included for exemptions for returning military veterans, previously

---

4. *Mollere* v. *Southeastern Louisiana College*, (U.S.D.C., La.), 304 F. Supp. 826 (1969).

married persons, and cases of significant hardship. A companion resolution established priorities for the granting of additional exemptions when feasible.

The majority of the court, in an opinion by Chief District Judge Benjamin C. Dawkins, Jr., sustained the validity and constitutionality of the rules. The board had argued that dormitory living has unquestionable educational values, and submitted affidavits from eminent educators in many parts of the country to support this plea. Judge Dawkins responded with a paragraph which is reminiscent of the words of the federal district court in Oklahoma of 18 years earlier, quoted previously in this chapter:

"When one considers the fully adequate facilities that are provided by such rules and the thousands upon thousands of students throughout the country who are able to obtain a higher education only because of such facilities, reasonably priced, and thus the national objective toward achieving a better educated society is fulfilled more easily, certainly it can not be seriously contended that the parietal rules are unreasonable, arbitrary or capricious."

As to the argument that compulsory dormitory living would be a violation of the Fourth Amendment right of privacy, he continued: "Even assuming, however, that a 'fundamental' right is involved, we believe there is a compelling state interest to assure that its college-age citizens are properly educated; and if housing, eating, and student life facilities are a vital part of that process, as we think they are, we hold there is no violation of the equal protection clause."[5]

District Judge Edwin F. Hunter, Jr., wrote an opinion concurring in the result, stating that he did not believe there was enough color of a federal question to justify a three-judge court. An acrid dissent was entered by Circuit Judge Robert A. Ainsworth, Jr., who thought the board rules in question "violate the First Amendment right of students to come and go as they please, associate with whomever they desire, and live with whom they choose. . . . As to those students under 21 years of age who are still minors and therefore under parental authority, the

---

5. *Pratz* v. *Louisiana Polytechnic Institute,* 316 F. Supp. 872 (U.S.D.C., La.) 1970. Summarily affirmed by the United States Supreme Court, 39 *U.S. Law Week* 3433 (April 6, 1971): "Louisiana State Board of Education's parietal regulations requiring students in state-supported colleges and universities to live and eat their meals in facilities provided by these institutions are constitutional. (Judgment affirmed.)"

mandates are an unwarranted interference with the right of parents to decide whether they wish their college-age children to live in campus dormitories or off-campus. Communal life is therefore imposed by a state agency and is involuntary. . . ."

It should be noticed that the facts and the pleadings in this case were not precisely the same as those in the *Mollere Case* of 1969, previously cited. Therefore it is not possible to say there is a direct clash between the opinion of Judge Cassibry in that case and those of the two majority judges in this Pratz Case, though they reach opposite results on the "equal protection" issue.

Private Developers of Student Housing Have No Recourse Against a University

In earlier decades it was restaurateurs and keepers of rooming houses who complained in vain that college rules were ruining their businesses. In 1970 it was builders of huge private dormitories. The partners in such a firm, having in 1964 invested substantial sums to build and operate a 300-bed private "Student House" near the campus of Northern Illinois University, came into court five years later lamenting that they were losing money, and claiming that the university had told them that if private capital would meet the student housing needs, the university would not build any more dormitories; but instead, each year the university-owned student housing capacity had been increased by 1,000 beds, and that the university was presently negotiating for the purchase of an existing 1,000-bed dormitory. With straight faces, they asked the court to enjoin the university from building or otherwise acquiring any more housing space.

It turned out that there was no evidence that they had ever had communication with the university's governing board or any member thereof, or with its presidents. The alleged promises had come only from certain middle- and lower-echelon staff members who were quite obviously without authority to make any such representations. Judge Samuel B. Epstein of the Cook County circuit court rendered summary judgment for the university; and on direct appeal to the supreme court of Illinois the outcome was the same.[6]

---

6. *Student House, Inc.* v. *Board of Regents of Regency Universities*, (Ill.), 254 N.E. 2d 496 (1969).

Challenges to Dormitory Rules

A United States District Court decision in Massachusetts was unequivocal. A student challenged three dormitory rules at Westfield
State College, all unsuccessfully.

One rule required all students either to live in a dormitory, or with
parents or relatives, or "in a situation previously approved by the college." The college had reached this conclusion after making a detailed
study of housing conditions in its vicinity. The district court said: "The
regulation is one made in good faith and on rational grounds, is reasonably related to valid educational purposes, and involves no arbitrary
and unreasonable classification."

Another rule provided for search of students' rooms by an official
of the college when deemed necessary. Said the court: "Of course a
student can not be required, as a condition for attending college, to
waive either expressly or impliedly his rights under the Fourth Amendment. However, that amendment forbids not all searches, but only unreasonable ones. Clearly there may be circumstances in which the college authorities are entitled to exercise a right of reasonable search. The
regulation in question is on its face no more than a notice that the
authorities reserve the right to conduct such a search in special circumstances." (For decisions regarding searches and seizures, see Chapter 10,
herein.)

Another rule prohibited residents of the dormitories from "associat-
ing with persons of the opposite sex in their rooms." The court recognized that this regulation was stricter than the similar regulations at
some other educational institutions, yet its subject matter was clearly
a proper one for some regulation by the college; the college has "the
right and indeed the duty to adopt reasonable regulations to maintain
order and discipline and promote an environment conducive to the educational development of the students"; and found that the rule was
for valid purposes relevant to the educational purposes of the institution, and imposed a reasonable limitation on student activities."[7]

Students at the College of William and Mary in Virginia, after having been suspended for two violations of the "no intervisitation" rule
for the college dormitories, sought from the federal district court a
permanent injunction to restrain the college from excluding them. Said

---

7. *Lynch* v. *Savignano*, (U.S.D.C., Mass.), Civ. Action No. 70-375-F (October
6, 1970).

the opinion: "This Court specifically finds no substantial invalidity of a properly drawn 'no visitation' rule. And this Court in no wise doubts the right of the College to discipline a violation, even to the extent of suspension from school, if the extent of the penalty is made the subject of proper notice."

However, it was decided that in this case the suspensions, having been made in a near-summary manner, had not met the requirements of due process as recently defined; which is a quite different matter from the substantive rights of the parties: "After a lengthy hearing, involving many witnesses, . . . this Court finds that procedural due process, guaranteed to petitioners under the Fourteenth Amendment, has been violated and that the injunction . . . should issue." Thus the students, defeated on the substantive issue, in this case won reinstatement on the point of defective disciplinary procedure alone.[8]

For decisions defining procedural due process in disciplinary cases, see Chapter 17 herein.

What of the Custodial, Proctorial, or Chaperonage Responsibility of the College Through Its Dormitory Supervisors?

Occasionally the parents of college students allege that their offspring have come to disaster as a proximate result of some negligence on the part of dormitory supervisors, and seek damages either for breach of contract or in tort.

A girl student of minor age at the University of Cincinnati, it was alleged, lived in a university dormitory in which supervision was so loose that she was continuously absent for several successive days before the fact was noticed; and it eventually turned out that she had been murdered. Her father sued the university for damages, asserting that it had negligently allowed his daughter to become associated with criminals, to be seduced, to become a drug user, and had failed to return her to the custody of her parents on demand.

The Common Pleas Court of Hamilton County, Ohio dismissed the suit: "In our opinion plaintiffs completely misconstrue the duties and functions of a university. A university is an institution for the ad-

---

8. *Buehler* v. *College of William and Mary*, (U.S.D.C., Va.), Civ. Action No. 62-70-NN, Eastern District of Va., April 6, 1971.

vancement of knowledge and learning. It is neither a nursery school, a boarding school, nor a prison. No one is required to attend. Persons who meet the required qualifications and who abide by the university's rules and regulations are permitted to attend and must be presumed to have sufficient maturity to conduct their own personal affairs.

"We know of no requirement of the law and none has been cited to us placing on a university or its employees any duty to regulate the private lives of their students, to control their comings and goings and to supervise their associations." (An appeal was noted, March 24, 1971.)[9]

The father of a 20-year-old girl student at Mills College in California complained that the college represented in its catalog and student handbook that students would be required to adhere strictly to rules governing signing in and out of the dormitories when away from campus between 6 p.m. and closing hours, and completing a card when they planned to be away from campus overnight. Actually, he alleged, these rules were not enforced; and upon his discovery of that fact, the college failed to release his daughter to his custody to live in the family home. For these reasons, he averred, the college had intentionally inflicted emotional distress upon him, unlawfully interfered with the father-daughter relationship, and engaged in intentional misrepresentation and fraud.

The college responded with a demurrer (an answer stating that even if all the allegations of fact in the complaint be taken as true, they are insufficient to constitute a cause of action). The court sustained the demurrer and gave the plaintiff 20 days in which to amend his complaint if he so chose.[10]

Relaxing of Parietal Rules

The reluctance of courts to invade the realm of discretion of the college authorities when no question of constitutional rights is involved is illustrated in a 1969 case in which the mother of certain female students at Vassar College was much disturbed by the change in parietal rules to allow unlimited visiting hours by males, and sued for a declaratory judgment and injunctive relief to prevent Vassar from adopting

---

9. *Hegel* v. *Langman*, Hamilton County, Ohio, Common Pleas No. A-245986, March 23, 1971. Appeal noted, March 24, 1971.

10. *Gunston* v. *Mills College of Oakland*, Alameda County, Cal. Superior Court, No. 411661, April 28, 1971.

that change. The case was summarily dismissed by Justice W. Vincent Grady of the Dutchess County supreme court, who said:

"Vassar College, like other previously all-female institutions, has succumbed to the trend of co-education and with the advent of males, new difficulties will be encountered by the college administration. It is the privilege of the college, through its Student Government Association, to promulgate and enforce rules and regulations for the social conduct of students without judicial interference."

A declaratory judgment would not be justified, he thought, because the court could not substitute its judgment as to the propriety of the rules for that of the administrative body; and an injunction forbidding unlimited visiting hours for males could not be issued because there was no showing of any immediate or prospective irreparable damage, and mere speculation as to possible consequences is not sufficient.[11]

Temporary Detention of a Young Girl Resident of a Dormitory for Her Own Safety May Be a Tort

Saralee Maniaci, a girl of 16 years, left her home in Windsor, Ontario, Canada, in September 1966 to become a student at Marquette University in Milwaukee. She carried a check for $2,000 to be used to pay the year's expenses. She was immediately installed in Heraty Hall, a dormitory. During the ensuing weeks she became increasingly dissatisfied. She was bored with her courses, unhappy with the social life. Frequently on week-ends she traveled to her home in Windsor in the company of a 32-year-old former priest whom she had known since childhood. Repeatedly she told her parents of her desire to leave Marquette. Her father persuaded her that things would get better, and advised her to give the school another chance.

Apparently, after such a visit at the end of October, she returned with the idea that if things did not work out, she would have her parents' permission to come home. November 2 she decided to go home, and told her closest friend, Jean Huby, whereupon Jean wanted to leave too, and asked to go with her to her home in Windsor, because she thought if she went to her own home her father would send her back to Marquette. Saralee acceded and promised Jean she would not tell anyone where they were going. The next morning she withdrew her

---

11. *Jones* v. *Vassar College*, 59 Misc. 2d 296, 299 N.Y.S. 2d 283 (1969).

$1,300 deposit at the bank, went to the railroad station and purchased two tickets to Detroit (Detroit and Windsor are virtually twin cities), and returned to her dormitory and began packing.

Word soon reached the dean of women and the dormitory head resident, who immediately notified her father that his daughter was intending to run away from school to marry an older man. Her father, upon learning that the "older man" was the former priest, said there must be some mistake, and declared he would approve whatever plans the former priest had.

The next morning the head resident told Saralee to report to the office of the dean of women. When she failed to report, the dean and an assistant dean went to Heraty Hall to persuade her to continue in school. She admitted that she intended to leave by train that evening and refused to state her destination. She did not say that she had, in fact, her father's permission to leave. She gave many reasons for leaving, including a desire to act, sing, and write, and a belief that she was more mature than the fellow-students whom she knew. About noon the dean of women decided that the student health physician should be called, and at 1:30 he arrived, accompanied by a nurse.

At 3:30 the physician suggested that Saralee be hospitalized. City police were called and asked to bring the papers for her temporary detention under the emergency provisions of a Wisconsin statute that permits such detention for not to exceed five days, of any person certified by a physician and two other persons as "having a mental illness, is in need of hospitalization, and is irresponsible and dangerous to himself and others." She was taken to the Milwaukee County General Hospital, to a locked ward, where she was confined with several other females for mental observation. The police officers said they had intelligent conversation with her and that she was cooperative and showed no tendencies toward violence.

She persuaded a social worker at the hospital to notify the former priest of her predicament. He arrived at the hospital at 11 p.m. and was allowed to talk with her when she told the nurse he was her fiancé. He immediately relayed the message to her father, who promptly telephoned the physician and insisted that his daughter be released. She was released at about 9:00 the next morning. She went to her dormitory, gathered up her belongings and departed for Windsor.

Later a suit for damages for false imprisonment was begun against four defendants—Marquette University, the dean of women, the physician, and the nurse. A jury gave a general verdict for the plaintiff, and after the awards of damages had been somewhat reduced by the judge, they stood as: compensatory damages, $5,000; punitive damages, Marquette University, $12,000; the physician $2,000; the dean of women, $1,000; and the nurse, $1. Appeal was taken to the supreme court of Wisconsin.

Justice Nathan S. Heffernan's review reached the conclusion that the complaint did not state a cause of action for false arrest, nor for malicious prosecution. The complaint, the court decided, could only be for the tort of "abuse of process," which is defined as "use of a legal process, whether criminal or civil, against another to accomplish a purpose for which it is not designed." This creates liability for the pecuniary loss caused thereby. Hence the judgment in favor of Saralee was reversed and remanded for a new trial on the newly pleaded cause of action.[12]

---

12. *Maniaci* v. *Marquette University*, (Wis.), 184 N.W. 2d 168 (1971).

CHAPTER 10

UNREASONABLE SEARCHES
AND SEIZURES

"THE RIGHT OF THE PEOPLE to be secure in their persons, houses, papers, and effects, against unreasonable searches and seizures, shall not be violated . . ." What is the application of the Fourth Amendment guarantee to searches of dormitory rooms occupied by resident students, or lockers, automobiles, or personal luggage used by students?

The recent classic litigation occurred in a federal district court in Alabama. Without a search warrant, two state narcotics agents, acting upon information regarding the possible presence of marijuana in certain dormitory rooms at Troy State University, searched a student's room in his presence and without his consent. They were accompanied by the dean of men. Marijuana was found in the room, and university disciplinary proceedings followed. The student went to court to challenge these *disciplinary proceedings;* not to challenge any arrest or criminal process. Here again the sharp distinction between the university's disciplinary power and the state's criminal jurisdiction is important.

Distinction Between College Discipline and Criminal Investigation

Sustaining the reasonableness of the search in this case, Chief

District Judge Frank M. Johnson, Jr., decided that a balance must be struck between the student's Fourth Amendment rights and the interest of the institution in maintaining discipline in the educational process:

"The student is subject only to reasonable rules and regulations, but his rights must yield to the extent that they would interfere with the institution's fundamental duty to operate the school as an educational institution. A reasonable right of inspection is necessary to the institution's performance of that duty even though it may infringe on the outer boundaries of a dormitory student's Fourth Amendment rights." He also said: "The constitutional boundary line between the right of the school authorities to search and the right of a dormitory student to privacy must be based on a reasonable belief on the part of the college authorities that a student is using a dormitory room for a purpose which would otherwise seriously interfere with campus discipline . . ."; and, "This standard of 'reasonable cause to believe' to justify a search by college administrators—even when the sole purpose is to seek evidence of suspected violations of law—is lower than the constitutionally protected criminal law standard of 'probable cause.' This is true because of the student-college relationship and because college disciplinary proceedings are not criminal proceedings in the constitutional sense."[1]

Two years later this decision was followed by another by the same judge, and involving the same institution, in which the foregoing distinction was made all the more clear. The facts of this 1970 case were somewhat different. After asking for and obtaining the cooperation of the university, the search was made by state agents accompanied, in one instance, by city police; marijuana was found, and the students were arrested, prosecuted, and convicted. The students then asked the federal court to set aside their convictions because the evidence used against them in their trial had been unlawfully obtained. District Judge Johnson decided that the state and city police officers making the search should have first obtained search warrants from a magistrate, and could not "ride in" on the strength of the consent of the university officials. Therefore, for the purpose of obtaining evidence to

---

1. *Moore* v. *Student Affairs Committee of Troy State University*, (U.S.D.C., Ala.), 284 F. Supp. 725 (1968).

be used in a criminal prosecution, the search was unreasonable and unlawful; and the criminal convictions based on it were unlawful.[2]

Judge Johnson's words were lucid: "As this Court emphasized in *Moore*, students and their college share a special relationship, which gives to the college certain special rights including the right to enter into and inspect the rooms of its students under certain situations. However, the fact that the college has this right—for a restricted purpose—does not mean that the college may exercise the right by admitting a third party."

Also, "Even though the special relationship that existed between these petitioners and Troy State University officials conferred upon the University officials the right to enter and search petitioners' dormitory rooms, that right can not be expanded and used for purposes other than those pertaining to the special relationship. The right conferred by the special relationship must be very narrowly construed, and with such a construction the University's right to enter and search could not in this instance be delegated to the state investigators."

Maine Cases: Maritime Academy and Job Corps Center

Another 1970 case involved a cadet at the Maine Maritime Academy, a state institution. The cadet's Volkswagen bus had two large American flags and several smaller flags draped in the windows. After academy officials suggested that the flags be removed, the cadet removed only two; whereupon the Commandant ordered the academy security officer to search the bus. This was done in the presence of the cadet and with his consent. Some frayed flags, a can of beer, and some marijuana were found. Academy regulations make possession of alcohol or narcotics punishable by dismissal.

The Commandant dismissed the cadet. Upon the advice of counsel, the board of trustees set aside the dismissal and held a full-scale *de novo* hearing, with advance notice to the accused, and with proceedings recorded in writing, after which it voted the dismissal and made a written record of its findings and conclusions. The cadet then asked the federal district court to invalidate the dismissal, on the

---

2. *Piazzola and Marinshaw* v. *Watkins*, (U.S.D.C., Ala.), 361 F. Supp. 624 (1970); affirmed by U.S.C.A., 5 Cir., No. 30332 (April 27, 1971) in an opinion by Judge Rives joined by Judge Thornberry, with Judge Clark dissenting in part.

grounds that the search was unreasonable and in violation of the Fourth Amendment, and the evidence produced by it should have been inadmissible at the disciplinary hearing. District Judge Edward Thaxter Gignoux held that the search was proper because it was a reasonable exercise of the school's disciplinary authority and was "solely for the purpose of enforcing the Academy Rules and Regulations and of insuring proper conduct and discipline on the part of the cadet."[3]

The search had not been made by federal or state police or criminal investigative officers, and the question of the admissibility of the evidence produced in any criminal proceeding was not at issue. The opinion seems to be consistent with the two decisions of District Judge Johnson in the Troy State University cases.

The same federal district court in Maine had decided an earlier case in 1969 in which an administrative officer of a Job Corps center had, without a search warrant, searched the suitcase of a corpsman and found marijuana; and the court found that the search was a reasonable exercise of supervisory authority needed to maintain proper standards of conduct and discipline.[4] The court also held that the marijuana thus discovered was admissible as evidence in a subsequent criminal proceeding. This latter part of the decision is obviously not consistent with the opinions in the *Moore*, *Piazzola*, and *Keene* cases; and since it preceded them, perhaps it may now be regarded as of greatly diminished persuasive weight, if any.

To conclude the story as of this writing, let it be repeated that the Fourth Amendment applies to criminal cases; and that somewhat less rigorous standards of justification preceding a search appear to be countenanced when the search is by the school authorities only and of the dormitory room or personal property of a student, with a view toward maintaining the necessary decorum of the school, and not by federal, state, or local police or criminal investigators, with intent to use any pertinent evidence obtained in a criminal trial, where evidence thus obtained without a search warrant should be inadmissible. In other words, criminal courts observe somewhat stricter standards of admissibility of evidence than is required of disciplinary bodies in educational institutions.

---

3. *Keene* v. *Rodger*, (U.S.D.C., Me.), 316 F. Supp. 217 (1970).
4. *United States* v. *Cole*, (U.S.D.C., Me.), 302 F. Supp. 99 (1969).

Cases in Pennsylvania, New York, and Arizona

A 1970 decision of a Pennsylvania Superior Court seems to be in accord with the foregoing principles. Marijuana had been found in the dormitory room of a student at Bucknell University when his room was entered and searched by a narcotics agent, a state trooper, the university's dean of men, and the head resident of the dormitory. It was agreed that there had been "no announcement of identity or purpose" prior to the entry into the room by using a passkey. Soon thereafter the student, Roy Wilson McCloskey, was arrested and convicted of possession of the drug in the local trial court.

Setting aside the conviction because the evidence on which it was based had been unlawfully obtained, the Superior Court said: "There is no evidence in this case of any exigent circumstances justifying entry into McCloskey's locked room without announcement of identity or purpose. . . . A dormitory room is analogous to an apartment or a hotel room. . . .

"The (student) rented the dormitory room for a certain period of time, agreeing to abide by the rules established by his lessor, the university. As in most rental situations, the lessor, Bucknell University, reserved the right to check the room for damages, wear, and unauthorized appliances. Such right of the lessor, however, does not mean McCloskey was not entitled to have a reasonable expectation of freedom from governmental intrusion, or that he gave consent to the police search, or gave the university authority to consent to such search."[5] The court correctly distinguished this case from the Troy State University cases. The distinction is between the admissibility of evidence in university disciplinary cases, and in criminal prosecutions; and it is an important distinction.

The matter is further illustrated in an instance wherein, in the summer of 1970, two law enforcement employees of the town of Normal, Illinois, obtained entrance to a dormitory room at Illinois State University without a warrant and observed a quantity of marijuana while rifling a dresser drawer; then later obtained a warrant for its seizure. In the ensuing criminal prosecution for illegal possession of marijuana, James Walker, attorney for the defense, filed a motion for suppression of evidence in which he was quoted as saying: "One of

---

5. *Commonwealth* v. *McCloskey*, (Pa. Super.), 272 A. 2d 271 (1970).

the few methods available to deter this type of unlawful police activity and to guarantee individuals the right to be secure in their persons, houses, papers and effects against unreasonable searches and seizures is to suppress the use of any such items as evidence in criminal actions against individuals whose rights have been violated."[6]

Hofstra University, apprehensive about marijuana in the dormitories, invited the police to participate in a "survey." Accompanied by two university officials, police officers entered a room in a residence hall without announcing their purpose and without a search warrant. The odor of marijuana in the hallway led them to the room. Once inside, they found marijuana and seized it. There was no consent to the entry by the occupants of the room. Justice Beatrice S. Burstein of the Nassau County supreme court commented: "Even if the doctrine of implied consent were imported into this case, the consent is given, not to police officials, but to the University; and the latter can not fragmentize, share, or delegate it.

"It seems self-evident that the dormitory room of a college student is not open for entry at all times for all purposes. Hence it must be ruled that the search in this case was unlawful and the evidence must be suppressed (inadmissible in criminal trial).

"University students are adults. The dorm is a home and it must be inviolate against unlawful search and seizure. To suggest that a student who lives off campus in a boarding house is protected but that one who occupies a dormitory room waives his Constitutional liberties is at war with reason, logic, and law."

The Appellate Division, affirming, was terse; 30 words sufficed:

"The sole argument presented by the People upon this appeal is that the search was incidental to a lawful arrest. The arrest, however, followed the search which was itself illegal."[7]

At Cochise College in Arizona, a public junior college, a dormitory resident was suspected of having marijuana in his room. An informer told a U.S. customs agent that he had actually seen the marijuana; whereupon the agent made an affidavit of "probable cause" and obtained a search warrant from a local magistrate, directed to two local deputy sheriffs who accompanied him to the college. The three

---

6. Quoted in the *Daily Pantagraph* of Bloomington-Normal, August 26, 1970.
7. *People* v. *Cohen*, 57 Misc. 2d 366, 292 N.Y.S. 2d 706 (1968); affirmed in 61 Misc. 2d 858, 306 N.Y.S. 2d 788 (1968).

UNREASONABLE SEARCHES AND SEIZURES117

obtained a key to the room, knocked on the door and announced their presence and purpose. Receiving no response, but hearing suspicious noises inside, they unlocked the door and entered and made the search and seizure. It was held that the process was not unreasonable or unlawful, and that the evidence thus obtained was not inadmissible in criminal proceedings, even though the search was after dark and the face of the warrant contained the word "day" and had not been marked explicitly to authorize a night-time search.[8]

Search Following Lawful Arrest; and the "Plain View" Rule

"Unquestionably, when a person is lawfully arrested the police have the right, without a search warrant, to make a contemporaneous search of his person and of a motor car in which he is a passenger, for evidence of a criminal offense in violation of the law," said District Judge Walter L. Nixon, Jr., in his decision denying injunctive relief to four students at the University of Southern Mississippi who had been suspended for trying to exacerbate disruption of the campus by distributing large numbers of leaflets falsely announcing that the university would be closed during the last week of May 1970.

These students had been arrested by campus security officers for running a stop-sign while driving on the campus; and at that time the officers observed a bundle of some 200 of the leaflets protruding from under the seat of the microbus they occupied. The officers seized the leaflets and they were admitted in evidence at the subsequent disciplinary hearings. The plaintiffs contended unsuccessfully that this was an unreasonable and unlawful seizure, and that the hearings were invalidated by failure to exclude the leaflets as inadmissible evidence.

Explaining that college disciplinary procedures are to be distinguished from criminal prosecutions, Judge Nixon aptly quoted from the *per curiam* pronouncement of the U.S. District Court for Western Missouri *en banc* (45 Federal Rules Decisions 133, 1968):

"The discipline of students in the educational community is, in all but the case of irrevocable expulsion, a part of the teaching process. In the case of irrevocable expulsion for misconduct, the process is not punitive or deterrent, but the process is rather the determination that

---

8. *State* v. *Dudgeon*, 13 Ariz. App. 464, 477 P. 750 (1970).

the student is unqualified to continue as a member of the educational community. . . . The attempted analogy of student discipline to criminal proceedings against adults and juveniles is not sound."

However, he said, "for purposes of resolving this search and seizure question, this Court will nevertheless consider the question as if it were raised in a criminal prosecution."

He quoted the "plain view" rule as stated in several U.S. Supreme Court decisions:

"It has long been settled that objects falling in the plain view of an officer who has a right to be in a position to have that view are subject to seizure, and may be introduced in evidence."[9]

The memorandum opinion of some 18,000 words is one of the longest extant in this field. It deals with many issues, including due process, specificity of university rules, and others. It cites many pertinent recent decisions. It is generally lucid and well-documented.

Search of High School Lockers: Kansas and New York

Decisions of state courts in Kansas and New York have held school lockers of high school pupils may not only be searched by the school authorities, but that police or other law enforcement officers may use evidence thus obtained without a warrant, in criminal prosecutions. In this manner a pupil in Kansas was convicted of burglary. Justice John Fontron of the Kansas supreme court spoke convincingly of the power and responsibility of school authorities to maintain control of school lockers; but made no comment on the question of allowing police officers to search without a warrant and use evidence thus obtained against the accused pupil in a criminal trial. In this case, no comment was bad news for the accused pupil.[10]

In New York the school vice principal permitted police detectives to search a pupil's locker for marijuana without a warrant, and the court allowed them to use what they found as evidence against the pupil in a criminal action. The New York Court of Appeals also dwelt on the importance of control over the lockers as necessary to

---

9. *Speake* v. *Grantham,* (U.S.D.C., Miss.), 317 F. Supp. 1253 (1970).
10. *State* v. *Stein,* 203 Kas. 638, 456 P. 2d 1 (1969); *certiorari* denied by U.S. Supreme Court.

the discipline of the school, and said "this interest . . . empowered the (school officer) to consent to the search by the detectives."[11]

The high school cases appear to be relatively less solicitous regarding constitutional rights than the decisions involving college students. One may suppose that this is because the judges are inclined to be more concerned about the state's "compelling interest" in fostering order and decorum in the schools for pupils who are largely under the age of 18, than in colleges where the students are adults by present-day standards. Here, as in other civil rights issues, the task of the courts is to strike a balance between the legitimate interests of the state and the constitutional liberties of individuals.

---

11. *People* v. *Overton*, 283 N.Y.S. 2d 22, 20 N.Y. 2d 360, 229 N.E. 2d 596; *Overton* v. *New York*, 301 N.Y.S. 2d 479, 24 N.Y. 2d 522, 249 N.E. ad 366 (1969).

CHAPTER 11

CONFIDENTIALITY OF
STUDENT RECORDS

EVERY UNIVERSITY OR COLLEGE must keep individual records of its students. There seems to be a paucity of statutes and judicial decisions regarding what types of information in these records must be kept confidential, and to whom and how and under what conditions the different kinds of data may be properly released.

Fortunately Illinois State University keeps current a brief written "Policy on Student Records" which may be presumed to be in harmony with what is known of the law of the subject. Only some of the basic essentials of this policy are indicated here.

First, the principle of parsimony or Occam's razor: "Unless a demonstrable need for a record is established which is reasonably and justifiably related to the basic purposes and necessities of the University, no records should be made or maintained." Thus it is sought to prevent the institution from being inundated in a maelstrom of paper.

Basic is the distinction between "public" or "directory" information, and all other data. "Public" information is that which is of public record or found in publications available to the general public. Some examples are: student's name, parent's name, home address and telephone number, campus address and telephone number, dates of attendance at the University, full or part-time enrollment status, major subject, degree earned, age, citizenship, date and place of birth, and portrait photograph. These may be released without the student's knowledge or consent on an individual basis. In usual practice, all inquirers except other educational institutions are simply referred to the *Student-Faculty Directory*, which usually satisfies them.

Encapsulated Principles Regarding Non-Directory Information

Requests from prospective employers for non-public or non-directory types of data will be complied with only with the written consent of the student concerned.

The same applies to requests from *other educational institutions* for reports of academic and disciplinary standing and transcripts.

Investigators from private or governmental agencies are subject to the same policy. They are told that non-public or non-directory information will not be disclosed without written consent of the person being investigated. If such an investigator comes with such authorization in hand, he should be referred to the Dean of Students.

"*A faculty member* may request information contained in permanent academic records when needed in the discharge of his official duties. A faculty member may request confidential information with the student's consent or when a counselor, dean or other person is mutually involved with the student."

"*Parents and guardians* are recognized as having legitimate interest in the academic and personal well-being of their sons, daughters, and wards; and may consult with the professional staff, keeping such consultation consistent with the basic policy regarding confidential student records."

Academic eligibility of students for honors, awards, or scholarships may be furnished the committee responsible for making the awards. (Specific grade-point averages can only be released at the request of the student.)

Research data should be collected and handled in ways which clearly respect the right of privacy and anonymity. When there is any doubt about the safeguarding of the data or the identity of those to whom it appertains, the consent of the persons should be formally obtained.

Student organizations are expected to provide the university with names and addresses of their current officers to whom communications can be directed; but the university does not maintain records of membership in student organizations.

Student affiliations and beliefs, including political associations, which become known to faculty members in the course of their work as instructors or counselors should be considered confidential; and there is a professional obligation against improper disclosure.[1]

Regarding disclosure of the identity of officers and members of organizations, the issue was illuminated in three decisions of the United States Supreme Court in the early 1960's, climaxing approximately a decade of protracted litigation in state and federal courts in certain southern states which were attempting to circumscribe or prohibit the activities of the National Association for the Advancement of Colored People within their borders.

In *NAACP* v. *State of Alabama* a state court order to reveal the names of all rank-and-file members of the organization in that state was reversed as "a substantial restraint upon the exercise by the members of their right to freedom of association," based on "an uncontroverted showing that on past occasions revelation of the identity of the rank-and-file members has exposed these members to economic reprisal, loss of employment, threat of physical coercion, and other manifestations of public hostility."[2]

The NAACP in Alabama had previously revealed, under court order, the names of its officers and employees; but successfully resisted disclosure of its membership lists.

A California appellate court decision of 1969 was in harmony with that result. A law student at the Berkeley campus of the University of California was an officer of a student organization engaged in the advocacy of dissident ideas. The organization was registered with the university and entitled to the privileges accorded registered student organizations. One of the requirements for such registration was submission to the university of a statement of the purposes and the names of the officers. When a member of the public sued the university for

---

1. The foregoing nine paragraphs are partly quoted and partly paraphrased from *Policy on Student Records.* Normal, Ill.: Illinois State University, Office of the Vice President for Student Affairs.

2. *NAACP* v. *State of Alabama,* 377 U.S. 288, 84 S.Ct. 1302, 12 L.Ed. 2d 325 (1964).

access to the names of the officers and stated purposes of all registered student organizations, the university yielded to her request without defending the suit.

The law student then sued in the superior court of Alameda County to enjoin public inspection of the records in question, on the ground that this would invade his right to freedom of association. The court dismissed the petition after a hearing, saying: "Public policy as framed within the law of this State requires disclosure of the subject records, such public policy being dominant and controlling to the right of associational privilege." The judgment of dismissal was affirmed by a California Court of Appeal, concluding: "Here the compelling interest of the public in being able to ascertain the information contained in the registration statement outweighs any minimal infringement of plaintiff's First Amendment rights."[3]

Investigative Resolution of Wisconsin Senate

An earlier decision by a federal district court in Wisconsin was somewhat similar as to facts and law, but involved the scope of the investigative power of a state legislative body.

One sequel to the Commerce Building disturbance of October 1967 at the University of Wisconsin was the adoption, two days thereafter, of a resolution of the Wisconsin Senate setting up an investigative committee of six senators charged with finding facts about the W.E.B. DuBois Club and the Students for a Democratic Society on the Madison campus, and their connections, if any, with the October disturbance "and any prior or further such activities."[4]

When this committee subpoenaed officers of the two student organizations named, two of them—David L. Goldman and Robert S. Cohen—asked the federal district court to declare the resolution violated the United States Constitution, and to enjoin the committee from compelling them to testify. A three-judge court was convened (Circuit Judge Thomas E. Fairchild and District Judges Myron L. Gordon and James E. Doyle). Judge Doyle wrote the opinion of the court,

---

3. *Eisen* v. *Regents of University of California*, (Cal. App.), 75 Cal. Rptr. 45 (1969).

4. Substitute Amendment 1 to Senate Resolution 13, as adopted October 20, 1967.

denying any declaratory judgment or injunctive relief and dismissing the case.

In his 7,000-word opinion, however, Judge Doyle emphatically characterized the resolution as "hastily drafted" and "not a model of explicitness or clarity," but concluded that "The primary subject of the investigation authorized was sufficiently understood by all concerned."

Noting that the resolution was broad enough to permit questioning concerning the identity of the members of the two organizations —which would run counter to constitutional protection of freedom and privacy of association, unless the state's interest in the primary subject was "so subordinating, compelling, and overriding as to justify this invasion"—the court concluded that the evidence before it was not sufficient to support that purpose. Thus the resolution would seem to fall on account of overbreadth, but, while characterizing it as peripherally vague and overbroad, nevertheless the court observed that up to the time of trial the committee had not actually operated in a manner to imperil the constitutional privacy of association; and that "The threat of unconstitutional application is insufficiently imminent, on the present record, to warrant intervention." This reluctance was due, at least in part, to the fact that the resolution was not a criminal statute, but an exercise of the investigative power of a legislative body.[5]

U.S. Senate Committee's Subpoena of Student Records

The Permanent Subcommittee on Investigations of the U.S. Senate Committee on Government Operations was authorized by the Senate on February 17, 1969, to delve into the causes of riots and other disorders in the United States, and the means necessary for their prevention. The subcommittee issued *subpoenas duces tecum* to various colleges and universities, including Columbia, Cornell, California at Berkeley, and The City University of New York.

Requested were the names of persons and organizations who had participated in campus disorders, the names of officers and faculty advisors of campus organizations, and the extent to which the persons

---

5. *Goldman* v. *Olson*, (U.S.D.C., Wis.), 286 F. Supp. 35 (1968).

named were receiving aid from the federal government or any tax-exempt agency. There was general compliance, but on June 17, 1969, some remonstrants asked the U.S. District Court for the District of Columbia to declare the *subpoenas* invalid and to enjoin the subcommittee and its staff from using the documents thus obtained. The action was dismissed by District Judge Howard F. Corcoran; and the judgment affirmed by the Court of Appeals, with Circuit Judges Harold Leventhal, Roger Robb, and Malcolm Richard Wilkey.[6]

The court thought there were "only the vaguest allegations of anticipated harm—a hypothetical speculation that on some indeterminate future occasion a student will decline to join, or a faculty member to advise, some campus organization; or that a Congressional blacklist will be used to cut off governmental benefits to those named." There was no showing, said the judges, of any current activity by the committee or its staff which would constitute an actual threat, or otherwise give immediacy to the claim that constitutional freedoms were being infringed or jeopardized.

"There are doctrines of judicial restraint which operate to avoid the possibility of unwarranted inteference with a coordinate branch of government, by requiring dismissal of applications not substantiated by a showing of need arising out of immediate threats to constitutional rights." The court's view was that there was only a remote danger of governmental action against the students on the basis of the information in the records; and that there was insufficient showing of probable governmental harassment.

Investigative Activities of Committee on Internal Security of U.S. House of Representatives

When a house committee prepared a 25-page report of "A Limited Survey of Honoraria Given Guest Speakers for Engagements at Colleges and Universities" by collecting from a number of institutions, without using any coercive process, some 1168 names of speakers and a scattering of data on compensation paid them, and checking these against its own files on twelve organizations,[7] thus

---

6. *Cole and the University Senate of The City University of New York,* (U.S.C.A., D.C.), 439 F. 2d 534 (1970).

7. The Nation of Islam, the Communist Party, the National Committee to Abolish HUAC, three Moratorium Committees to End the War in Vietnam

turning up a "blacklist" of 65 persons, some of the 65 sued for an injunction against publication of the report, as obviously tending to inhibit freedom of speech and assembly, and thus violating the First Amendment.

District Judge Gerhard A. Gesell of the District of Columbia, while he could not prevent the printing of the report in the *Congressional Record*, nor enjoin any member of Congress from disseminating it in his own way, could and did issue a permanent injunction restraining the Public Printer and the Superintendent of Documents from publishing it. "It is alien to any legitimate Congressional function," he said, "for any Committee of the Congress to disseminate lists designed to suppress speech. Members of the Committee may speak their minds, and their words will carry added weight because of the great prestige of their high office. They can not, however, by the mere process of filing a report devoid of legislative purpose, transform these views into official action of the Congress and have them published and widely distributed at public expense."[8]

Communications Between High Schools and College Admissions Officers

College admissions officers commonly ask high school principals or counselors to forward their personal appraisals of their graduates who are applying for admission at the college. These communications are mutually understood to be confidential; and indeed it seems likely that they would be held to be "privileged" as between educational officers for a legitimate purpose, thus protecting them from libel vulnerability unless proved to be wantonly or maliciously false. As to whether they are protected from disclosure in court, there is uncertanty, added to by a 1968 decision of a county superior court in Maine.

In 1964-65 a high school student in Connecticut applied for admission to Bates College in Maine and three other colleges, and was rejected by all four. His parents believed this resulted from unfavor-

---

(designated respectively National, New, and Spring), the Socialist Workers' Party, the Black Panther Party, Students for a Democratic Society, the Student Non-Violent Coordinating Committee, the Youth International Party, and Persons Cited for Contempt in the Chicago Seven Trial.

8. *Hentoff* v. *Ichord*, (U.S.D.C., D.C.), 318 F. Supp. 1175 (1970).

able reports by his school officers, and they asked the high school principal to correct or withdraw the reports, which they assumed were "arbitrary and capricious" and "not based on fair and proper procedure." The school officials refused, and the parents then asked a Connecticut court to order them to grant the request. The school officials said they had no copies of the reports and declined to tell the parents what was in them; whereupon the parents, after Bates College refused to release copies, asked the Maine court to order it to do so.

As illustrative of a long-entrenched procedure, the attorney for Bates College argued: "It is most important that this court acknowledge and protect the confidentiality of the documents and recommendations sent to college admission staffs by secondary school officials. If secondary school officials are to be put in fear of suits for defamation and lesser forms of intimidation with respect to such comments, they will be inhibited and will tend to shade their remarks toward the noncontroversial. The resulting lack of candor and objectivity will be of great detriment to the colleges, and their admissions procedure will be severely impeded."

The University of Maine was persuaded to file, as *amicus curiae*, a similar statement: "To reveal the information received from secondary or preparatory schools would constitute a breach of trust, and would make meaningless our admissions procedures. If disclosure of such information were made mandatory, no school could safely send us meaningful recommendations, nor would we request such information in writing."

The court ordered Bates College to produce the papers. It had found no authority for the proposition that such documents are "privileged against disclosure under proper judicial process." Conceding that "It may be true that such communications are privileged in the sense that no libel or slander suit may be maintained thereon," and that it "may also be true that colleges could require, as a matter of contract, that applicants agree to respect the confidential nature of such evaluation," the court saw no reason why Bates College should not be ordered to release to the parents the papers at issue in this case.[9]

Subsequent to that decision some New England colleges have

9. Maine Superior Court Civ. Action, Docket No. 3572, Androscoggin County (May 8, 1968). Discussed in *College Board Review*, No. 71 (Spring 1969), p. 21.

placed clauses in their application forms such as the following: "The undersigned agree that the information furnished on this form, together with all information received by the admissions office as a result of this application from any source whatever, shall be completely confidential and shall not be disclosed to anyone, including the candidate and his family, except that the Dean of Admissions may, in his sole and uncontrolled discretion, disclose any part or all thereof to such person or persons as he deems advisable." The exact legal effect of these clauses has not been fully determined.

Meantime, the parents of the student in the Bates College case, having won their suit in the Maine court as recounted above, filed a $135,000 damage suit in a Connecticut court against the counselor and principal of their son's Connecticut high school, for allegedly having transmitted unjustified negative recommendations which caused the college to reject his application. The outcome of this action had not been reported in time for inclusion herein.

CHAPTER 12

TORTS AGAINST STUDENTS

When a student is injured in his person or property as a proximate result of the negligence or willful intent of an officer or employee of a college or university while engaged in his duties as an agent of the college, the civil wrong thus arising is a tort. Whether and in what circumstances the student can sue the college and recover indemnity for the injury has given rise to much litigation in the past. Generally during the latter half of the nineteenth century such suits were barred, in the case of public colleges, by the doctrine of "governmental immunity"; and in the case of private colleges, by the doctrine of "charitable immunity." For half a century these theories have been slowly eroded, and entirely repudiated in some states; but in a minority of the states they continue to prevail.

Negligence of State and Other Public Colleges and Universities

Irrespective of any question of immunity, it is essential in any tort suit that the injured party allege and prove the fact of negligence as the proximate cause of the injury. Failure to do this will result in dismissal of the case.

A 1968 Delaware decision illustrates. The University of Delaware soccer team was being transported to Philadelphia for a match with

Temple University, in two motor vehicles. The leading vehicle was driven by the coach who was in charge of the expedition. The second vehicle, a minibus owned by the University of Delaware, was driven by Gary Richard Adams, a student and member of the team. When the first vehicle slowed down on the approach to a traffic light, the minibus collided with it from the rear, and Adams was injured.

He alleged that the minibus brakes were defective, and that fact should have been known and corrected by the university's agents, including the coach, Loren Kline; and that their failure in this respect was negligence, making Kline and the university liable for damages on account of his injury. On this issue recovery was denied, and partial summary judgment was granted in favor of both the coach and the university. There was some testimony to the effect that the malfunctioning of the brakes was due to the fact that the minibus was overloaded considerably beyond its capacity, rather than to any discoverable defect in the brakes. The court thought both the coach and the university might have been negligent in permitting the vehicle to be overloaded, if that were shown to be the proximate cause of the collision. Therefore the court denied the motion for summary judgment on that issue.[1]

When Carmela Morrone, a girl student at the State University of New York College at Potsdam, fell and was injured on hard-packed snow and ice on the walk leading into her dormitory residence, the testimony was that the accident occurred at about 1:30 p.m. Carmela had walked on the same walk at least once during the forenoon of the same day. Another resident of the same dormitory testified that during the same afternoon she had fallen twice on the same walk, at approximately the same spot, and that in the second instance she had been helped to her feet by Carmela.

The Court of Claims held that Carmela had failed to demonstrate the absence of contributory negligence on her own part, and therefore dismissed the case. On appeal, the five-judge Appellate Division approved this judgment and also added that any finding of negligence on the part of the state would be contrary to the weight of the evidence. Thus the judgment of dismissal was affirmed.[2]

---

1. *Adams* v. *Kline and the University of Delaware,* (Del. Super.), 239 Atl. 230 (1968).

2. *Morrone* v. *State of New York,* (N.Y. App. Div.), 294 N.Y.S. 2d 236 (1968).

Paula Vreeland, a student at the University of Arizona, had a scheduled class on an upper floor of the engineering building on the campus. She entered on the main floor and began to ascend the marble stairway, which was about 80 inches wide and equipped with a handrail only on the left-hand side, which was used by descending traffic, and there was no handrail available to persons going up on the right-hand side. Mrs. Vreeland, on her way up, stepped upon and slipped on one or more metallic-colored heavy-duty thumb-tacks of the type used on nearby bulletin boards. She fell and sustained injuries.

Ordinarily, when notices were removed from the boards, the tacks were left on the board. Although for "official" use, the boards were not glass-enclosed, and were accessible to anyone. The stairway was cleaned only once a day, at night, when the building was unoccupied. The court of appeals of Arizona decided, in view of all the circumstances, that neither the absence of a handrail nor the presence of the tacks on the steps was sufficient to justify submission of the question of negligence to a jury, since no allegation was made that any agent of the university knew of the presence of the hazard and had opportunity to remove the tacks, but failed to do so. Accordingly the trial court's judgment directing a verdict for the university was affirmed.[3]

The direction in which the law of the tort responsibility of public universities and colleges tends to move is indicated by a decision of the supreme court of Nebraska in 1969. Jack Johnson, participating in a track meet on the premises of the University of Omaha (then a municipal university), while pole-vaulting, fell upon a wooden box which had been placed by the university beneath the pole-vault standards, and was injured. His suit for damages was dismissed by the trial court, but this judgment was reversed and remanded by the state supreme court, making a lucid statement about the doctrine of governmental immunity from tort liability:

"The traditional common law rule of sovereign or governmental immunity has been subject to both legislative and judicial modification and reshaping. The reasons supporting a broad-brush application of the traditional common law doctrine in its old form are no longer defensible. This court has adopted a course of reexamination and gradual transition, rather than sweeping and complete abrogation."

---

3. *Vreeland* v. *Arizona Board of Regents of State Universities,* (Ariz. App.), 449 P. 2d 78 (1969).

Declaring that the court intended to treat this issue by a "process of inclusion and exclusion, case by case, and step by step," Justice McCown, speaking for the majority (Justices Spencer, Smith, and Walter H. Smith, a district judge sitting in the place of Justice Carter, concurred without opinion; Chief Justice White and Justices Boslaugh and Newton dissented without opinion), announced a new rule covering this case:

"We now hold that cities, counties, and all other governmental subdivisions, and local public entities of this state, including municipal universities, are not immune from tort liability arising out of a physical condition, affirmatively and voluntarily created by the public body on its premises, where the existence of the condition is not reasonably visible or apparent, and where the condition constitutes an unreasonable risk of harm to persons authorized to use and reasonably using the premises for the purposes intended."[4]

He added: "This holding applies to all causes of action arising after a date one month following the filing date of this opinion. In respect to other causes of action, the new rule applies if, but only if, the city, governmental subdivision, or local public entity was insured against such liability on the date the claim arose, and then only to the extent of the maximum applicable amount of its insurance coverage. This holding is applicable to the case at bar."

Lawrence Brown, a student at North Country Community College at Saranac Lake, New York, alleged that February 27, 1969, he was walking on the main campus and slipped and fell on mounds or ridges of ice and snow, and that the negligence of the college in failing to remove the hazard was the proximate cause of the injuries he sustained, for which he sued for damages.

The college attempted to challenge the jurisdiction of the Essex County supreme court, and also contended that the complaint was insufficient to state a cause of action. Justice Harold R. Soden denied these motions, but gave permission to file an amended answer within 20 days. Although the board of trustees of the college, sponsored by two adjoining counties, is a corporate entity, it is not a municipal corporation as defined in the statutes, nor is it a part of the corporation known as the State University of New York. Its relationship to the

---

4. *Johnson* v. *Municipal University of Omaha*, (Nebr.), 169 N.W. 2d 286 (1969).

state, said Justice Soden, is not such as would require under existing statutes that a tort action against it would have to be brought in the state Court of Claims.[5]

When an individual occupies, at one and the same time, the dual status of student at the university and employee of the same university, this puts a different face on the question of compensating him for an injury sustained while about his duties as employee.

A full-time student in the agricultural practice course at the University of Hawaii signed, at the time of his enrollment a contract specifying the place, weekly hours, and wages for his concurrent job on the university farm. Subsequently he was killed by the overturn of a tractor while working at the farm. It was held that since his contract satisfied the requirements of the Workmen's Compensation Law, the exclusive source of indemnity for his accidental death would be under that statute.[6]

Other workmen's compensation cases involving employees of the university or college other than students will appear in the next volume in this series, dealing with faculty and staff members and other employees.

Negligence by Private Colleges and Universities

Private nonprofit institutions were formerly very generally held to be immune from tort liability on the theory that all their assets were dedicated to the charitable educational purpose, and not to be diverted to the indemnification of mere private grievances. The funds and property of such charitable corporations were guarded from "the hungry maw of litigation." During the past half-century this doctrine of immunity has been heavily restricted or abolished entirely in nearly all the states.

A landmark in that progress was the lengthy and scholarly opinion of U.S. Circuit Judge Wiley Rutledge in *President and Directors of Georgetown College* v. *Hughes*, (U.S.C.A., for D.C.), 130 F. 2d 810 (1942), in which he advocated convincingly the total abolition of the immunity theory. Strangely enough, nearly a quarter of a century

---

5. *Brown* v. *North Country Community College*, (N.Y. Misc.), 311 N.Y.S. 2d 517 (1970).

6. *Evanston* v. *University of Hawaii*, (Hawaii), 438 P. 2d 187 (1971).

later the same institution raised unsuccessfully the same defense in a somewhat similar case.

At Georgetown University there was a custom of allowing the sophomore students to haze the freshmen in a ceremony in which the freshmen were required to leave their dormitory and march in a long line in an ungainly posture known as the "elephant walk" to the athletic field, where they were subjected to a "mud bath." On one of these annual occasions (in 1956) the "elephant march" broke formation and Richard F. Heimbuch, a freshman, was violently tackled from the rear by a sophomore, knocking him to the ground and causing a fracture of the femur, damage to a hip joint, and other injuries. Heimbuch sued the university for indemnification, charging negligence in countenancing the affair.

U.S. District Judge Burnita Shelton Matthews had only to decide the single issue of whether any vestige of the doctrine of immunity for charitable corporations prevailed in the District of Columbia; specifically, whether Georgetown University would be immune from this suit under the theory that the student is a "beneficiary" of the institution, and barred from biting the hand that feeds him, as had formerly been held in some jurisdictions.

Judge Matthews concluded by reaffirming the earlier position of Circuit Judge Rutledge, to the effect that in the District of Columbia it makes no difference whether the injured party is a "beneficiary" or a "stranger to the charity"; the doctrine of immunity simply does not prevail. Before reaching that conclusion, however, she observed that the injured student was paying a total of $1,808 in charges and fees for the academic year; and although Georgetown University alleged that this sum did not compensate it fully for the expenses attributable to the education of one student, it failed to prove this to the satisfaction of the court, and doubt remained in the mind of the court that the student was really a "beneficiary of the charity."

It was also noted that the university was carrying liability insurance on which the total premiums amounted to $30,000 to $40,000 a year. The order of the court was that the defense of charitable immunity would not prevail, and the question of negligence in this case must be tried by a jury.[7]

---

7. *Heimbuch* v. *President and Directors of Georgetown College*, (U.S.D.C. for D.C.), 251 F. Supp. 614 (1966).

Different questions, mainly of fact rather than law, were at issue in the case of Richard W. Cramer, a student at St. Lawrence University who was severely injured in football practice, resulting in paralysis below the chest. He had been hospitalized with German measles, and the injury occurred a few days after his release. In his suit for indemnity, the university, the hospital, and several individuals involved were joined as defendants. One Dr. Erich Schaefer, who appeared to have been an employee of the hospital and a contract physician for the university, was alleged to have been responsible for his discharge in an ill and physically weakened condition, and also for failure to notify the university that he was unfit to participate in football practice. Ronald C. Hoffman, the university's football coach, was alleged to have been negligent in allowing him to play in football practice, and this negligence was imputed to the university.

At the trial in U.S. District Court (because of diversity of citizenship) there was a jury verdict in favor of all defendants; and District Judge Edmund Port, denying a motion for judgment notwithstanding the verdict, gave judgment for the defendants. On appeal, Circuit Judge Leonard P. Moore (with Chief Circuit Judge J. Edward Lumbard and Circuit Judge Henry J. Friendly also sitting) concluded that the jury's verdict was supported by the weight of the credible evidence, and affirmed the judgment.[8]

A Wisconsin case, decided in state courts, touches upon the degree of care which a private college is bound to exercise in the maintenance and regulation of its campus to avoid liability for tortious injuries to its invitees (among whom are its students).

Larry Stamberger, a student at Carthage College at Kenosha, Wisconsin, was injured when, riding his motorbike on a two-way private road on the campus, he collided with an automobile which had been parked facing oncoming traffic (parked on the east side of the road, facing south), and which moved out into his traffic lane, confronting him head-on.

The gist of the complaint against Carthage College was that it was negligent in not promulgating and enforcing a regulation prohibiting "left-hand parking" on a two-way road. A Wisconsin statute forbids such parking on public streets, but it is held not to apply to

---

8. *Cramer* v. *Hoffman and St. Lawrence University*, (U.S.C.A., N.Y.), 390 F. 2d 19 (1968).

private roads; and the state supreme court, in an opinion by Justice
Bruce F. Beilfuss, decided that as a matter of common law the parking
in this case did not constitute a hazardous condition sufficient to support an allegation of breach of the duty of ordinary care on the part of
the college.

Consequently the order of the county court sustaining demurrers
to the pleadings (asserting no cause of action) was affirmed.[9]

A Kentucky case was brought by a girl student who was injured
by a fall on the gymnasium floor during a running game in a regular
class period. Evidence showed that at the time there were three or
four spots (perhaps four inches in diameter) from six inches to a foot
apart, of an unknown dark sticky substance on a small area of the floor,
and that this caused the fall. Apparently the presence of the substance
was not noticed by anyone prior to the fall, and there was no evidence
that the instructor or anyone connected with the college was aware
of it.

In the county court a jury awarded the injured girl $10,000
damages, and the court entered judgment accordingly; but the state
court of appeals (court of last resort in Kentucky) reversed this and
directed judgment for the college, holding that in a case such as this
there is insufficient proof of negligence unless it is proved that some
officer, agent, or employee of the college had known of the existence
of the hazard in advance and had failed to remove it.[10]

In a North Carolina case involving a proprietary dancing school, a
thirteen-year-old girl pupil, who had had instruction there for six
years, fell and injured her knee when attempting a series of "pique
turns" at the request of her teacher. The floor had been freshly waxed,
but six or seven of her classmates executed the same step ahead of her
without mishap; and on these facts the trial court granted a judgment
of nonsuit; and this was affirmed by the Court of Appeals, pointing out
that the use of wax on dance floors is an established custom, and that
in this case the teacher had warned the pupils about the fresh waxing.
None of the fourteen other pupils in the class had any mishaps. All
were wearing the same type of dancing shoes on the same floor, and
there was no evidence that anything done or left undone by the pro-

---

9. *Stamberger* v. *Matthaidess and Carthage College*, (Wis.), 155 N.W. 2d 88
(1967).

10. *Cumberland College* v. *Gaines*, (Ky.), 432 S.W. 2d 650 (1968).

prietors was the proximate cause of the accident. "The cause," said the court, "is left in the realm of conjecture."[11]

The same result was reached in a similar New York case. Here a dance student who was injured by a fall while under instruction alleged that the floor was highly polished and that no powdery substance or "traction" had been placed upon it as had often been done in the past. She was awarded a judgment on a jury verdict in the trial court, but this was curtly reversed and vacated by the five-judge Appellate Division, holding that the testimony made no case against the proprietor.[12]

---

11. *Hedrick* v. *Tigniere's School of Dancing*, (N.C.), 147 S.E. 550 (1966).

12. *McArthur* v. *Elad Conservatory, Inc., a Dale Dance Studio*, (N.Y. App. Div.), 270 N.Y.S. 2d 977 (1966).

CHAPTER 13

FREEDOM OF SPEECH
AND ASSEMBLY

"CONGRESS shall make no law . . . abridging the freedom of speech, or of the press; or the right of the people peaceably to assemble and to petition the Government for redress of grievances."

For half a century the highest tribunal in the land has held that freedom of speech must not be cut off unless what is being said constitutes a clear and present danger of causing immediate violence, or injury to persons or property, or invasion of the rights of others. The doctrine is also accepted that peaceable gathering in crowds, marching, parading, singing, handclapping, banner-carrying, picketing, and bearing of placards are classified as "symbolic speech" coming under the same rule.

Peaceable Assemblies Off-Campus

Observe first two landmark decisions of the United States Supreme Court, in 1963 and 1965, involving peaceable off-campus demonstrative activities by students in southern black colleges. Both involved incidents occurring in 1961.

At Columbia, South Carolina, a large number of "high school and college students of the Negro race" demonstrated on the two-block grounds of the Statehouse. Some 30 or more law enforcement officers were present on the grounds when the marchers arrived, and they informed the marchers that they would be arrested if they did not disperse within 15 minutes. The conduct of the marchers on the grounds was quiet and orderly, with no disorder or disruption of pedestrian or vehicular traffic. They listened to a "religious harangue" by one of their leaders and sang loudly "The Star-Spangled Banner" and other patriotic and religious songs, while stamping their feet and clapping their hands. A crowd of some 300 onlookers collected, but there was no evidence of any threatening remarks, hostile gestures, or offensive language on the part of any member of the crowd.

After 15 minutes the police arrested 187 of the demonstrators and marched them off to jail. When this case reached the United States Supreme Court, the gist of the opinion of the court, written by Mr. Justice Stewart, was that the arrests for breach of the peace by marching peacefully on the sidewalk around the statehouse, to publicize the marchers' dissatisfaction with discriminatory actions against Negroes, infringed their constitutionally protected rights of free speech, free assembly, and freedom to petition for redress of their grievances. He said, "The Fourteenth Amendment does not permit a State to make criminal the peaceful expression of unpopular views."[1]

On December 14, 1961, 23 students from Southern University, a Negro college, were arrested in downtown Baton Rouge, Louisiana, for picketing stores that maintained segregated lunch counters. The Reverend Mr. B. Elton Cox, an ordained Congregational minister and a field secretary of CORE, was an adviser to this movement. On the evening of December 14 he and Ronnie Moore, student president of the local CORE chapter, spoke at a mass meeting at the college. The students resolved to demonstrate the next day in front of the courthouse in protest of segregation and the arrest and imprisonment of the picketers, who were being held in the parish jail located on the upper floor of the courthouse.

The next day some 2,000 students marched from the college to the downtown area. At various points along the way they were met by police patrolmen who tried unsuccessfully to persuade them to turn back. They assembled on the sidewalk at the old statehouse, and

1. *Edwards* v. *South Carolina*, 372 U.S. 229, 83 S.Ct. 680, 9 L.Ed. 2d 697 (1963); reversing 239 S.C. 339, 123 S.E. 2d 247 (1961), after granting *certiorari*, 369 U.S. 870, 82 S.Ct. 1141, 8 L.Ed. 2d 274 (1962).

from there marched in orderly procession the distance of about two blocks to the sidewalk along the courthouse, where they were met by a somewhat flustered chief of police who had not expected them to reach that point. He hastily ordered them to "get over on the other side of the street." This was interpreted to mean oral permission to conduct a brief demonstration on the sidewalk at the opposite side of the street, which was somewhat more than 100 feet from the courthouse; but the point was disputed in later court proceedings, and was the cause of some differences of opinion among the judges as to whether the demonstration was in violation of the Louisiana statute prohibiting such activities "in or near a Courthouse."

The demonstration consisted of loud singing, praying, handclapping, and listening to a short speech by Reverend Cox, in which he advised that after the demonstration some of the students should go to the four eating-places and ask to be served, and sit for one hour if not served. Within a few minutes police and sheriff's officers dispersed the assemblage with tear-gas. Later Reverend Cox was arrested and charged with disturbing the peace, obstructing a public passage, and conducting a demonstration near a courthouse, all of which were violations of Louisiana statutes. Louisiana courts convicted him on these charges, and the convictions were affirmed by the state supreme court. On appeal to the Supreme Court of the United States, the convictions were reversed.

The opinion of the majority of the court was by Mr. Justice Goldberg. He said explicitly that Reverend Cox's adjuration to the students to conduct sit-ins in segregated places of business "obviously did not deprive the demonstration of its protected character under the Constitution as free speech and assembly." As to the charge of "obstructing public passages" he added that "the practice in Baton Rouge of allowing unfettered discretion in local officials in the regulation of the use of the streets for peaceful parades and meetings is an unwarranted abridgment of freedom of speech and assembly secured by the First Amendment, as applied to the States by the Fourteenth Amendment."

Justices Black, Clark, White, and Harlan concurred in part and dissented in part from the majority opinion, according to their separate views of the three charges of which Reverend Cox had been convicted.

The ultimate result turned out that though the high tribunal was not unanimous, the prevailing majority reversed all the convictions and exonerated Reverend Cox of the charges. This was a triumph for the principle of orderly and peaceable freedom of speech and assembly.[2]

Disruptive Action Is Not Protected

Freedom of speech is subject to lawful limitations as to "time, place, and manner"; and it is not to be confused with violent *action* or direct incitation thereto. The *Edwards* and *Cox* cases were criminal proceedings. We turn now to matters of university discipline. It is important not to overlook the difference. State and federal criminal jurisdiction is universal within the appropriate geographic areas, and no university or college is a sanctuary in which crimes may be committed with impunity, or into which accused criminals may flee from justice. No university or college has any criminal jurisdiction. It does not impose criminal penalties such as fines or imprisonment. It has only its own disciplinary authority, within which the severest possible penalty is suspension or expulsion.

At the University of Colorado a number of students staged a protest demonstration against the recruiting activities of an agent of the United States Central Intelligence Agency. They physically blocked and prevented entrance to the University Placement Service offices by standing in the doorways. Having been subjected to disciplinary action by the university, some of them went to the federal district court with a plea that their constitutional rights had been infringed. Dismissing the case, the court remarked: "Plaintiffs engaged in overt physical acts which effectively interfered with one of the normal activities of the University, namely interviewing students for employment," and "Their conduct in the Court's opinion was much more than is fairly understood to be embraced within the term 'political activity.'

"We do not subscribe to the notion that a citizen surrenders his civil rights upon enrollment as a student in a university," said the court, "as a corollary to this, enrollment does not give him the right to violate the constitutional rights of others."[3]

---

2. *Cox* v. *State of Louisiana*, 379 U.S. 536, 85, S.Ct. 453, L.Ed. 2d and 379 U.S. 559, 85 S.Ct. 476 L.Ed. 2d (1965); reversing 244 La. 1087, 156 So. 2d 448 (1963) and 245 La. 303, 158 So. 2d 172 (1963).

3. *Buttny et al* v. *Smiley, President, and Regents of University of Colorado*, (U.S.D.C., Colo.), 281 F. Supp. 280 (1968).

During the recent episode at Berkeley wherein "street people" and students attempted to seize and hold a university-owned park, the president-elect of the student association of the University of California addressed an outdoor gathering of students on the campus, exhorting them to "make it costly for the University to have put up the fence around the park," and commanding them to "go down and take the park," whereupon about a thousand students trooped down Telegraph Avenue to the park and engaged in violence which culminated in the death of one person and injuries to others.

When he sought the aid of the federal district court in resisting university discipline on civil rights grounds, he was met with the court's decision that his words had transcended a mere expression of opinion entitled to constitutional protection, and had become conduct for which he could be called to account under university regulations, "whatever his claim as to his subjective purpose and intent."[4]

In litigation which had followed the earlier Berkeley disorders of 1964, a California state court of appeal had held "In this case the University's disciplinary action was a proper exercise of its inherent general powers to maintain order on the campus and to exclude therefrom those who are detrimental to its well-being," and refused a writ of *mandamus* to reinstate four suspended students.[5] This doctrine of inherent general disciplinary authority was also enunciated by a New York court.[6] It is basic and indispensable; but it is limited to an extent by the accepted principle that the rights of students, as protected under the First and Fourteenth Amendments, must not be disregarded.

For example, one would scarcely doubt that a university could lawfully prohibit any demonstration or protest within an athletic facility during the time it is reserved for an authorized athletic event; and such was the holding of the United States District Court in a Colorado State University case of 1971, where the president had promulgated that policy on the day after a near-riot in the gymnasium at half-time during a basketball game with Brigham Young University, when individuals, who had been given permission to stage a demonstration *out-*

---

4. *Siegel* v. *Regents of University of California*, (Cal. App.), 57 Cal. Rptr. 463 (1967).

5. *Goldberg* v. *Regents of University of California*, (Cal. App.), 57 Cal. Rptr. 463 (1967).

6. *Schuyler* v. *State University of New York at Albany*, (N.Y. App. Div.), 297 N.Y.S. 2d 368 (1969).

side the building (against the attitude of the Mormon Church toward
Negroes), had invaded the basketball court and triggered a fight in
which missiles were thrown and a press photographer was hit on the
head with a heavy piece of angle-iron.

District Judge Fred M. Winner said, "Balancing the rights in this
case, this court concludes that the University must prevail. This is not a
Tinker situation where the school officials had mere apprehension of
trouble. Colorado State University was already in trouble. . . . School
regulations and policy statements need not meet all of the standards
of certainty required of criminal statutes; they must be reasonable and
understandable. This policy statement is understandable and, under the
facts and circumstances here present, the policy is reasonable."[7]

Compare this decision with that of the U.S. District Court in
Wyoming in the case of *Williams* v. *Eaton,* discussed herein in Chapter 8, "Various Facets of Student Life."

This present chapter is concerned with rights of speech, assembly,
and petition for redress of grievances. Other chapters herein deal with
the right to invite and hear speakers, the freedom of the student press,
due process in disciplinary proceedings, and unreasonable searches and
seizures. Issues of constitutional civil rights also infiltrate into other
chapters at various points. In fact, they are so ubiquitous that they may
well be said to form the principal *motif* of this present volume. For
that reason a quotation of Section 1983 of Title 42, *United States Code,*
will be found as the frontispiece.

Assemblies on Campus Can Not Be Made Wholly
Contingent on Advance Permission

A federal district court in South Carolina held in 1967 that a college rule broadly prohibiting students from joining in "parades, cele-
brations, and demonstrations," without first getting approval of the
college authorities, was a prior restraint on the right of freedom of
speech and assembly, incompatible with the First Amendment, and
invalid. Hence suspension of students for violating the rule was unlawful.[8]

---

7. *Evans* v. *State Board of Agriculture,* (U.S.D.C., Colo.), 39 *U.S. Law
Week* 2685 (June 1, 1971).

8. *Hammond* v. *South Carolina State College,* (U.S.D.C., S.C.), 272 F. Supp.
974 (1967).

In the course of that opinion U.S. District Judge Robert W. Hemphill remarked: ". . . The power of the president to oversee, to rule, is an integral part of the mechanism for providing and promoting education at State College. Be that as it may, colleges, like all other institutions, are subject to the Constitution. Academic progress and academic freedom demand their share of Constitutional protection. . . ."

This decision could easily be overestimated as to its effect. The college rule here was a textbook case of an unconstitutionally overbroad and too sweeping regulation. A college can make precise and reasonable rules governing the time and place of meetings on the campus without colliding with the constitution.

Up to the present, the federal courts are not always in agreement as to exactly what rules satisfy the constitutional requirements and what do not. This lack of consensus is shown by the frequency of reversals and dissenting opinions.

The difficulties sometimes experienced by federal courts in establishing firm precedents in this area are illustrated by a 1971 decision of the U.S. Fourth Circuit Court of Appeals which reversed a thoughtful and well-reasoned opinion of a U.S. District Court in Virginia.

The Madison College Case

Madison College in Virginia has rules regarding "demonstrations," in pertinent part:

"A demonstration is considered to be a public manifestation of welcome, approval, protest or condemnation as by a mass meeting, procession, picketing, or occupation or premises. (Exhibitions commonly associated with social or athletic activities are not within the purview of this definition and its supporting regulations.)"

. . . . .

"1. The demonstration is to be registered with the Office of Student Activities 48 hours in advance."

. . . . .

"4. Demonstrations are forbidden in the areas of the Health Center, inside any buildings, and in the locations of fire hydrants. The appropriate areas for demonstrations will be determined at the time of the request."

. . . . .

"When an assembly of students not authorized . . . has been requested to disband . . . those students refusing to comply will be subject to immediate suspension."

In April 1970 numbers of students were inclined to express their dissent from the college's decision not to retain various members of the teaching faculty. On April 23 they held a meeting in the Blackburn Hall Auditorium and a gathering near Gibbons Hall. Each of these assemblies was billed as a "free university" or "teach-in" concerning broad issues of campus governance. Both were conducted in accord with college rules—the outdoor meeting having been "registered" as prescribed in Rule 1, and the indoor meeting-space having been "requisitioned" in advance as required by another rule.

Immediately after these meetings some of the participants decided to move on to Wilson Hall, the administration building, and assembled there at about 11 p.m., without advance arrangements. The building was not locked, and about 25 persons decided to enter the lobby and corridor and remain there until morning to dramatize their concern and to meet with President G. Tyler Miller when he arrived at his office. The group was quiet and orderly.

At 12:35 a.m., the dean of student services, James Fox, came in and warned the group that they were conducting an unregistered demonstration in violation of the college rules, and would be subjected to immediate suspension if they did not leave within 15 minutes. Soon most of the group departed. The dean returned at 1:15 a.m. accompanied by a photographer who took pictures. The dean carried a tape recorder. He announced to the eight or nine persons present that a violation of regulations had occurred. They listened quietly and all departed within a few minutes.

On April 24, a number of students sought, more than 48 hours in advance, to "register" a "vigil" in Wilson Hall. Dean Fox disapproved this request because it would authorize a "demonstration" inside the building, contrary to Rule 4. Two days later a group of about 50 students and 3 professors assembled again in the Wilson Hall lobby at 8:50 p.m. with the same intentions as before. At 9 p.m. campus police began to lock the doors, and advised all the occupants to leave within five minutes. About half of the 50 left. Dean Fox arrived at 9:29 p.m. and gave the 27 persons present 15 minutes in which to leave. He said the students present would be subject to college disciplinary action, including suspension, and that nonstudents might be arrested.

Forty minutes later he returned and announced that the students were subject to suspension. With him were other administrators who took names and photographs. The group remained in the building, and over the next two hours was approximately doubled in size. (The campus police had not locked all doors; and some students entered through unlocked windows.) There was no destruction of property, no disorder, no disturbance of any of the educational functions of the college.

Around midnight the police arrived and arrested about 30 of those in the Hall. The students offered no resistance, and swept the floor clean of litter before leaving. From here on our story follows only the college disciplinary proceedings. Lewis H. Sword and other leaders of the student group asked the federal district court for a declaratory adjudication as to the constitutionality of the pertinent college regulations.

District Judge Robert R. Merhige, Jr., declared in his memorandum opinion that both Rule 1 and Rule 4 (previously quoted) were "facially unconstitutional" (the latter insofar as it forbade demonstrations inside any building); that the same was true of the operative definition of a "demonstration"; and that the penalty provision allowing suspension of students who refused to comply with an order to disband an unauthorized demonstration was invalid as here applied.[9]

An order was issued to the effect that "the plaintiffs may not be subjected to discipline by the college for their participation in unregistered demonstrations in Wilson Hall on the nights of April 23 or 26, nor for their failure to disband such activities when directed to do so by a college official." The case was retained on the docket for consideration of such further requests for relief as might be made.

The kernel of the lengthy and scholarly opinion, citing many recent federal decisions, is "*Apprehension alone will not justify repression.*"

On July 1, 1971, the foregoing decision was reversed by the Fourth Circuit Court of Appeals, and remanded with instruction to dismiss the complaint.

Key statements from the Circuit opinion:

"In our opinion, the regulation proscribing the use of college

---

9. *Sword* v. *Fox*, (U.S.D.C., Va.), 317 F. Supp. 1055 (1970); reversed in Fourth Circuit Court of Appeals, July 1, 1971. (40 U.S. Law Week 2059).

buildings for demonstrations, especially as applied to the particular building involved here, is a valid and reasonable exercise of the authority of the college to promulgate and enforce rules and regulations, and does not represent an unreasonable limitation upon the First Amendment rights of the appellees and the class they represent. . . .

"A regulation which prohibits demonstrations within the college buildings 'measurably contributes to the maintenance of order and decorum within the educational system' and represents 'a reasonable exercise of the power and discretion' of the college authorities. . . . It is immaterial whether those in violation of the regulation were violent or peaceful. . . . The decision of the District Court is accordingly reversed and the action is remanded with instruction to dismiss the complaint."[10]

Observe next a judgment of the Fifth Circuit Court of Appeals which was cited with approval.

"The Student Expression Area" on Campus

The Students' Rights chapter of the Southwest Texas State University handbook (popularly known as "Hill Hints") contained a regulation governing the holding of meetings on campus:

"Students and University personnel may use the Student Expression Area located on the grass terraces in front of Old Main between the hours of 12 noon to 1 p.m., and from 5 to 7 p.m. Reservations for the Student Expression Area are made through the Dean of Students Office and must be made at least 48 hours in advance.

"Rules . . . :

1. No interference with free flow of traffic.

2. No interruption of the orderly conduct of University affairs.

3. No obscene materials.

4. Person making the reservation is responsible for seeing that the area is left clean and in a good state of repair.

"When a registered student organization plans to invite a non-University person to address a meeting, his name must be submitted to the Dean of Students at least 48 hours before the event."

The Vietnam Moratorium held its first public protest October 15,

---

10. *Sword* v. *Fox*, (U.S.C.A., Va.), 40 U.S. Law Week 2059 (1971).

1969. Southwest Texas State University authorized a local program to take place in the Fine Arts Auditorium from 11 a.m. to 12 noon.

Without authorization and contrary to regulations, demonstrations were held from 10 to 11 a.m. and from 12 noon to 1:15 p.m. in the Huntington Statue area which is between two classroom buildings. Faculty and students subsequently complained that the demonstration disturbed and disrupted regularly scheduled classes; but no disciplinary action was taken as a result of the October events.

For the mid-November meeting, the Moratorium group insisted on 10 a.m. to 2 p.m. in the Huntington Statue area. Both the time and the place requested were outside the handbook rule quoted above. About 50 students congregated in the statue area at 9:45 a.m. on November 13. The dean of students, Floyd Martine, arrived and told them to leave. Only 10 refused and remained. They sat on the grass. They caused no injury to property. They attracted a crowd of onlookers. The university officials, believing they could not maintain order if they allowed this situation to continue for four hours, summarily suspended the recalcitrants until the fall of 1970, beginning at once, November 13, 1969.

The suspended students made no complaint about due process. They attacked nothing but the validity of the rules quoted herein from the handbook. U.S. District Judge Jack Roberts refused to grant an injunction to prevent their suspension; but on interlocutory appeal the Fifth Circuit stayed the refusal of an injunction and enjoined the suspension pending final disposition of the case—on the ground that the students would suffer irreparable injury if wrongly suspended. Circuit Judges John Minor Wisdom and Bryan Simpson concurred in this; but Circuit Judge James P. Coleman filed a dissent in which he said he was of the opinion that no substantial federal question was presented in this case.

Six months later the same court, with the panel then being composed of Circuit Judges Homer Thornberry, David W. Dyer, and Charles Clark, disposed of the case in accord with Judge Coleman's view. This decision vacated the stay and injunction, affirmed District Judge Roberts' original order, and remanded the case for completion of the proceedings.[11]

Judge Clark: "Appellants (students) contend that the Hill Hints

---

11. *Bayless* v. *Martine*, (U.S.C.A., Tex.), 430 F. 2d 872 (1970).

regulation on its face amounts to an impermissible prior restraint upon the exercise of First Amendment rights. It can not be read so broadly. . . . The Student Expression Area regulation in Hill Hints is a valid exercise of the University's right to adopt and enforce reasonable, non-discriminatory regulations as to the time, place and manner of student expressions and demonstrations."

Judge Thornberry: "The crucial fact in this case is that the university did not prohibit this demonstration. It merely regulated the time and place at which it could be held. My concurrence is based upon my judgment that the demonstrators knowingly and intentionally violated a lawful direction of the Dean of Students that prohibited them from using this particular time and place for their demonstration, after being specifically warned by the dean that they would be suspended if they persisted in this particular course of action."

Temporary Emergency Prohibition
of All Campus Assemblies

San Fernando State College in southern California was troubled by various disorders in the winter of 1969. There was on the campus a designated place, the Open Forum, which was understood to be the approved place for large student assemblies. The disorders were intensified during January 7 and 8, 1969. It was said that during those days a daily habit was developing—the students would gather at the Open Forum in the forenoons and be harangued by activist speakers until their psychic temperature was raised to boiling, and then about noon they would proceed *en masse* to the administration building and engage in disruptive activities. There was a tendency for the disturbances to continue through the afternoon and night.

Acting President D. T. Oviatt had agreed to address a meeting at the Open Forum at noon January 9; but at 2 a.m. on that day the situation appeared so desperate to him that he decided to prepare an emergency order, which was widely disseminated about the campus by various effective means between 6:30 and 7 that morning. After describing the escalation of disruptive activities through the winter and especially during the preceding few days, and explaining that the emergency measure was temporary only and hopefully would be in effect only briefly, the order said:

"During the emergency all demonstrations, assemblies, rallies, and meetings in the Open Forum or elsewhere, except for classes, are pro-hibited. The meeting in the Open Forum for 12 noon today has been cancelled."

By 9:30 a.m. many students were assembled in the Open Forum, waiting for speeches, apparently ready to repeat the routines of the preceding days. At that time one Captain Lembke of the city police de-partment appeared with some college administrators. Many city patrol-men were in the immediate vicinity. Captain Lembke decided that the meeting was unlawful, and ordered the assembly to disperse, warning that any persons who did not leave would be arrested.

Soon large numbers were arrested and taken to jail, charged with violation of *California Penal Code* section 409, which makes it a crime to remain present at a place of unlawful assembly after being lawfully warned to disperse. Eventually some were convicted, and appeals from the convictions were carried up in at least two suits.[12] In both cases the convictions were affirmed. In the *Hairston* case the three judges of the California court of appeal were unanimous. (Judges Smith, James G. Whyte, and Beach Vasey.) In the *Uptgraft* case Judges Smith and Vasey concurred, but Judge Delbert E. Wong entered a persuasive dissent:

"Received into evidence were five reels of motion picture films, four taken by police photographers and one taken by a cameraman from a television station. . . . Three reels which were taken January 9 minutely depict the gathering of the students in the Open Forum, the giving of speeches, the giving of the order to disperse, and the arrests. The students were cooperative and submitted to arrest peacefully and without incident. Some of the women students were crying as they were being arrested, or waiting to be arrested. There were many tear-streaked faces and determined looks, but no resistance. After viewing the films, one can only conclude that the students were submitting to arrest because they believed that they had a right to assemble peace-fully in the Open Forum area.

"I do not think that a college administrator, a police officer, or even a legislative body can ignore the 'clear and present danger test' and prevent people, including students from peacefully assembling, at a place where they have a right to be, merely because those responsible

---

12. *People* v. *Hairston*, 8 Cal. App. 3d Supp. 19, 87 Cal. Rptr. 470 (1970); and *People* v. *Uptgraft*, 8 Cal. App. 3d Supp. 1, 87 Cal. Rptr 459 (1970).

for making the administrative or legislative decision *suspect* or *fear* that the assembly may at some future time become unlawful."

In other words, to Judge Delbert E. Wong, this was a police break-up of a lawful assembly. Regarding the necessity of safeguarding free speech and assembly for students and teachers, he quoted an eloquent passage from a recent California decision concerned with teachers.[13]

The convicted student leaders received jail sentences or other criminal penalties. Hairston, who was sentenced to 60 days in jail, took a petition for *habeas corpus* to the federal district court, but this was denied by District Judge Robert J. Kelleher.[14]

Speech, Actual or Symbolic, Distinguished from Disruptive Action

On April 15, 1970, several hundred students at Pennsylvania State University, led by a group known as the Coalition for Peace, staged a rally in front of "Old Main." This culminated in a march to the Ordnance Research Laboratory. The activities of the laboratory were not hindered, and university authorities did not interfere with either the rally or the march.

Later in the day the students returned to Old Main and surged into the building in a combative mood, and executed a "sit-in" or "take-over" which resulted in personal injuries to some members of the university staff and some damage to property. The board of trustees appointed a special three-member disciplinary panel to hear charges brought against 40 of the students for violation of university rules. (The panel was composed of Robert E. Woodside, former superior court judge; Genevieve Blatt, former state secretary of internal affairs; and William T. Coleman, a Philadelphia lawyer).

After several days of hearings, during which the accused students were "afforded a wide range of constitutional rights," a majority of the panel (Mr. Coleman submitting a minority report), recommended penalties ranging from permanent suspension (for five students adjudged most culpable) to probation for selected lengths of time for a dozen others. The recommendations were to President Eric A.

---

13. *Los Angeles Teachers' Union* v. *Los Angeles City Board of Education*, 71 A.C. 572, 78 Cal Rptr. 723, 455 P. 2d 827 (1969).

14. *Application of Hairston*, (U.S.D.C., Cal.), 323 F. Supp. 784 (1971).

Walker who approved them and ordered the penalties prescribed. The first litigation was by Geoffrey Sill and Steven D. Weiss, graduate students, who received final notices of permanent dismissal June 30, one day after the beginning of the summer term.

Still and Weiss asked U.S. District Judge William J. Nealon, Jr., for a preliminary injunction to reinstate them immediately to attend the summer term pending final decision on the merits. The petition was denied on the ground that they had not established that they would suffer irreparable damage if injunctive relief were not forthcoming. Specifically, they would have access to the university libraries, even if not as students; no report would be made of their disciplinary troubles to their respective draft boards pending a final decision on the merits, hence no change in their selective service status; their fellowship or assistantship for the next academic year would be held open; and their major professors would give them academic advice on request. A biologic science laboratory would even preserve and keep alive a living microbiologic culture that had been developed by Weiss for his research purposes.[15]

In the later decision on the merits, Judge Nealon noted that Section II(A) of the *University Guide* (rules and regulations) "recognizes the right of lawful assembly and demonstration. However, while recognizing that these rights must be protected by the university, the regulation excludes any *action* or combination of actions which *unreasonably* interferes with the *operation* of, and right of *access* to physical accommodations used in the performance of teaching, research, and administrative functions and related adjunct activities of the university, or infringes upon the rights of others to freely participate in its programs and services.

"Whether it is speech-connected or stems solely from an aim to physically confiscate University property, it is not constitutionally protected and need not be tolerated."[16]

The opinion holds that the requirements of due process as in *Dixon* v. *Alabama* (see Chapter 17 herein) need not be followed when the disciplinary penalty is anything lighter than temporary suspension. (This is in accord with the more common expression of the same point:

15. *Sill* v. *Pennsylvania State University,* (U.S.D.C., Pa.), 315 F. Supp. 125 (1970).

16. *Sill* v. *Pennsylvania State University,* (U.S.D.C., Pa.), 318 F. Supp. 608 (1970). Preceded by (U.S.D.C., Pa.), 315 F. Supp. 125 (1970).

the requirements of due process are simpler in cases of less gravity, where relatively small or trivial offenses are disposed of with less time-consuming formality.) It also holds that the appointment of the special disciplinary panel, even though after the offenses had been committed, was no violation of due process.

The opinion also speaks of vagueness and overbreadth of rules, and expressly favors the degree of generality approved by the Eighth Circuit in the *Esteban* case over the "meticulous specificity" espoused by District Judge James E. Doyle of the Seventh Circuit. (See Chapter 18 herein, on "How Specific Must Disciplinary Rules Be?")

Non-Disruptive Demonstration on Campus
Is Protected as Symbolic Speech

Reversal of a U.S. District Court judgment by the Circuit Court of Appeals was necessary to reinstate a student at the Virginia Polytechnic Institute and State University who had been excluded from readmission in the fall of 1969 for disciplinary reasons.

Thomas J. Saunders was described as a bright young man who "through two and one-half years at the school had maintained an unusually high academic average and an unblemished disciplinary record." Saunders was active in the local Committee for Peace in Vietnam, which planned and executed a peaceful demonstration against war at the commissioning exercises for the ROTC units on the campus June 7, 1969, where General William G. Westmoreland, Chief of Staff of the Army, was the featured speaker. The demonstration did not disrupt the ceremonies. No person who engaged in it was arrested, and none other than Saunders was disciplined in any way.

VPI requires all students (except summer school) to apply for readmission each year, and responds with a letter of tentative acceptance, to be followed by notice of acceptance in August. Students thus accepted are called "matriculated students" in the parlance of the registrar. It happened that Saunders, overloaded with curricular and extra-curricular work and ambitious to maintain his high scholastic record, had "resigned" April 28 and at the same time applied for readmission at the next fall term. He received his notice of tentative admission May 6, and signed and returned his acceptance May 7. Technically he was not a "matriculated student" at the time of the demonstration in June.

There was a VPI rule, in part as follows: "If there are any individuals who are not matriculated students or staff of the University participating in picketing, demonstrations, or similar activities . . . on campus . . ., these individuals will immediately be asked to leave. On refusal, they will be subject to arrest." On this basis the institution undertook to discipline Saunders by refusing him readmission.

Chief District Judge Ted Dalton denied Saunders preliminary injunctive relief and dismissed his complaint; but because classes were about to begin, Circuit Judge John D. Butzner, Jr., stayed the effect of the order and enjoined the university from excluding Saunders until further order of the Court of Appeals. On review of the merits, Circuit Judge Harrison L. Winter, sitting with Circuit Judges Butzner and J. Braxton Craven, Jr., held that denial of readmission for participating in the peaceful, orderly, and non-disruptive demonstration was unconstitutional invasion of Saunders' right to free speech.[17] The hassle about technical "matriculation" was brushed aside as inconsequential, as it deserved to be.

Judge Dalton confronted another case from VPI in May 1970, of which the facts and conclusions of law have not yet been reported. He set a hearing for May 22, and said tersely: "This court desires to fully preserve the right of peaceful and orderly dissent, but it will not overturn the decisions of the college administration in suspending those who seek by force to thwart not only the operation of the institution, but also their own education and that of their fellow-students."[18]

Use of University Facilities for Anti-Draft Meeting

Another example of divided judicial opinion is afforded by a California case which reached the Ninth Circuit Court of Appeals. An unincorporated association at the University of California at Berkeley, known as Campus Draft Opposition, a recognized and registered campus organization, applied for the use of the Greek Theatre for a "Viet Nam Commencement" on May 17, 1968.

The purpose of the occasion was to honor those young men who, "for reasons of conscience, believe that the actions of the United States in Viet Nam are unjust and immoral and who therefore can not

17. *Saunders* v. *Virginia Polytechnic Institute,* (U.S.C.A., Va.), 417 F. 2d 1127 (1969); reversing 307 F. Supp. 326 (1969).

18. *Jane Ruth Seymour* v. *Virginia Polytechnic Institute and State University,* (U.S.D.C., Va.), 313 F. Supp. 555 (1970).

participate in the Armed Forces." The purpose of the association was to provide support for such men in various ways.

The regents rejected the application, pointing to their rule: "University facilities shall not be used for the purpose of organizing or carrying out unlawful activity." They reached this decision after the distinguished University Counsel, Thomas C. Cunningham, had advised them that the proposed assembly would be in violation of the federal Selective Service Act, while a group of five professors in the law school had submitted a memorandum to the contrary.

When certain members of Campus Draft Opposition requested an injunction against enforcement of the rule, U.S. District Judge Lloyd H. Burke dismissed the complaint. This judgment was affirmed by the Court of Appeals, in an opinion by Circuit Judge John F. Kilkenney, joined by Circuit Judge Ozell M. Trask. District Judge Warren J. Ferguson, sitting by designation, entered a vigorous and lengthy dissent, in which he said no decision should have been made by a single judge at the district court level, but a special three-judge federal court should have been convened to decide the constitutional issue.

Judge Ferguson regarded the regents' resolution as an unconstitutional prior restraint on speech and peaceful assembly. He cited the words of Mr. Justice Potter Stewart in a 1968 decision of the United States Supreme Court[19] in which it was said the power of government could not be used "to deny or unwarrantedly abridge the right of assembly and the opportunities for the communication of thought . . . immemorially associated with resort to public places."[20]

Demonstration on Campus Chiefly by Non-student Adults and Children

In the spring of 1966, from early March until mid-June, black students and others at Alcorn Agricultural and Mechanical College near the small town of Lorman, Mississippi, carried on several successive marches and demonstrations against J. D. Boyd, president of the College, demanding his removal. The activities were led by Charles Evers, field director for the National Association for the Advancement

---

19. *Shuttlesworth* v. *City of Birmingham*, 394 U.S. 147, 89 S.Ct. 935, 22 L.Ed. 2d 162 (1968).

20. *Sellers* v. *Regents of University of California*, (U.S.C.A., Cal.), 432 F. 2d 493 (1970).

of Colored People. On March 4, 250 Negro adults, marching in order-ly fashion on the campus to present a statement of grievances to the president, were halted by the college police chief, the county sheriff, and a force of state highway police, and about 235 of the marchers were arrested.

On the same day the demonstrators filed a complaint in the United States district court, seeking adjudication of their right peacefully to assemble and petition the college president regarding redress of griev-ances concerning the operation of the college. The court issued a tem-porary restraining order permitting, on March 12, 200 marchers to proceed from an entance of the campus to the Administration Building and send a committee into the president's office to present a petition of grievances, then return to the point of assembly. This took place as planned, with no interference or disorder. President Boyd promptly transmitted the grievances to the Board of Trustees of State Institutions of Higher Learning at the state capital (Jackson), which governs all state colleges and universities; and, on March 24, the leaders of the demonstrators submitted to the court a request to withdraw their com-plaint, but without any drafted order, and no order was made or signed by the court.

On April 1 and 2, Charles Evers spoke to crowds at the nearby town of Port Gibson, announcing a large demonstration on the Alcorn campus for April 4, and urging attendance, including school children who were to stay out of school for the purpose. April 4 was a day of considerable disorder, with children circling the president's house, clapping, singing, and calling out obscenities to the patrolmen present. Students joined the disturbance, cursing the patrolmen from classroom and dormitory windows. As the day wore on the police arrested 35 persons, but the same level of disorder continued until after a mass meeting just off one edge of the campus at 9:30 p.m., where Evers urged all to continue the same activities the next day.

The state police had obtained an injunction from the local state court, forbidding any marching on the campus; but some 60 children climbed over and through the fences and again surrounded the presi-dent's house, where the campus police chief tried to disperse them with hoses that had insufficient water pressure and with tear-gas that blew in his own face. At 8:40 p.m. Evers assembled his crowd for a march on the campus contrary to the injunction and the orders of the police. At this point the police were physically between Evers' assembly of

1,200 persons just outside the campus, and some 200 students on the other hand. The highway was totally blocked, and when the police began efforts to clear it they were surrounded. Bottles were thrown, and five shots fired (allegedly none by police, who threw tear-gas). One patrolman had his rifle and 30 rounds of ammunition taken from him, while a loaded rifle was taken from one of the demonstrators. Some persons on both sides were injured, but fortunately none seriously.

On the night of April 7, windows and doors were broken and some other damage done to college buildings. On April 13, at the request of the state attorney general, the federal court held a second hearing, where Evers appeared with his counsel and moved for a continuance and voluntarily agreed not to lead, participate in, or advise further demonstrations pending a full hearing on the merits. The court granted the continuance and set trial for May 5. There was some sporadic disorder on the campus April 18, and on April 22, a contractor's temporary construction building on the campus was burned, and some damage was done to the exterior and interior of the Student Union Building.

April 27 the college authorities filed their answer, as had been directed by the court, and asked for an injunction against further demonstrations, and for money damages of $16,000 for damage to buildings and equipment, $33,000 for expense to the highway patrol, and $2,000 for costs to the county sheriff. May 23 a group of elementary and high school students appeared on the campus shouting and singing and disrupting the annual commencement exercises.

Additional continuances were granted, so that finally the trial was begun July 8, and lasted six days. In the opinion of the court, District Judge Dan M. Russell, Jr., stated the main question: "To what extent can either side be restrained, on the one hand without interfering with the rights of the plaintiffs to peaceful assembly and presentation of grievances, and on the other without judicial usurpation of administrative functions of school officials and the duty of law enforcement officials to maintain order?"

After considering the facts, Judge Russell remarked with acerbity that "there is nothing in the constitution or law for lawlessness, violence, or destruction of property under the guise of petition and protest. The right of free speech, assembly or protest has never been so judicially enlarged as to permit disruption of a school and destruction of its property." Accordingly the court dismissed the action of the plaintiffs (demonstrators) and permanently enjoined them from "inciting, leading, participating in or counseling any marches, demonstrations or disturbances on the campus."

No damages were awarded in the absence of evidence that those who caused the damage were identifiable members of the plaintiffs' class as defined by the court. This case is apparently unique because the plaintiffs were the leaders of the demonstrations, asking the court for an order against the defendants (college authorities and civil authorities) leaving the plantiffs free to continue to present their demonstrations unhindered, indefinitely. They were not protesting the arrests made March 4, or at other times; and there was no college disciplinary action involved in the complaint. In view of the circumstances, though dismissal of the complaint may seem to have been justified by the facts, possibly the permanent injunction against "any marches, demonstrations, or disturbances" may have been too sweeping. Would it have been more in accord with the constitutional rights of the plaintiffs if the court had declared their right to assemble, march, and present grievances, so long as these actions did not cause, or create a clear and present danger of, any material disruption of the operation of the college?

It seems that the demonstrations which occurred in this case were originated and led by adult citizens, not students; and that the disputes were exclusively between members of the Negro race, with no racial discrimination as a factor. To what extent were parents of students, alumni, and other citizens having a legitimate interest in the welfare of the college, involved? What was the substance of the grievances? These matters do not appear in the published report of the decision.[21]

Exhibit of Art as Free Expression

The concept of speech as comprehended in the wording of the First Amendment to the United States Constitution comprehends not only oral utterances, but also "symbolic speech" as demonstrated by picketing, placard-carrying, and parading; all forms of written or printed communication; and also expression through the arts such as music, painting, and sculpture.

---

21. *Evers* v. *Birdsong*, (U.S.D.C., Miss.), 287 F. Supp. 900 (1968).

At the University of Massachusetts there developed a well-established custom of scheduling successive art exhibits on the walls of a much-used corridor on the first floor of the Student Union Building—a corridor along which daily large numbers of students, faculty members, and visitors to the university passed to and from the dining facilities and other parts of the building. It was also frequented occasionally by persons of the general public, sometimes including children.

The custom of hanging art exhibits on the wall existed only by the tacit consent of the university authorities, and there was no written rule or regulation on the subject; but it was sufficiently well-received that the corridor had been redesigned and somewhat remodeled for the specific purpose of displaying exhibits of art.

By the usual informal procedure, involving the chairman of the department of art and a representative of the student union board, an exhibition of the works of Charles Close, then an art instructor, was scheduled for January 8 to January 31, 1967; and 31 of his paintings and drawings were put in place on the evening of January 7, under his supervision. Some were completed major works, while others were preliminary drawings or studies, included for educational purposes. Some of the paintings showed nude or partially nude figures and bathroom scenes. It was said that some of the male and female figures depicted the genitalia "in clinical detail"; "a skeleton was fleshed out only in this particular"; and two of the captions were: "I'm only 12 and already my mother's lover wants me," and "I am the only virgin in my school."

Immediately the exhibit gave rise to some unfavorable discussion and controversy, and several meetings including the president, the provost, the secretary of the university, and on some occasions the chairman of the art department were held to consider the matter. The artist-instructor was not present at any of these meetings, although on one occasion he was sitting in the anteroom but was not invited inside. On January 13 it was decided to remove the exhibition, and on that evening the paintings were taken from the walls without notice to the artist. His paintings were returned to him several days later. He sued in federal district court for a mandatory injunction to compel the university to restore the exhibit for the duration of the unexpired portion of the scheduled period. His contention was: "Art is as fully protected by the Constitution as political or social speech."

United States District Judge Francis J. W. Ford issued the desired order. "The University had adopted the policy of allowing such exhibitions. It had provided an area open to the public, and had moreover taken steps to adapt this area for that particular purpose. Plaintiff had fully complied with the procedure for scheduling a time for his exhibition and the works had been placed on display. In these circumstances, the court agrees with plaintiff that his right to maintain his exhibitions for the scheduled period came within the protection of the First and Fourteenth Amendments. Thereafter defendants could terminate the exhibition and remove his paintings only in accordance with the regulations narrowly drawn to serve the legitimate interests of the University."

In other words: "having chosen to permit and even to encourage expression in the form of exhibitions of art, the University can not by arbitrary or discriminatory action bar plaintiff from exhibiting his work for the period to which under the existing procedure he had become entitled to do so."

Judge Ford did not hold that, having no written regulations on the subject, the University could not have terminated the exhibition of art under any circumstances; but he held that it could do so only if there existed any grounds sufficient to justify under the Constitution such a restraint of freedom of expression. No such grounds appeared in this case, he said. "There was nothing in the evidence to show that the continuance of the exhibition for the scheduled period would have in any way resulted in any substantial interference with any legitimate interest of the University. At most the exhibition seems to have displeased some persons who saw it, and to have given rise to some lively discussion. There was also some vague evidence of a few complaints made to officials of the University. There was also evidence of one anonymous threat to damage the paintings, and evidence that one of the paintings had been stolen." (Here the judge inserted a footnote that security guards were available for assignment to protect the exhibition, as had been done on earlier occasions in the case of earlier exhibitions threatened by theft or vandalism.) "There was nothing to indicate any possibility of disorder or of interruption of the University's activities. At most the exhibition was a source of some annoyance or embarrassment, but this is far from providing adequate justification for infringement of plaintiff's constitutional right to free expression." Here the court cited *Tinker* v. *Des Moines* and *Hammond* v. *South Carolina State College.*

Finally, said Judge Ford: "There seems to have been no formal finding or statement by the defendants as to the reason why the paintings were removed. From the evidence it appears only that the officers who decided that they should be removed were agreed that this should be done because the paintings were 'inappropriate.' It needs no discussion to find that mere 'inappropriateness' not further explained or defined is far too vague a standard on which to base any limitation of freedom of expression."[22]

The university appealed from this decision, and it was flatly reversed by the United States court of appeals in an opinion by Chief Judge Aldrich, in which Circuit Judges McEntee and Coffin concurred without opinion. Noting that the holding "was not grounded upon a finding that defendants were unreasonable in their opinion," and that District Judge Ford had not thought it necessary to see the paintings himself, "apparently taking the position that, at least in the absence of express regulations as to what was impermissible, defendants had no right to censor simply on the basis of offensiveness which fell short of unlawful obscenity," the Circuit Judges said emphatically, "We disagree."

First, the court of appeals downgraded the importance of the artist's interest in exhibiting and the interest of students and the public in seeing what he had to show, as compared with the analogous interest of a possibly unpopular speaker in being permitted to speak, and the right of students and others to hear what he has to say. "Cases dealing with students' rights to hear . . . involve a medium and subject matter entitled to greater protection than plaintiff's art. Even as to verbal communication the extent of the protection may depend upon the subject matter. . . . We consider plaintiff's constitutional interest minimal."

Turning then to the university's interest, all persons passing through the corridor were viewed as a "captive audience," entitled to protection "against assault upon individual privacy, short of legal obscenity," quoting the United States Supreme Court decision in *Redrup* v. *New York;*[23] and also quoting from Professor Charles Alan Wright: "There are words that are not regarded as obscene, in the constitutional sense, that nevertheless need not be permitted in every

---

22. *Close* v. *Lederle,* (U.S.D.C., Mass.), 303 F. Supp. 1109 (1969). Reversed in same (U.S.C.A., 1 Cir.), 424 F. 2d 988 (1970).
23. *Redrup* v. *New York,* 386 U.S. 767, 87 S.Ct. 1414, 18 L.Ed. 2d 515 (1967).

context. Words that might properly be employed in a term paper about *Lady Chatterley's Lover* or in a novel submitted in a creative writing course take on a very different coloration if they are bellowed over a loudspeaker at a campus rally or appear prominently on a sign posted on a campus tree."[24]

"Freedom of speech must recognize," said the court, "at least within limits, freedom not to listen." The opinion concluded acridly, "With all respect to the district court, this is a case that should never have been brought," and ordered the judgment reversed and the case dismissed.

It is possible to feel that the opinion of the court of appeals met that of the district court rather obliquely, and that in this case we have an instance of opposite judgments traceable in part to the philosophical and social predilections of the different courts.

Looking at the university, it might also be possible to regard this case as a classic instance of imperfect communication on the campus. In view of the fact that the artist was apparently never once consulted about the difficulty, and never allowed to attend any administrative meeting in which it was discussed, and the fact that his paintings were removed from exhibition without any notice to him, might well have caused him to think the treatment accorded him personally was summary and perfunctory, not to say shabby, and caused him to think of litigation in defense of his constitutional rights. It is conceivable that had he been openly and cordially invited as a participant in the process, he might have voluntarily withdrawn all or part of his own exhibit under the circumstances.

Distributing Handbills or Publications on Campus as Protected Communication

In November 1965, Ashton Jones, wearing a sandwich board, "Help Stop Viet Nam War Now For Peace and Freedom," stood near the student union building on the campus of the University of Arizona at Tucson, and distributed handbills critical of the Vietnam

---

24. In Charles Alan Wright's article in *Vanderbilt Law Review*, October 1969, cited elsewhere herein. At this point the court of appeals also cited Emerson, "Toward a General Theory of the First Amendment," 72 *Yale Law Journal*, 877-938 (1963).

engagement to passers-by who would accept them. Campus police officers informed him of a university regulation:

"No hand-out items, including handbills, may be distributed on the campus grounds or in the campus buildings at any time, except programs and other informational items which are officially related to authorized meetings, and which are distributed in the room or rooms assigned to the events in question."

When Jones refused to leave the campus, the officers removed him forcibly. He immediately returned. A small crowd then gathered. There was some conversation about Vietnam. Eventually two bystanders seized the sandwich boards and destroyed them. Jones departed, but returned twice the next day, each time being removed by the campus police.

He then went to the U.S. district court for an injunction against enforcement of the rule. His complaint was dismissed, but on appeal to the Ninth Circuit court of appeals this judgment was reversed; and while the court of appeals issued no injunction, it directed the district court to "restrain permanently the Board of Regents of the State Universities from interfering with Jones' right to speak and to distribute handbills on areas of the Tucson campus which are open to the public generally."[25]

"The challenged regulation," said Circuit Judge Walter Ely, for the court, composed of Senior Circuit Judge Gilbert H. Jertberg and Circuit Judge James R. Browning in addition to himself, "completely prohibits the distribution of any handbills, at any time, in places open to the public generally. Such a blanket prohibition is clearly unrelated to any valid regulatory purpose when applied to public property generally open to the public at large." It seemed to be a classic case of an overbroad rule for purposes which could be accomplished by more specific regulation of the time, place, and manner of the exercise of the constitutionally protected rights of communication.

The Board of Curators of the University of Missouri has a rule prohibiting: "indecent conduct or speech." A graduate student in journalism, classified as a non-resident of Missouri, was expelled for participating in the distribution of indecent publications on and near the campus. She asked the federal district court to declare the rule

---

25. *Jones* v. *Board of Regents of University of Arizona*, (U.S.C.A., Ariz.), 436 F. 2d 618 (1970). Preceded by (U.S.C.A., Ariz.), 397 F. 2d 259 (1968).

unconstitutionally vague and overbroad and in impermissible limitation of free speech; and for injunctive relief to reinstate her on the theory that attendance at the state university partook of the nature of a civil right.

Rejecting her petition, the court said "indecent conduct or speech is definite enough for purposes of university regulations." Noting that she was not a resident of Missouri, the Judge also declared: "It has long been held . . . that one state can not be held responsible for the education of citizens of another state. . . . In the absence of exceptional circumstances not present in this case, no violation of plaintiff's federal rights of due process or of equal protection can therefore be predicated on her dismissal from the University of Missouri when she was not a domiciled resident of Missouri."[26]

This would seem to mean that an out-of-state student in a state university has no more rights as against the university than has a student in a private institution—which appears surprising, because the alleged wrong for which relief is sought is plainly "state action."

26. *Papish* v. *Board of Curators of the University of Missouri*, (U.S.D.C., Mo.), Western District of Missouri, Civ. Action No. 1466 (May 7, 1971).

CHAPTER 14

THE "SPEAKER BAN" FUROR[1]

CHARLES ALAN WRIGHT, professor of law at the University of Texas who delivered the Oliver Wendell Holmes lectures at the Vanderbilt University School of Law in April 1969 said:

"I cannot find a single case decided on its merits in this decade in which a speaker ban has been upheld by a court. . . . I am strongly tempted to believe that the only good speaker ban is one that has not yet been tested in court."[2] The record has continued unspoiled.

North Carolina and Illinois

In 1963 North Carolina enacted a measure prohibiting any person known to be a member of the Communist party, or any person who had pleaded the Fifth Amendment in a loyalty investigation, from being invited to speak on the campus of any state-supported university or college. Controversy ensued, and Governor Dan Moore appointed a special "speaker policy study commission" which recommended that speakers as described in the statute should be allowed to appear only

---

1. Major parts of this chapter were first published in *The Educational Forum,* Vol. 35, No. 4, pp. 471-478 (May 1971), under the title "Speaker Bans and the Courts."

2. At pages 1050, 1051 of Charles Alan Wright, "The Constitution on the Campus." *Vanderbilt Law Review* XXII, No. 5 (October 1969), pp. 1027-1088.

"infrequently" and only "when it would serve educational purposes." All the institutional governing boards then adopted these recommendations, and in 1965 the legislature amended the act of 1963 to delegate authority in the matter to the boards.

In 1968 the duly elected president of the student body at the Chapel Hill campus of the University of North Carolina, and other officers and members of recognized student organizations, wishing to invite Herbert Aptheker (avowed Communist) and Frank Wilkinson (outspoken advocate of abolishing the U.S. House Un-American Activities Committee who once pleaded the Fifth Amendment) to speak on the campus, found their invitations repudiated and the speakers rejected by Acting Chancellor J. Caryle Sitterson, backed by President William Friday.

The students, joined as plaintiffs by the prospective speakers, then sued in federal district court to have declared unconstitutional the statute of 1965 and the rules of the trustees adopted under it in 1966. The court granted the injunction sought, and pronounced the statute and the rules null and void, because of vagueness. They ran afoul of the First Amendment protection of free speech and assembly because a prohibitory statute must be worded with sharp precision so that a reasonable interpretation will not leave doubt as to what is forbidden and what is not, thus actually limiting the freedom of prudent or timid persons who will stay far away from the area of doubt.

"In order to withstand constitutional attack," such statutes, said the court, "must impose a purely ministerial duty upon the person charged with approving or disapproving an invitation to a speaker falling within the statutory classifications, or contain standards sufficiently detailed to define the bounds of discretion. Neither criterion has been met with respect to the procedures and regulations in question."

Said U.S. District Judge Edwin M. Stanley: "It is beyond question that boards of trustees of state-supported colleges and universities have every right to promulgate and enforce rules and regulations consistent with constitutional principles, governing the appearance of all guest speakers. . . . No one has an absolute right to speak on a college or university campus, but once such institution opens its doors to visiting speakers it must do so under principles that are constitutionally valid."[3]

---

3. *Dickson* v. *Sitterson*, (U.S.D.C., N.C.), 280 F. Supp. 486 (1968).

In 1947 the Illinois legislature enacted a measure known as the Clabaugh Act, providing that "No trustee, official, instructor or other employee of the University of Illinois shall extend to any subversive, seditious, and un-American organization, or to its representatives, the use of any facilities of the University for the purpose of carrying on, advertising, or publicizing the activities of such organization."

Students at the Chicago Circle campus of the University of Illinois brought a class action before a special three-judge federal court to have this statute declared unconstitutional and void. Among the plaintiffs was a group known as Illinois Humanists, whose proposed invitation to a guest speaker (Louis Diskin, a Communist) had been rejected by the administration, the court found, "Solely on the basis of the speaker's associations and the views to be espoused." It was clear that the standing policy of the university was to allow any guest speaker who had been invited by a recognized student group to speak at a reasonable time, space permitting.

"We hold," said District Judge Alexander J. Napoli, "that the Act, both on its face and as applied to these plaintiffs, had denied them due process of law, because it lacks the precision of language required for a statute regulating an area so closely intertwined with First Amendment liberties; because it is an unjustifiable prior restraint to speech; and because it lacks the procedural safeguards required for a form of regulation amounting to censorship."

He went on to explain that speech may be suppressed only when it presents a clear and present danger that substantive evil may result. "A statute which fails to provide an ascertainable standard of conduct and which because of its vagueness inhibits the exercise of constitutionally protected freedoms of speech and assembly is void. . .

"A statute purporting to regulate expression may not be so broad in its sweep as to hazard the loss or impairment of First Amendment freedoms by appearing to cover speech which may not constitutionally be regulated . . .

"Any system of prior restraint comes to this Court bearing a heavy burden against its constitutional validity . . .

"Viewed against the backdrop of these constitutional principles, the Act, and the regulations made pursuant to it, are abhorrent to the Constitution of the United States."[4]

---

4. *Snyder* v. *Board of Trustees of University of Illinois*, (U.S.D.C. Ill.), 286 F. Supp. 927 (1968).

In Alabama and Tennessee

Auburn University in Alabama had rules barring as a guest speaker "any person convicted of a felony," and also apparently anyone having "ideas Auburn could not sanction." These rules were presumably written by the former President Harry H. Philpott and administered by him.

The Human Rights Forum, a student organization duly recognized as such, invited William Sloan Coffin, the controversial Chaplain of Yale, to address it; whereupon the administration forbade his appearance. Representatives of the forum asked the United States district court to enjoin the university from interfering, and to declare the rules unconstitutional.

District Judge Frank M. Johnson granted the injunction, and pronounced the rules invalid. Quoting the First Amendment, "Congress shall make no law . . . abridging the freedom of speech . . . or the right of the people peaceably to assemble," he pointed out that the United States Supreme Court has recognized that hearers and readers have rights under that provision. "There can no longer be much doubt that constitutional freedoms must be respected in the relationships between students and faculty and their university . . . Indeed, it could be argued that an open forum is even more important on a campus than among the public generally."

Quickly noting that "an institution might provide for procedures permitting an orderly scheduling of facilities, and it might preclude conflicts with academic events," the court then declared "the regulations may not be used to deny either the speakers or the listeners equal protection of the laws by discriminating among speakers according to the orthodoxy or popularity of their political or social views."

After observing that at the time of this suit Chaplain Coffin had been convicted of a felony in a federal district court in Massachusetts, but that conviction was then on appeal, Judge Johnson remarked that lawyers would not apply the word "convicted" until after all appeals had been exhausted. (The conviction was in fact later reversed.)

Further, said Judge Johnson, "That part of the regulation which would bar speakers whose views Auburn could not sanction also sweeps overbroadly, although it is difficult for this Court to see why a university administration should be thought to have the authority to approve the ideas of a campus speaker as a condition to the speaker's appearance at the invitation of students and faculty. If this is a legitimate concern, it can be dealt with in ways other than totally barring the speaker.

"The vice in these regulations, however, is really far more basic than their just being vague and overbroad. These regulations . . . are not regulations of conduct at all . . . The State of Alabama can not, through its President of Auburn University, regulate the content of ideas students may hear . . . Such action . . . is unconstitutional censorship . . . While it can be said that President Philpott has the ultimate power to determine whether a speaker is invited to the campus, the First Amendment right to hear of the students and faculty of Auburn University means that this determination may not be made for the wrong reasons or for no reason at all.

"The evidence in this case does not reflect any likelihood of disruption of the academic functions and mission of Auburn University by reason of the appearance and lecture of the Rev. Coffin."[5] Five months later this decision was affirmed by the United States Court of Appeals, Fifth Circuit, in an opinion by Circuit Judge Griffin B. Bell.

The University of Tennessee had an officially sanctioned organization exclusively of students, known simply as "Issues," which operated a lecture series on an annual budget of $12,000, allotted from student activities fees. During the academic year 1968-69 this organization's proposed invitations to Dick Gregory, Negro civil rights activist, and Timothy Leary, of hallucinogenic drug fame, were rejected by the university administration.

Rules in the student handbook included: "An invitation to a speaker who is to be sponsored by a student organization must be approved by the appropriate officers and faculty-alumni advisers to that organization and registered with and approved by the Dean of Students as meeting the following criteria:

"(1) The speaker's competence and topic shall be relevant to the approved constitutional purpose of the organization;

"(2) There is no reason to believe that the speaker intends to present a personal defense against alleged misconduct or crime which is being adjudicated in the courts;

"(3) There is no reason to believe that he might speak in a

---

5. *Brooks* v. *Auburn University*, (U.S.D.C., Ala.), 296 F. Supp. 188 (1969). Affirmed, (U.S.CA., 5 Cir.), 412 F. 2d 1171 (1969).

libelous, scurrilous or defamatory manner or in violation of public laws which prohibit incitement to riot and conspiracy to overthrow the government by force."

The aggrieved students attacked these rules as unconstitutionally broad and vague, and asked for an injunction and a declaratory judgment to that effect. Chief Judge Robert L. Taylor wrote the decision of the United States district court. He granted no injunction, because "The defendants are responsible citizens who occupy high positions in state government. We believe that they will abide by the declaration of this Court that the current policy of the University of Tennessee is not in accord with the plaintiffs' First Amendment rights because the standards fixed for the selection of outside speakers are too broad and vague . . . but plaintiffs may renew their application at an appropriate time if it becomes necessary.

"The University has made it its policy to allow recognized student groups to invite speakers and to make university facilities available to both speaker and audience. The regulations by which the University denies permission for the appearance of speakers are required by the Constitution to be clearly and narrowly worded. The existing regulations in the Student Handbook do not satisfy those requirements." (Because they are susceptible of arbitrary determination.)

Citing the North Carolina, Illinois, and Auburn University decisions of recent months, and observing that they are in general harmony with established definitions of First Amendment rights by the United States Supreme Court, District Judge Taylor added: "The interchange of ideas and beliefs is a constitutionally protected necessity for the advancement of society."[6]

Mississippi

In Mississippi, the Board of Trustees of State Institutions of Higher Learning governs all the state universities and colleges. Its rules regarding guest speakers, applicable to all campuses, were challenged as to constitutionality by student organizations at the two principal universities. A faculty association and other interested persons joined as plaintiffs.

6. *Smith* v. *University of Tennessee*, (U.S.D.C., Tenn), 300 F. Supp. 777 (1969).

The rules adopted at various times during recent years were first examined by a special three-judge federal court in January 1969, and found unconstitutionally vague on their face "for lack of objective measurement, thus falling within the compass of those decisions of the Supreme Court holding that a law forbidding or requiring conduct in terms so vague that men of common intelligence must necessarily guess at its meaning and differ as to its application, violates due process of law."[7]

Among the causes for rejection found in these rules were clauses apparently barring "speakers who will do violence to the academic atmosphere," "persons in disrepute in the area from whence they come," "those charged with crime or other moral wrongs," "any person who advocates a philosophy of the overthrow of the government of the United States," "any announced political candidate or any person who wishes to speak on behalf of a political candidate," or "sectarian or political meetings on the campuses, conducted by organizations outside the college complex." These, said the court, "obviously must be, and are, condemned under the void-for-vagueness doctrine."

The board of trustees, wishing to submit new regulations for the approval of the court, was allowed sixty days in which to do so, and did so on March 10, 1969, only to see them held to be "either invalid for vagueness under the Due Process Clause, as were the former regulations, or in clear violation of the Free Speech and Assembly provisions of the First and Fourteenth Amendments as well as the Equal Protection Clause of the Fourteenth Amendment." This was the finding of the three-judge court composed of Circuit Judge Coleman and District Judges Russell and Keady, the opinion being written by Chief District Judge William C. Keady. The court patiently set out each of the thirteen new regulations separately and explained why it could not stand. Although this was succinctly done, it required about five thousand words, and space forbids its full reproduction here, desirable as that might be. Only two salient examples can appear:

1. Barring a person who "advocates" violent overthrow of the government, without differentiating between "the mere abstract teaching of the moral propriety or even moral necessity for a resort to force

---

7. Citing *Baggett* v. *Bullitt,* 377 U.S. 360, 84 S.Ct. 1316, 12 L.Ed. 2d 377 (1964), in which the opinion by Mr. Justice Byron R. White invalidated "loyalty oath" statutes of Washington State.

and violence, and preparing a group for violent action by steeling it to such action," is defective. Quoting from a Supreme Court decision: "The essential distinction is that those to whom the advocacy is addressed must be urged to *do* something, rather than merely to *believe* in something."[8]

Further, "Not only must there be advocacy to action, there must also be a reasonable apprehension of imminent danger to organized government."[9]

2. "Any classification which bans political speeches is arbitrary and unreasonable and was unequivocally condemned by the Supreme Court, holding that political discussion must be free and open."[10]

Evidently skeptical of the ability of the board of trustees to produce valid "speaker rules," the court then took the unusual step of drafting a set of rules, and decreeing that they be in force until repealed or amended by the board. Perhaps the motive was to allay any panicky feeling of being without rules and without confidence to draw up a set that would pass the judicial test.

The court-drafted code comprised about 1,500 words. After declaring that the constitutional freedoms of speech and assembly shall be enjoyed by the students and faculties of the state institutions of higher learning as respects the opportunity to hear off-campus, or outside speakers on the various campuses, and affirming that free discussion of subjects of either controversial or non-controversial nature shall not be curtailed, it repeats that there is no absolute right to assemble or to make or hear a speech at any time or place, regardless of the circumstances, content of speech, purpose of assembly, or probable consequences of such meeting or speech.

Covering various essential procedural matters incident to the approval and issuing of invitations, and to reviews and appeals related thereto,[11] the rules make their main point in a section defining the only conditions under which a request to invite a designated speaker may be refused. "A request made by a recognized organization may be denied

---

8. Quoting Mr. Justice Harlan in *Yates* v. *United States,* 354 U.S. 298, 77 S.Ct. 1064, 1 L.Ed. 2d 1356 (1957).

9. Citing *Herndon* v. *Lowry,* 301 U.S. 242, 57 S.Ct. 732, 81 L.Ed. 1066 (1937).

10. Citing *Mills* v *Alabama,* 384 U.S. 214, 86 S.Ct. 1434, 16 L.Ed. 2d 484 (1966).

11. To forestall dilatory tactics which might defeat its purpose, the code provides at pertinent points that if a request is not acted upon within a specified brief number of days, it shall be regarded as granted or approved.

only if the head of the institution, or his authorized designee, determines, after proper inquiry, that the proposed speech will constitute *a clear and present danger* to the institution's orderly operation, by the speaker's advocacy of such *actions* as": (wordage abbreviated)

1. Violent overthrow of government.

2. Willful damage or destruction, or seizure and subversion, of the institutional buildings or other property.

3. Forcible disruption or impairment of, or interference with, the institution's regularly scheduled classes or other educational functions.

4. Physical harm, coercion, intimidation, or other invasion of lawful rights, of the institution's officials, faculty members or students.

5. Other campus disorder of a violent nature.

In this fashion the three-judge federal court instructed the board of trustees in the pertinent constitutional law.[12]

Only a few months later occasion arose for another application of the foregoing principles. A Young Democratic student organization at the University of Mississippi at Oxford sought to invite Tyrone Gettis, president of the student body at Mississippi Valley State College at Itta Bena (a predominantly black institution) to speak at Oxford on the recent campus disorders at Itta Bena as he saw them. Gettis had been a leader in the student protests at Itta Bena which had led to some violence and a temporary closing of the college; but he was not accused of injuring any persons or property. Chancellor Porter D. Fortune, Jr., of the University of Mississippi, twice refused permission for Gettis to be invited to speak at Oxford, believing that such an event would constitute a clear and present danger to the orderly operation of the university; and a campus review committee voted 4 to 1 to disapprove the request.

United States District Judge Orma R. Smith, after providing a hearing *de novo* on the matter, concluded with an order: "The decision of the committee will be reversed and University officials will be directed to approve the request." Disavowing an adverse criticism of the chancellor and the committee, the judge merely said they were overly cautious. Gettis had agreed to speak on nothing but the subject

---

12. *Stacy* v. *Williams*, (U.S.D.C., Miss.), 306 F. Supp. 963 (1969). Circuit Judge James P. Coleman and District Judges Dan M. Russell, Jr., and William C. Keady; opinion by Keady.

assigned. The campus at Oxford had only about 200 black students among a total of 6,000. Three professors at the university (one of English and two of law) had testified that they saw no "clear and present danger" in the proposed speech by Gettis. In these circumstances "The students at the University should not be deprived of the right to hear speakers espousing controversial matters."[13]

The Stance of the Federal Courts

The foregoing decisions are by United States district courts (or by specially convened three-judge federal courts) in the Fourth, Fifth, Sixth, and Seventh Circuits. One of them (the Auburn University case) has been affirmed by the United States Court of Appeals for the Fifth Circuit. No case directly involving a "speaker ban" has reached the United States Supreme Court; but the strong trend indicates that statutes and regulations of this type are far along toward the fate recently suffered by the "loyalty oath" statutes in many states—ultimate extinction—except in forms that strictly abstain from invasion of the civil rights of students and teachers.

There are some decisions of state courts of the same general tenor as the federal decisions recited here. Fear of ideas and prohibition of their expression are not compatible with education, nor permissible under the Constitution of the United States. Formerly the courts generally refrained from taking a hand in the affairs of colleges and schools; now they are willing to intervene to protect civil rights. The change is beneficent.

A 1970 decision of the First Circuit Court of Appeals turned only on what might appear to be a trivial technicality, but illustrated the tendency of the court to be scrupulously fair. Mark Wefers, president of the student government at the University of New Hampshire, contracted with three of the "Chicago Seven" to speak on the campus May 5, 1970, at 7 p.m. On May 1 the board of trustees voted to allow the use of the Field House only until 5 p.m., ostensibly to reduce the danger of violence. Wefers obtained from U.S. District Judge Hugh H. Bownes an injunctive order to the trustees, directing them to permit Abbie Hoffman, David Dellinger, and Jerry Rubin to speak between 3:30 and 6:30 p.m.

---

13. *Molpus* v. *Fortune*, (U.S.D.C., Miss.), 311 Fed. Supp. 240 (1970).

The speakers arrived at about 3:30, but refused to speak until 7:30. The court, having intended that its order would prevent any speaking after 6:30, was outraged when the meeting was held after that hour, and found Wefers guilty of criminal contempt. Wefers felt no responsibility, because the court's order was directed to the trustees, not to him. The Circuit Court of Appeals agreed with this view, exonerated Wefers, and vacated his conviction. The opinion was by Chief Circuit Judge Bailey Aldrich, sitting with Circuit Judges Edward M. McEntee and Frank M. Coffin.[14]

A California State Court Is in Accord

The principles adhered to by the federal courts are echoed in a California court of appeal decision of 1969. A Grossmont College student organization, the Open Forum, arranged a debate on Vietnam between a member of the Communist Party, U.S.A., and a member of the John Birch Society. The college governing board refused to allow the Communist to speak. Charles Dunbar, a student leader, and John Feare, faculty adviser to the Forum, asked the San Diego superior court for a writ of *mandamus* against the board. The court sustained a demurrer by the college and dismissed the action.

The Court of Appeal, through Presiding Justice Gerald Brown, with Justices Martin J. Coughlin and Ault (assigned) concurring, decided that the issue must be tried on the facts and the law.

"The question here is not whether the Board could close the campus to all guest speakers. The issue is the extent of the Board's control over who will, and will not, speak once it has invited as part of its educational program, student groups to arrange discussions of controversial subjects by guest speakers. Once the Board has opened a forum for the free expression of ideas, it may not exceed constitutional limitations in picking the ideas it wishes to be freely expressed."[15]

The Issue at a Private University

Private universities and colleges, save in the rare instances where

---

14. *United States* v. *Wefers*, (U.S.C.A., N.H.), 435 F. 2d 826 (1970).
15. *Dunbar* v. *Governing Board of Grossmont Junior College District*, (Cal. App.), 79 Cal. Rptr. 662 (1969).

they have been adjudged to have been, for one reason or another, extraordinarily transformed into institutions having a predominant color of governmental agency, do not come within the constitutional limitations on "state action" regarding individual civil rights.

Southern Methodist University at Dallas scheduled a dedication program for a new law library April 29 and 30, 1971. The main speaker was Attorney General John N. Mitchell. A student who was local chairman of the Student Mobilization Committee, imbued with the idea that there should be one or more other speakers on campus prepared to answer the anticipated remarks of the admittedly conservative attorney general, on April 19 requested space in the main quadrangle for April 29. On April 21 his request was refused, and he was advised that nothing would be permitted to detract from the events surrounding the dedication program. On April 22 he got special permission from the Student Center Committee to use a lounge and patio of the Student Center April 29; but the next day he was specifically forbidden by the central university administration to hold a program in the center or anywhere else on the campus any time April 29 or before 6 p.m. April 30.

He got no relief from the federal district court because Southern Methodist University is a private university and the remedies provided against state action in the well-known *42 U.S. Code Section 1983* do not apply to it. Moreover, the two-day ban was a reasonable limitation of time and place, under the existing circumstances, the court believed.[16] This was affirmed by the Fifth Circuit April 30.

Although the federal court judgment was favorable to it, the university, determinedly bent on preventing any competition with the dedication ceremonies, sought and obtained a temporary injunction in the local state court against the student and his group, on the ground that threatened acts of the group would interfere with the right of the university to make and enforce reasonable regulations as to time, place, and character of the use of its personnel and facilities.[17]

---

16. *Story* v. *Tate*, U.S.D.C., Northern District of Tex., No. CA-3-4719-C, April 29, 1971.

17. *Southern Methodist University* v. *Story*, 101st Jud. Ct. Dallas County, No. 71-4372, April 29, 1971.

CHAPTER 15

STUDENT ORGANIZATIONS

The recognition and regulation of a great variety of organizations of students is one of the responsibilities of the administration of a university or college. There is a duty to foster and encourage those that contribute to education, recreation, health, and general well-being, without interfering with the main operation of the institution itself; that is, its regular operation of libraries, laboratories, and classroom activities; its research and public service work, and a host of other efforts that are integrated or closely related to any of these.

A state or other public college or university has an obligation to proceed with careful regard for the recently freshly-defined constitutional rights of the individuals involved, even when it may seem that the organization in question may be of a tendency inimical to the orderly operation of the educational functions of the institution; but this does not mean that the administration can not refuse "recognition," or must refrain from enforcing valid institutional rules, or abstain from invoking applicable state statutes when the facts justify it.

Denial of Recognition

When the president of Central Connecticut State College refused recognition of a local group of students whose application asserted that they were to be known as a local chapter of Students for a Democratic Society, but also indicated that the group would not be subject to direction from the national organization, the U.S. District Court decided that the college must afford the students a hearing on their application, prior to the president's action on it.

Said the court: "No student group is entitled, *per se,* to official college recognition. Rather, once a college allows student groups to organize and grants these groups recognition, with the attendant advantages, constitutional safeguards must operate in favor of all groups who apply. This requires adequate standards for recognition and the fair application of these standards. It is the procedural application of the existing college standards that is in issue here.

"A student organization can not be denied college recognition on the *ex parte* findings of the recognizing authority, where those findings have no basis in the organization's application for recognition. Where ambiguity exists in such an application, and such ambiguity, if resolved against the applicants would result in their non-recognition, constitutional due process requires that a timely hearing be scheduled with advance notice and the petitioners be given at least an opportunity to be heard."[1]

The court added some trenchant comments: "Where it is found that a club's objectives are designed to encourage and foster campus disruption and violence so as to frustrate and destroy the college's established educational policies, it is not only the lawful right of the colege administration, but it is its duty to act with firmness and decision. . . . When the climate of civility in the academic community is once destroyed, the intellectual interchange of ideas ceases and academic freedom with its dispassionate search for truth is destroyed."

The foregoing decision was made prior to and pending another action by the same parties before a special three-judge federal court, in which it was held that the denial of the students' application for rcognition as a campus organization did not constitute any cognizable interference with their personal ideas or beliefs, nor have any "chilling effect" on academic freedom; and that it would not prevent the students from forming such an organization off campus.[2] Accordingly they were granted no redress.

---

1. *Healy* v. *James,* (U.S.D.C., Conn.), 311 F. Supp. 1275 (1970); and 319 F. Supp. 113 (1970).
2. *Healy* v. *James,* (U.S.D.C., Conn.), 319 F. Supp. 113 (1970). Affirmed by Second Circuit Court of Appeals, 40 *U.S. Law Week* 2071 (August 3, 1971).

A different result was reached in a decision by a U.S. district court in Virginia when the Radford College Senate denied the application of a student group for recognition as a campus chapter of the American Civil Liberties Union. A committee of the senate reported that "recognition entitles an organization to the use of all forms of campus publicity, sponsorship of activities, and the use of college facilities." The same report made clear, however, that nonrecognition did not necessarily preclude the use of such facilities; and in the senate resolution refusing recognition in this instance there was the express statement that "Radford College may make available to this organization, as it has to other organizations not recognized by the college, campus facilities including publicity media and physical facilities as college facilities permit."

It appeared that the college regularly refused recognition to all religious societies and clubs, out of respect for the traditional separation of church and state, but denominational clubs flourished off campus, and were occasionally granted temporary use of campus facilities. The college habitually recognized local chapters of Young Republicans and Young Democrats. The senate resolution in this case said: "The Senate of Radford College feels that the role and purpose of the American Civil Liberties Union lies basically outside the scope and objectives of this tax-supported educational institution."

Chief District Judge Ted Dalton considered this statement to be so vague as to be overbroad, and pointedly compared it with the similar statement in the rules of Hunter College of The City University of New York which were invalidated in the 1962 case of *Buckley* v. *Meng*, 35 Misc. 2d 467, 230 N.Y.S. 2d 924: "Programs offered by outside organizations insofar as they are determined to be compatible with the aims of Hunter College as an institution of higher learning." Accordingly the court granted declaratory relief to the petitioner, the American Civil Liberties Union of Virginia, but granted no injunction, "in the belief that the administration of Radford College will comply in good faith with the final judgment rendered in the cause by this court or on appeal"; and suspended execution of the declaratory judgment pending appeal.[3]

Judge Dalton readily decided that the Virginia state-wide branch

---

3. *American Civil Liberties Union of Virginia, Inc.,* v. *Radford College,* (U.S.D.C., Va.), 315 F. Supp. 893 (1970).

of the American Civil Liberties Union had standing to bring this suit jointly with individual students at Radford College because several of the students were members of the state-wide organization; though he was careful to say, "What is involved in this case is not the right of the ACLU to come on a college campus and seek to form a local chapter, but the right of interested students on that campus to form such a chapter and gain official college recognition for it."

The court noted in passing that at least two other state institutions of higher education in Virginia; namely, the College of William and Mary and Old Dominion University, had recognized ACLU groups of students as campus organizations; made a good thumbnail description of the national ACLU, quoted Voltaire's famous aphorism, and concluded: "The judgment of this court is that the ACLU students have a right to be recognized as a campus organization."

The opinion is notable for a concise disquisition on numerous recent decisions defining the new balance between the rule-making authority of college and university administrators and the constitutional rights of students, including the groups of cases bearing on the invitation of outside speakers of unorthodox or controversial views to the campuses, and upon the freedom of the college student press, discussed in other chapters herein, especially Chapter 16.

Invasion of the Civil Rights of Organizations

The rights guaranteed under the First Amendment apply to organizations as well as to individuals, wrote U.S. Circuit Judge Gerald W. Heaney in a footnote to his opinion in the case of *Pickings* v. *Bruce* (1970), in which Circuit Judges Charles J. Vogel and Myron H. Bright concurred.[4] This was a case in which the administration of Southern State College at Magnolia, Arkansas, undertook twice to discipline or penalize a recognized student organization, for two separate acts.

A small bi-racial group of students known as Students United for Rights and Equality (SURE) was officially recognized by the college in October 1968. Its stated purposes were "to provide an organized program of leadership and participation among representatives of all

---

4. Reversing and remanding the prior decision of the U.S. District Court by Chief Judge Oren Harris, dismissing the complaint without prejudice.

races, nationalities and religions," "to provide members with an opportunity to develop philosophies regarding human relations," and three other well-expressed and laudable related goals.

In December 1968 when five female black students attended Sunday religious services at the College View Baptist Church, an off-campus, all-white church, they were asked to leave, being told that the congregation was not racially integrated and was not ready for integration. When officers and members of SURE learned of this, they were disturbed by it, and the student publicity chairman, on behalf of the organization, wrote a courteous but pointed letter to the pastor of the church, suggesting that racial exclusion violated the basic tenets of Christianity, and inquiring whether the congregation had any official policy concerning the freedom of college students to join in its worship without regard to race, creed, color, or national origin.

The letter had the prior approval of two faculty members who were advisers to the club, and a copy of it was sent to the college president, Imon Bruce. The president criticized all college personnel connected with the incident; asked the student publicity chairman of SURE and both the faculty advisers to resign their offices, and later directed one of them to confine his college work to teaching and to refrain from sponsoring any college organization or program; and ordered that SURE, as an organization, be placed on probation for the remainder of the academic year because of this incident, the implied terms of probation being that the organization would confine its activities to the campus.

On the foregoing issue the Circuit Court of Appeals spoke plainly: "Students and teachers retain their rights to freedom of speech, expression and association while attending or teaching at a college or university. They have a right to express their views individually or collectively with respect to matters of concern to a college or to a larger community. . . . It follows that here the administrators had no right to prohibit SURE from expressing its views on integration to the College View Baptist Church or to impose sanctions on its members or advisers for expressing these views."

The second incident, about three months later, was an invitation by SURE to Mr. and Mrs. Joe Neal, representatives of the Southern Students' Organizing Committee, to attend the regular monthly meeting of SURE, to show a film, "The Face of the South," produced by the AFL-CIO, and to discuss the film after its showing. At that time Southern State College casually allowed student groups to bring outside speakers to the campus, but the college had no policy, written or otherwise, regarding such events.

President Bruce learned of the projected appearance of the Neals only the day before it was scheduled to occur. He immediately requested SURE's president and its two new faculty advisers to cancel the invitation. They refused. The Neals appeared and performed as scheduled. There were no campus disorders or disruptions of any kind attributable to their visit. Within a few days the dean of students advised SURE's president both orally and in writing that because of the failure to cancel the invitation to the Neals, SURE's charter was immediately temporarily suspended. The suspension, he said, would be reviewed in turn by the student senate and by the student affairs committee of the faculty and administration, after which he would make the final decision, subject to appeal to the president of the college and the board of trustees.

The student senate voted against the suspension; and without waiting for further proceedings, several officers, advisers, and members of SURE began an action in the U.S. district court asking for a declaratory judgment and injunctive relief. Named defendants were the president, the dean of students, and the members of the board of trustees of Southern State College. Dismissal of the suit was followed by appeal to the U.S. Court of Appeals, wherein Circuit Judges Gerald W. Heaney, Charles J. Vogel, and Myron H. Bright concluded: "We hold that under the circumstances of this case, the defendants had no right to demand that the speaking invitation to the Neals be withdrawn nor to impose sanctions for refusal to withdraw it." Accordingly the judgment of dismissal by the district court below was reversed and the case remanded.[5]

Circuit Judge Heaney aptly included in the opinion a quotation from the familiar leading case of *Tinker* v. *Des Moines Community School District*, 393 U.S. 503, 89 S.Ct. 733, 21 L.Ed. 2d 731 (1969): "In our system, undifferentiated fear or apprehension of disturbance is not enough to overcome the right to freedom of expression. Any departure from absolute regimentation may cause trouble. Any variation from the majority's opinion may cause fear. Any word spoken, in class,

---

5. *Pickings* v. *Bruce*, (U.S.C.A., Ark.), 430 F. 2d 595 (1970).

in the lunch room, or on the campus, that deviates from the views of another person may start an argument or cause a disturbance. But our Constitution says we must take this risk . . . and our history says that it is this sort of hazardous freedom—this kind of openness—that is the basis of our national strength and of the independence and vigor of Americans who grow up and live in this relatively permissive, often disputatious, society."

State University May Decline to Be Host to a Regional Conclave of Thousands of Protesters from Half a Dozen States

At Clemson University in South Carolina the local Vietnam Moratorium Committee staged a demonstration on the campus October 13, 1969. Disorder was narrowly averted, partly through the efforts of the vice president for student affairs and his staff, and partly because of a timely rain which chilled the proceedings.

The same organization asked the university to approve and co-operate in its plans to hold a regional meeting of protesting students from six southeastern states November 14. Plans were inchoate but it was thought this might attract as many as 3,000 "outsiders" over whom the university would have no disciplinary authority. It would require many large and small meeting-rooms, and various other facilities, and well-devised arrangements for police protection. The intervening time was too short to permit the plans to be perfected. The university rejected the scheme, whereupon the organization asked U.S. District Judge Donald Russell for a restraining order directing that it be approved.

The judgment had to be made November 11, only three days before the desired event. Judge Russell reflected that there would hardly be time for invitations to reach most of the recipients. Denying the requested order, he said: "The University is entitled to protect itself from such difficulties, created by persons to whom it owes no responsibility. Its requirement to accord constitutional rights may well be deemed to extend merely to its own students."[6]

---

6. *Clemson University Vietnam Moratorium Committee* v. *Clemson University,* (U.S.D.C., S.C.), 306 F. Supp. 129 (1969).

Seizing and Occupying a Meeting-Room Is Action
Beyond the Limits of Protected Speech

The circuit court of Leon County, Florida, issued a temporary order enjoining members of the local chapter of Students for a Democratic Society from holding any meetings or rallies in any buildings on the campus of Florida State University at Tallahassee, until further order of the court. This order had been obtained by the acting president of the university on evidence that the SDS intended to seize and occupy a room in the Student Union Building in the evening of that day, and was served by law enforcement officers in that room after the meeting had begun (March 4, 1969).

Later the same court denied a motion to dissolve the temporary order; and an interlocutory appeal was taken to the Court of Appeal, on federal and state constitutional grounds. Justice James C. Adkins, with the four other justices concurring, dismissed the appeal:

"When the interest of SDS members in seizing a part of a campus building in open defiance of known University regulations is balanced against the need of the University to maintain order and respect for fair rules, and its need to pursue educational goals without undue disturbance, it is apparent that the equities clearly lie with the University and that the activities of SDS and its members fell beyond the limits of protected speech."[7]

To emphasize the public interest, Justice Adkins also said: "A college education is no longer a luxury for the wealthy, but is regarded as a necessity for most high school graduates."

Phantom Organization Has No Claim on
Free Use of University Facilities

In May 1970, while attending a rally at New Haven, Connecticut, in support of the Black Panthers, a small group of students from Brandeis University at Waltham, Massachusetts conceived the idea that a National Center for (Student) Strike Information should be operated. Returning to the Brandeis campus, they appropriated to their own use certain desk-space and office equipment in the Union Building, and attempted to compile and distribute a periodical newsletter. The enter-

---

7. *Lieberman* v. *Marshall,* (Fla. App.), 236 So. 2d 120 (1970).

prise was never financially solvent, and after a few months it became apparent that the organization was virtually non-existent, and was parasitic, enjoying unauthorized use of university space, equipment, and supplies. When Brandeis University terminated this use of its valuable administrative equipment, the amorphous NSIC and five individual students asked the federal district court for an injunction to prevent what they averred to be denial of their constitutional rights. The petition, preposterous on its face, was denied by District Judge Andrew A. Caffrey.[8] Brandeis is a private university, not subject to the constitutional restraints on "state action"; and no university, private or public, is under any constitutional obligation to subsidize any particular student organization.

Right to Publish and Distribute Campus Newspaper

At Texas Tech University the Channing Club is a recognized student organization, unincorporated, which sponsors *The Catalyst*, a tabloid newspaper addressed primarily to students and faculty, and appearing irregularly. This is a nonprofit enterpise, drawing some income from advertising and some from newsstand sales. It was regularly distributed from two points on the campus—the student union building and the university book store.

On January 13, 1970, the university prohibited the distribution of Issue 6, Volume I of *The Catalyst* on the campus, acting under parts of the current Code of Student Affairs and Rules and Regulations which proscribe "lewd, indecent or obscene conduct or expression on University-owned-or-controlled property," and "selling and soliciting on the campus without official authorization." Representatives of the Channing Club then sued in federal district court for injunctive and declaratory relief, which was granted by District Judge Halbert O. Woodward, who said:

"Such direct regulation of expression must be founded upon substantial justification, some overriding governmental interest vindicating interference with First Amendment freedoms. Here, no such justification has been shown to exist. Testimony revealed no indication that the work of the university or any class was disrupted; there were no

8. *National Strike Information Center* v. *Brandeis University*, (U.S.D.C., Mass.), 315 F. Supp. 928 (1970).

hostile remarks, no threats or acts of violence, no infringement or restriction on the rights of other students, and no indication of that clear and present danger of a serious substantive evil necessary to justify invasion of constitutionally protected rights. It is not enough that administrative officials anticipated the possibility of some disturbance. Uncrystallized apprehension of disruption can not overcome the right to free expression."

Continuing on another point, he added: "numerous other publications, not banned, and sold from the same locations as *The Catalyst*, contained language identical to that objected to here, which does sustain the allegation of discrimination and denial of equal protection. The State does not become privileged to ban a publication merely because it is edited and published by students. This alone is sufficient to justify the issuance of the injunction." Accordingly it was ordered that "Plaintiffs may sell and distribute Issue 6, Volume I of *The Catalyst* in the same manner and at the same times and places in which it was formerly distributed and sold."[9]

Student Political Organizations May Solicit Members and Sell Materials on Campus

The New Left Education Project, then defendant in a state court suit for an injunction to restrain it from distributing a newspaper, the *Rag*, on the Austin campus of the University of Texas (in alleged violation of two University of Texas rules), asked the federal district court to enjoin further prosecution of the state court suit and declare the regents' rules on which it was based unconstitutional.

The federal court dismissed the original plaintiffs so there would be no interference with the state judge's adjudication of the proceedings pending against them in the state court; but allowed the Young Democratic Club, the Young Socialist Alliance, and a number of individual University of Texas students to intervene and proceed as joint plaintiffs.

Then a special three-judge district court was convened. Its judgment was in favor of the plaintiffs so far as the regents' rules were concerned.

---

9. *Channing Club* v. *Board of Regents of Texas Tech University*, (U.S.D.C., Tex.), 317 F. Supp. 688 (1970).

The two rules in question, which had the effect of preventing student political organizations from soliciting dues from potential members, and even from soliciting persons to become dues-paying members, and from selling political materials on campus, except as authorized by the administration, were held to be unconstitutionally overbroad and also invalid as licensing regulations affecting First Amendment rights without adequate guidelines.

In a commendably well-reasoned *per curiam* opinion Circuit Judge Homer Thornberry and District Judges Dorwin W. Suttle and Jack Roberts declared Sections 6.11 (commercial soliciting) and 6.12 (noncommercial soliciting) of the *Regents' Rules and Regulations* unconstitutional, and enjoined the regents from enforcing either section.[10]

"By broadly limiting all solicitation in the two rules, the Regents have simply failed to speak with that small calibre precision required of regulations touching First Amendment rights."

Moreover, "These regulations place standardless discretion in the institutional head or his agency-delegate to grant or withhold exercise of First Amendment rights. It is well-settled law that regulations can not be allowed to stand when they make enjoyment of First Amendment freedoms contingent upon the will of an administration."

Basic premises of the opinion were stated thus: "Soliciting dues-paying members for a lawful orginization—especially a political one—is speech and associational activity of a fairly high order . . ., as is distributing literature 'which communicates thoughts between citizens, and discusses public questions,' . . . especially when its content is primarily political."

Balance Between State Criminal Statutes and First Amendment Rights of Student Organizations

The Wisconsin Student Association, a non-stock corporation, was held to be a proper party in a suit in a federal court asking to have a Wisconsin statute declared unconstitutional and invalid. The statute in question was Section 36.49, *Wisconsin Statutes*:

"36.49. *Sound-Amplifying Equipment.* (1) Any person who

---

10. *New Left Education Project* v. *University of Texas System*, (U.S.D.C., Tex.), 326 F. Supp. 158 (1970).

utilizes sound-amplifying equipment in an educational or administrative building owned or controlled by a state institution of higher education . . . or upon the grounds of such institution without the permission of the adminstrative head of the institution or his designee, may be fined not more than $100 or imprisoned not more than 30 days, or both."

A three-judge federal court (Circuit Judge Thomas E. Fairchild and District Judges James E. Doyle and Myron L. Gordon) found the statute fatally defective because it was a delegation of unrestricted discretion without any specification or standards to guide its exercise. This, where freedom of speech is involved, is a violation of the First Amendment to the United States Constitution; and the statute was declared unconstitutional and void.[11] Judge Gordon spoke for the court.

The offending statute had been first published May 15, 1969. Thereafter three students were arrested and charged with violations, in the county court of Dane County. On January 1, 1970, before the three-judge federal court had been convened, District Judge James E. Doyle, acting as single District Judge, had ordered the county court proceedings temporarily stayed. Although there is some doubt as to whether federal courts may properly exercise this authority over state courts, Judges Fairchild and Doyle believed that "in a clear case involving the facial invalidity of a statute regulating freedom of speech, it is proper to stay pending state court proceedings." Judge Gordon thought otherwise, but the majority prevailed, and Judge Doyle's temporary order was made permanent. This halted all prosecutions under the invalid statute.

On August 22 and October 17, 1969, the board of regents had twice adopted rules to implement the statute. These rules, though they may have supplied some of the elements that the statute lacked, could not, of course, save it from being struck down by the three-judge federal court on October 13, 1970. Meantime, the board of regents, in June 1970, adopted a wholly new rule regarding sound-amplifying equipment, including an elaborate set of "governing principles" to guide local campus administrators in regulating its use. This new rule mentions no state statute and does not purport to be under the specific authority of Section 36.49, but is an exercise of the board of regents'

---

11. *Wisconsin Student Association* v. *Regents of the University of Wisconsin*, (U.S.D.C., Wis.), 318 F. Supp. 591 (1970).

general power to govern the University of Wisconsin. Hence it is presumably unaffected by the federal court decision. All three successive sets of regents' rules on sound-amplifying equipment are reproduced as appendices to Judge Gordon's opinion for the three-judge court.

At Michigan State University in May 1970 a student group known as the Action Group to Combat Racism (AGCR) and others asked President Clifton R. Wharton, Jr., to close the university for one day as an act of protest against the killing of black students by state and local police officers at Jackson State University in Mississippi. President Wharton decided against this and suggested that students and others take more constructive measures to express their various concerns.

Meantime, apparently prior to President Wharton's response, the AGCR had planned a meeting to discuss problems of racism, to take place at 8 p.m. May 18, 1970, in the Michigan State University Union. The normal process of reserving meeting space was not followed. President Wharton and other administrators were invited to attend, as were all other persons interested in the topic of discussion. At the appointed hour some 300 to 500 persons were assembled in the main lounge. Witnesses said the meeting appeared to be almost totally unorganized. There was much milling about and filtering in and out, continually. Only one speaker, a black student leader, addressed the whole assembly, and his remarks were concluded before 9 p.m. Thereafter there were various small-group discussions. As the hours passed, the filtering in and out continued, and there was no sign of an adjournment. An assistant manager of the union, present in his office in the building, made, over a public address system, appropriate announcements of the regular union closing hour, which was 11 p.m. and presumably well known to all students.

The meeting dragged on until 1:30 a.m., at which time it became apparent that about 150 policemen, summoned from various state and local jurisdictions, had surrounded the building and suddenly entered it with instructions to arrest all persons present. One hundred and thirty-two arrests were made. Prosecutions were instituted in the state courts, charging violations of the Michigan statute against trespass, and of a Michigan State University ordinance against loitering.

The AGCR, as an organization, and nine other individuals concerned brought an action in federal district court seeking federal intervention to prevent the prosecutions on the grounds that the arrests had not been made in good faith for a paramount state purpose, but that the criminal process had been purposely abused so as to deprive the students of their First Amendment rights of speech and assembly. No question was raised as to the constitutionality of the Michigan trespass statute, but only the good faith of its application in this particular case was attacked; therefore the issue was held to be not of sufficient importance to justify the convening of a special three-judge court.

District Judge Noel P. Fox denied any declaratory or injunctive relief. In his lengthy opinion he carefully reviewed in detail the context of facts preceding and surrounding the mass arrests. During the early months of 1970 there had been a considerable atmosphere of unrest and disruption on the campus. On several occasions there had been some minor destruction of property. Only three days before the meeting of May 18, a group of students and others had conducted a "sit-in" in the building housing the offices of the Army ROTC, and remained in the building after the 6 o'clock closing hour. At 8 p.m. the vice president for student affairs and the campus director of safety had successively informed them that if they did not leave within five minutes they would be arrested. When the police arrived, the protestors left the building. Immediately afterward rocks were thrown and windows broken on one side of that building. No arrests were made.

During the long progress of the inchoate meeting of May 18, some damage was done to the Administration Building and to an off-campus building owned by International Business Machines Corporation, and there was some suspicion that the culprits were among those who were constantly filtering in and out of the Union Building, though this connection was actually never alleged or proved; and all parties agreed that the meeting in the union itself was never disorderly or destructive, though certainly poorly organized. In this highly charged situation, President Wharton, the county prosecuting attorney, and the campus director of safety, with some advisers and assistants, stationed themselves at the headquarters of the campus department of safety and attempted to keep in touch with the night's occurrences by telephone, messenger, and other means. The arrests were at the request of President Wharton with the concurrence of the county attorney and other advisers, and the plan was determined upon at about 11:30 p.m. During the ensuing two hours the 150 policemen were assembled and deployed.

In the federal district court the students attacked the constitutionality of the Michigan State University ordinance against loitering, under which they were also charged; but here again won no recourse.[12] Judge Fox deemed it inappropriate to pass upon that question, and declined to do so, believing it should first be tried in state courts; but he ordered that the U.S. district court retain jurisdiction of that issue.[13] This was presumably in anticipation of possible future events.

Recognizing that the well-known "loitering" statutes and ordinances have often been declared unconstitutional because they are so vague as to provide no ascertainable standards for administration, or so overbroad as to allow enforcement encroaching upon constitutionally protected areas, the sage Judge Fox permitted himself some quotable remarks:

"Loitering, reflecting, ruminating, recollecting, or reconnoitering, may in a sense in time and space, or in the intellectual or mind's eye, be interrelated concepts perfectly harmless and indeed desirable. Hopefully these are a part of a university's atmosphere and circumstances.

"These words have no sinister meaning and imply no wrongdoing or misconduct. They stand in sharp contrast to trashing, windowbreaking, and other miscellaneous acts of indiscriminate vandalism."

Honorary and Professional Societies of Students Are Private Associations Choosing Their Own Members

A different *genus* of student organization is exemplified by traditional associations which choose as their members only students nearing completion of a liberal or professional college or university course and whose standing indicates they will be among the few top members of their respective classes in academic rank. These are known generically as "honorary societies" and membership is prized; but it does not come automatically, because always the societies choose their own members, and high academic ranking does not guarantee selection.

Such an honorary society for law students is the Order of the

---

12. *Cholmakjian* v. *Board of Trustees of Michigan State University*, (U.S.D.C., Mich.), 315 F. Supp. 1335 (1970).

13. It turned out that the county attorney elected not to prosecute the charges of violating the university ordinance.

Coif, which has local chapters in many of the better law schools, including the school of law of the University of Southern California. There Meyer Blatt was a June 1967 graduate, standing fourth among a class of 135 graduates, he alleged. He had been a night student since September 1961. He was respected as a student by the law dean and faculty.

Disappointed at not being invited to the Order of the Coif, he allowed himself to hope a state court would intervene in his behalf. He asked for an order against the university and the local chapter to grant him membership. To no avail. Courts do not order the internal affairs of private nonprofit associations in the absence of the weightiest of reasons. In the nature of things, there can be no lawful contract or any binding promise of an invitation. There is always an uncertain element of hazard until the initiation ceremonies are concluded. One is again reminded of the lucid statement attributed to Karl Jaspers: "Every selection is an injustice."

The trial court sustained the demurrer of the defendants, finding no cause of action; and the Court of Appeal affirmed the judgment, in an opinion by Justice Harold W. Schweitzer, with Presiding Justice John J. Ford and Justice John R. Allport concurring.[14]

---

14. *Blatt* v. *University of Southern California*, 5 Cal. App. 3d 935, 85 Cal. Rptr. 601 (1970).

CHAPTER 16

FREEDOM OF THE STUDENT PRESS

AMONG OTHER CHANGES accompanying the current "revolution" in campus life are new court pronouncements of how far student editors and reporters can legitimately go in expressing controversial views or allegedly indecent words; and how far university and college administrators can go in censoring or suppressing student publications unacceptable to them.

One view is that a student newspaper should be a forum for many types of controverted social and political issues (within necessary limits of "time, place, and manner"); that it should be lively and intellectually challenging. Thus it may in itself be an important educational agency, not only for its own staff, but for all who read it thoughtfully.

An opposite belief is that the copy of student publications should be pre-censored by some faculty or administrative authority, and purged of anything that might be feared to be offensive to members of the "establishment" in the community or state, or contrary to strongly-held predilections of any influential class of readers. Someone has pointedly said, "Reading a student newspaper is often a good deal like being immersed in a vat of lukewarm molasses."

A *New York Times* story of December 2, 1969, under the byline of Robert Reinhold, bore the headline "Campus editors now say what they think." It reported primarily recent events at Fitchburg State

College in Massachusetts, but touched occurrences at many other institutions in other states. Nelly Jo Lee of the United States Student Press Association was reported to have said "Activist newspapers . . . are saying that there is no such thing as objectivity and that any story is going to be somewhat subjective. The college press is trying to give a side that frequently isn't given in the professional press."

Massachusetts State Colleges

At Fitchburg State College in Massachusetts the student newspaper was called *Kampus Vue* and was "primarily on student news and campus events" until John Antonelli was elected by the student body as editor-in-chief. He changed the name to *The Cycle* and broadened the focus, "to explore and comment on areas of broader social and political impact." The paper depended on an allocation of some of the receipts from compulsory student activity fees. Under a state statute these fees and any receipts from the activities themselves are retained in a revolving fund to be expended "as the president of the college may direct in furthering the activities . . ."[1]

On September 21, 1969, the copy of Eldridge Cleaver's article "Black Moochie" (originally published in *Ramparts Magazine*) was sent to the usual printer of *The Cycle* to be included in the forthcoming issue. The printer, whose daughter was a student at the college, objected to the theme and the four-letter words, refused to print the article and telephoned the college president, James J. Hammond. The president withheld payment for the printing of that issue of *The Cycle* and said he would refuse to allow future editions to be published unless he or his representatives gave prior approval to all the copy before it was printed.

In fact, the issue containing "Black Moochie" was printed by another printer, paid out of funds raised by students at four of the other state colleges in Massachusetts, and widely circulated. Antonelli agreed for the time being to cooperate with a board of two professors set by the president to censor materials intended for publication; but within a month or two he and his staff disagreed with these two professors over budget matters, and all submitted their resignations. Antonelli then sued in federal district court for an injunction and a

---

1. Massachusetts *General Laws*, chapter 73, sec. 1B.

declaratory judgment that the announced plan of censoring was unconstitutional under the First Amendment guarantee of free speech and press.

District Judge W. Arthur Garrity, Jr., granted no injunction against President Hammond, because he regarded him as a "highly placed and responsible public official, and there is no reason to believe he will not abide by the law as herein declared." He made the declaratory judgment, however: "The exercise of rights by individuals must yield when they are incompatible with the school's obligation to maintain the order and discipline necessary for the success of the educational process. However, any infringement of individual constitutional freedoms must be adequately related to this legitimate interest. No such justification has been shown in this case."

He continued: "The university setting of college-age students being exposed to a wide range of intellectual experience creates a relatively mature marketplace for the interchange of ideas so that the free speech clause of the First Amendment with its underlying assumption that there is positive social value in an open forum seems particularly appropriate."

The Massachusetts statute authorizing the president to direct the expenditure of student activity funds does not empower him to dictate directly the content or substance of the activities, decided Judge Garrity. Said he: "We are well beyond the belief that any manner of state regulation is permissible simply because it involves an activity which is a part of the university structure and is financed with funds controlled by the administration. The state is not necessarily the unrestrained master of what it creates and fosters."

He thought, "It may be lawful in the interest of providing students with opportunity to develop their own writing and journalistic skills, to restrict publication in a campus newspaper to articles written by students. Such a restriction might be reasonably related to the educational process. But to tell a student what thoughts he may communicate is another matter. Having fostered a campus newspaper, the state may not impose arbitrary restrictions on the matter to be communicated."[2]

This *ratio decidendi* was reinforced by a quotation from the opinion of the United States Supreme Court in the recent decision holding that high school students could not be prohibited from wearing black

---

2. *Antonelli* v. *Hammond*, (U.S.D.C., Mass.), 308 F. Supp. 1329 (1970).

armbands as a sign of mourning for the Vietnam war, so long as this was not shown to cause any disorder or disruption of the work of the school, or any invasion of the rights of other pupils:

"In our system, students may not be regarded as closed-circuit recipients of only that which the State chooses to communicate. They may not be confined to the expression of those sentiments that are officially approved. In the absence of a specific showing of constitutionally valid reasons to regulate their speech, students are entitled to freedom of expression of their views."[3]

The Case in Alabama

Some three years earlier a somewhat similar case had been decided by a federal district court in Alabama, with similar result. Troy State University in Alabama maintained a rule that the student newspaper should not publish anything adversely critical of the governor or the legislature of the state. Gary Clinton Dickey, student editor of the *Tropolitan*, the campus newspaper, wrote an editorial in support of President Frank A. Rose of the University of Alabama, who had taken a strong stand for freedom of speech and press at that institution, and as a result had become a target of criticism and harassment from some members of the legislature and some newspaper editors in the state.

Specifically, President Rose had defended the publication of a document which served as the program of a two-day meeting at the university on "A World in Revolution" and contained the names and excerpts from the words of such speakers as Dean Rusk (keynoter), James Reston, General Earle G. Wheeler, Roy Wilkins, Bettina Aptheker, and Stokely Carmichael.

Dickey's editorial was well-written and in good taste. It was entitled "A Lament for Dr. Rose," and concluded by saying "*The Tropolitan*, therefore, laments the misinterpretation of the program by members of the legislature, and the considerable harassment they have caused Dr. Rose. It is our hope that this episode does not impair his effective leadership at the University or discourage him in his difficult task."

A professor of English at Troy assured Dickey that the piece was

---

3. Quoted from *Tinker* v. *Des Moines Public School District*, 393 U.S. 511, 89 S.Ct. 739 (1969).

worthy of publication, but both the faculty advisor of *The Tropolitan* and President Ralph W. Adams forbade his publishing it, on the basis of the rule that the governor and members of the legislature are never to be criticized, because the institution belongs to the state, and a newspaper can not criticize its owners!

The faculty adviser gave Dickey some copy to use instead, under the caption "Raising Dogs in North Carolina." Dickey let his own caption stand and left the space below it blank except for the word "Censored" printed diagonally across it; and thus the paper appeared.

Troy State University first notified Dickey that he was suspended for "insubordination," without giving him any prior notice or hearing; and upon being ordered by the U.S. district court to rescind that suspension and afford him an administrative hearing, did so, with the same result. Dickey then asked the court for an injunction. Chief Judge Frank M. Johnson, after receiving the pleadings and taking evidence orally in court, declared the suspension unconstitutional and void, and ordered it rescinded. He also granted the injunction.[4]

The judge explained that Troy State University was under no legal obligation to permit Dickey to continue as editor, nor even under any compulsion to continue publishing a campus newspaper; but "Since this state-supported institution did elect to operate the 'Tropolitan' and did authorize Dickey to be one of its editors, they cannot as officials of the State of Alabama, without violating the First and Fourteenth Amendments, suspend or expel Dickey for his conduct as reflected in this case."

Put in another way: "State school officials can not infringe on their students' right of free expression as guaranteed by the Constitution where the exercise of such right does not 'materially and substantially interfere with requirements of appropriate discipline in the operation of the school.' "[5]

Troy State University, said Judge Johnson, "cannot punish Gary Clinton Dickey for his exercise of this constitutionally guaranteed right by cloaking his expulsion or suspension in the robe of 'insubordination.' " In short, Dickey was in fact suspended for his exercise of

4. *Dickey* v. *Alabama State Board of Education*, (U.S.D.C., Ala.), 273 F. Supp. 619 (1967).
5. Quoting *Burnside* v. *Byars*, (U.S.C.A., 5 Cir.), 363 F. 2d 744 (1966), upholding the right of black high school pupils to wear "freedom buttons" if this did not disrupt the school.

his right of free expression. The court also quoted from the "flag-salute" decision of the United State Supreme Court[6] on the responsibilities of state school authorities:

"The Fourteenth Amendment, as now applied to the States, protects the citizen against the State itself and all of its creatures—Boards of Education not excepted. These have, of course, important, delicate, and highly discretionary functions, but none that they may not perform within the limits of the Bill of Rights. That they are educating the young for citizenship is reason for scrupulous protection of Constitutional freedoms of the individual, if we are not to strangle the free mind at its source and teach youth to discount important principles of our government as mere platitudes."

The Alabama State Board of Education appealed the Dickey case, but the Fifth Circuit Court of Appeals hewed to the line of its perceived duty to dismiss it as moot after learning that Dickey did not intend to return to Troy State University. It refused to consider the merits, and ordered the judgment vacated, saying this was federal court custom in moot cases, and was not to be interpreted as an opinion for or against the judgment.[7]

Student Publications as Tools of Instruction

At Southern Colorado State College the student newspaper, *The Arrow*, was financed from student activity fees until July 1970, when it was agreed that the college would assume the printing costs while the student government continued to pay staff salaries and supplies. The college president announced that the college department of mass communications would supervise the operation as an "instructional tool" as in a "laboratory course." Soon thereafter the acting chairman of the communications department stopped publication of one article critical of the college president, and another critical of a local judge. These misstated facts, he said, were libelous and violated the ethics of journalism.

Soon the girl student who served as managing editor was removed from her position, whereupon she asked the federal district court for

6. *West Virginia State Board of Education* v. *Barnette*, 319 U.S. 624 (1943).
7. *Alabama State Board of Education* v. *Dickey*, postponed, (U.S.C.A., 5 Cir.), 394 F. 2d 490 (1968), and declared moot, *Troy State University* v. *Dickey*, (U.S.C.A., 5 Cir.), 402 F. 2d 515 (1968).

an order of reinstatement, back pay, and an injunction to restrain further interference with her freedom of speech. Chief District Judge Alfred A. Arraj granted the petition. Although the articles in question were said to be libelous, no proof of that was offered. The paper was supposed to be a forum for student expression, but the college exercised censorship over its content. A part of this faculty and administrative control was a vague direction not to use "controversial" material. Prior to July 1970 there had been no supervision of student writing. The new policy had not been defined with sufficient clarity, thus leaving the managing editor unsure of her responsibilities.

In the carefully chosen words of Judge Arraj: "We find it unnecessary to decide whether a state-supported college is free to establish a newspaper which it places under the control of its journalism department, whether such a college may decline to finance a newspaper for the expression of student opinion or whether, once established, such a project may be abandoned. We need not decide these questions because we have concluded from the evidence that prior to the summer of 1970 the *Arrow* did serve as a forum for student expression and the new policy of administration and faculty (control) was not thereafter put into effect with sufficient clarity and consistency to alter the function of the newspaper. As a result we find the *Arrow* continued to serve as a student forum, the restraints placed on plaintiff's writing did abridge her right of free expression, and her suspension was an impermissible punishment for the exercise of that right."

Further, "Nor can we uphold such conduct merely because it comes labeled as 'teaching,' when in fact little or no teaching took place. The administration and faculty may have had the best of intentions concerning the *Arrow's* future, but it is clear to us that they did not carry out their plans. . . .

"This decision only requires that school officials make a clear choice." The choice is between a student newspaper in which editorial policies are decided by the students, or a newspaper controlled by the administration. If the latter, then the policies must be clearly defined and supervised, and the instructional services actually provided.[8]

As a valued tool of instruction, many law schools operate a periodical *Law Review*, largely controlled by a student editorial board

---

8. *Trujillo* v. *Love*, Civ. Action No. C-2785 in U.S.D.C., Colo. (February 11, 1971).

manned by students senior in rank and high in standing. These scholarly, professional periodicals constitute an important segment of the literature of the law. They regularly publish many articles by studious professors and practitioners, as well as a good deal of high-quality student writing on legal developments and problems. As is true of all scholarly publications, the editors exercise a wide discretion in the acceptance and rejection of proffered articles.

A would-be contributor to the *Rutgers Law Review*, after his article was rejected, conceived the argument that a publication of a state university must be open to all writers, and that the rejection was an unconstitutional abridgement of his freedom of speech. His complaint was summarily dismissed by U.S. District Judge Robert Shaw, and the judgment was affirmed in the Third Circuit by Circuit Judge Albert Branson Maris, sitting with Circuit Judge Austin L. Staley and Circuit Judge Francis L. Van Dusen. "He does not have the right ... to commandeer the press and columns of the *Rutgers Law Review* for the publication of his article, at the expense of the subscribers to the *Review* and the New Jersey taxpayers, to the exclusion of other articles deemed by the editors to be more suitable for publication."[9]

Paid "Editorial Advertisements"

Distinct from the editorial and news content of a campus paper is the question of its acceptance of paid advertisements designed to promote social or political views. Of course the paper has a right to reject any and all paid advertising; but the courts have said that if it accepts paid commercial advertisements, then it can not refuse paid "editorial ads" without unconstitutionally restricting freedom of expression.

Students at the Wisconsin State University at Whitewater submitted three editorial advertisements to the campus newspaper, the *Royal Purple*, requesting that they be published at the usual rates. The three ads dealt respectively with (1) a university employees' union, (2) problems of discrimination, and (3) race relations and the war in Vietnam. The paper rejected all three.

When the case came before United States District Judge James E. Doyle at Madison, he concluded: "It is adjudged and declared that

---

9. *Avins* v. *Rutgers, the State University of New Jersey*, (U.S.C.A., N.J.), 385 F. 2d 151 (1967); *certiorari* denied, 390 U.S. 920, 88 S.Ct. 855 (1968).

defendants (Regents of Wisconsin State Colleges) have unlawfully deprived plaintiffs (the students) of their rights of freedom of speech and expression by refusing to print the editorial advertisements submitted by plaintiffs, or by sanctioning such refusal.

"Plaintiffs' right to express their views on vital issues of the day should not be restricted unless a 'clear and present danger' to society is apparent . . . Defendants have not claimed that they would prove the existence of a clear and present danger and it is highly doubtful that they could. The only danger present here is the threat posed to plaintiffs' right to free speech."[10]

This judgment was subsequently affirmed by the Seventh Circuit in an opinion by Circuit Judge Thomas E. Fairchild, sitting with Circuit Judge Otto Kerner and Senior District Judge William J. Campbell.

Earlier in the same year (1969) a parallel case involving a high school in New Rochelle had been decided by another United States district court. There District Judge Charles M. Metzner had said, of a proffered advertisement opposing the Vietnam war:

"There is no logical reason to permit news stories on the subject and preclude student advertising . . . The lawsuit arises at a time when many in the educational community oppose the tactics of the young in securing a political voice. It would be both incongruous and dangerous for this court to hold that students who wish to express their views on matters intimately related to them, through traditionally accepted non-disruptive modes of communication, may be precluded from doing so by that same adult community."[11]

Pamphleteering

A further variety of questions concerns the right of persons to put their views in writing and distribute them on the campus in the form of pamphlets, leaflets, or so-called "underground" newspapers.

Two such cases occurred in two state universities in Tennessee.

---

10. *Lee* v. *Board of Regents of State Colleges*, (U.S.D.C., Wis.), 306 F. Supp. 1095 (1969). Affirmed, (U.S.C.A., Wis.), 441 F. 2d 1257 (1971).

Showing that the doctrine of "clear and present danger" is not new, but long-established, Judge Doyle cited *Schenck* v. *United States*, 249 U.S. 407, 39 S.Ct. 247, 63 L.Ed. 470 (1919) and *Terminiello* v. *City of Chicago*, 337 U.S. 1, 69 S.Ct. 894, 93 L.Ed. 1131 (1949).

11. *Zucker* v. *Panitz*, (U.S.D.C., N.Y.), 299 F. Supp. 102 (1969).

Both were appealed to the United States Supreme Court; but certain circumstances in both instances caused the high tribunal to decline to review, so that at this writing there is no Supreme Court decision on this issue.

Kenneth Jones and other students at Tennessee State University at Nashville (then known as Tennessee Agricultural and Industrial University) were suspended for writing and distributing on the campus a pamphlet attacking the administrative officers in intemperate terms and directly urging all students to boycott the registration of the fall of 1967. They had been given notice of charges and a hearing at the university. Judge William E. Miller of the United States district court dismissed their complaint, and this judgment was affirmed by the United States Court of Appeals, in a short opinion by Circuit Judge Bert Combs.[12]

The Supreme Court granted *certiorari*, "primarily to consider the issues raised by Jones' claim that he had been separated solely because of his distribution of leaflets urging a boycott of fall registration"; but when the case came up a majority of the high court concluded: "after oral argument, and on closer review of the record, it emerges that Jones' suspension was based in part on a finding that he lied at the hearing. This sufficiently clouds the record to render the case an inappropriate vehicle for this court's first decision on the extent of First Amendment restrictions on the power of state universities to suspend students for expression of views alleged to be disruptive of the good order of the campus"; and dismissed the writ. Three of the justices held different views. Mr. Justice Hugo L. Black would have *affirmed* the decision. Justice William O. Douglas said the court should have reviewed the case, in a dissenting opinion in which he was joined by Justice William J. Brennan.[13]

The Douglas-Brennan dissent was cogent and convincing: "If he is to be expelled for lying, he is entitled to notice and opportunity to be heard on that charge. . . .

"The circulation did not disrupt a classroom or any other university function. It would seem, therefore, that it is immune from punishment, censorship, or any form of retaliating action.

---

12. *Jones* v. *State Board of Education of Tennessee*, (U.S.D.C., Tenn.), 279 F. Supp. 190 (1968); affirmed in (U.S.C.A., 6 Cir.), 407 F. 2d 834 (1969).

13. *Certiorari* granted, 396 U.S. 817 (1969): writ dismissed, (Feb. 24, 1970).

"Our failure to reverse is a serious setback for First Amendment rights in a troubled field.

"The leaflet now censored may be ill-tempered and in bad taste. But we recognize in *Terminiello* v. *Chicago* (337 U.S.1) that even strongly abusive utterances or publications, not merely polished and urbane pronouncements of dignified people, enjoy First Amendment protection: 'A function of free speech under our system is to invite dispute. It may indeed best serve its high purpose when it induces a condition of unrest, creates dissatisfaction with conditions as they are, or even stirs people to anger. Speech is often provocative and challenging. It may strike at prejudices and preconceptions and have profound unsettling effects as it presses for acceptance of an idea.' "

At East Tennessee State University at Johnson City there was a similar incident in which Marietta Norton and other students wrote and distributed harshly-phrased pamphlets allegedly designed to incite violent disruption of the operation of the institution; and were suspended. Here United States District Judge W. E. Miller dismissed the complaint of the students, and this judgment was affirmed by the United States Court of Appeals in an opinion by Circuit Judge Paul C. Weick. However, a vigorous and lengthy dissent was entered by Circuit Judge Anthony J. Celebrezze. The pamphlets in question urged the students to "stand-up and fight" and seemingly advised them to emulate the leaders of violent disorders at Berkeley and at Columbia University; and referred to local administrative officers as despots and "problem children" deserving to be reprimanded by students.

Though the language may have been false and inflammatory, there was no sufficient evidence that distribution of the papers on campus would lead to an eruption or riot, or cause any substantial interference with the normal activities of the university, said Circuit Judge Celebrezze; and he thought the words, and the time, and place, and manner of distribution were within the protection of the First Amendment.[14]

The United States Supreme Court declined to review this decision,[15] with Justices Thurgood Marshall, William O. Douglas, and William

---

14. Dissenting opinion in *Norton* v. *East Tennessee State University*, (U.S.C.A., 6 Cir.), 419 F. 2d 195 (1969), affirming judgment of dismissal by District Judge William E. Miller.

15. The recently-appointed Justice Harry Blackmun voted with the majority.

J. Brennan joining in dissent from the majority. Mr. Justice Marshall said the form, place, and manner of expression at issue here were within the protection of the Constitution, and the decision of the U.S. Court of Appeals should be reversed. He distinguished between "the burning of buildings and the peaceful but often unpleasantly sharp expressions of discontent."

Since there is as yet no Supreme Court decision based on a review of the merits of either of the cases that arose in Tennessee, the two decisions of the Court of Appeals stand as the law in the Sixth Circuit. Refusal by the Supreme Court to review these decisions does not imply that the high tribunal would affirm them; the sheer bulk of its business compels the court to reject most of the 3,000 requests for review that come to it each year.

In Illinois and Texas

Rather similar to the foregoing two cases is another in the Seventh Circuit, where a high school principal at Joliet, Illinois, handed his pupils a pamphlet "Report to Parents" with a request to deliver it to their parents at home. Two students, Raymond Scoville and Arthur Breen, subsequently wrote and distributed a caustic criticism of the principal, the dean, and the pamphlet, and in which they strongly advised all pupils to refuse to accept, or "destroy if accepted, any propaganda whatsoever from the administration," and advocated disregard of school regulations. For this they were suspended and subsequently expelled.

Expulsion for this offense was adjudged proper by United States District Judge Napoli, and his judgment was affirmed by a panel of the United States Court of Appeals; but the Court of Appeals subsequently granted a rehearing *en banc* and reversed and remanded the judgment in an opinion by Circuit Judge Roger J. Kiley. Circuit Judge Latham Castle entered a dissent.

Judge Kiley was convinced that the facts of this case afforded no basis for any reasonable inference that any substantial disruption of the operation of the school would result. Said he: "While recognizing the need of effective discipline in operating schools, the law requires that the school rules be related to the state interest in the production of well-trained intellects with constructive critical stances, lest students' imaginations, intellects and wills be unduly stifled or chilled. Schools are increasingly accepting student criticism as a worthwhile influence in school administration."

He concluded that further proceedings should be had in the district court to determine whether the "forecast" of disruption was justified in fact; and if not, then Scoville and Breen were entitled to the declaratory judgment, injunctive and damage relief sought.[16]

Much the same denouement occurred in the case of a high school in Houston, Texas, where Dan Sullivan and Mike Fischer, boys in the senior class, became concerned with what seemed to them to be unnecessary and capricious repression and low morale in the school, and so wrote and had printed and distributed (out of school hours and off the school premises) three issues of an "underground newspaper" called the *Pflashlyte* in which the administration of the school was rather crudely criticized and argument was made for more harmony among students, faculty, and administration. A case was also made for constitutional free speech and press, based on some research in the legal sources.

The distribution was apparently made in a public park near the school, and pupils were asked not to take the papers into the school; or if they did so, to keep them concealed. Nevertheless, some of the papers found their way into the building and a few were seen in the hands of pupils in classrooms, and in half a dozen instances teachers took them from the pupils without classroom disruption. In a few instances pupils asked a teacher to conduct a discussion of the paper during class time, and were refused.

After a few days of sleuthing the principal identified the two boys, who readily admitted they were the "editors." (The principal's alarm was somewhat escalated by the unfortunate fact that the printing was done at the University of Houston, a state university, on a work-order signed by the Students for a Democratic Society, then a recognized student organization at the university; and that, contrary to the wishes of the two boys and without their order or consent, the initials "S.D.S." were printed on the issues.)

Without further process the principal immediately told the two boys and their parents that they were suspended for the remainder of the year, and advised them that their only recourse would be to try to

---

16. *Scoville* v. *Board of Education of Joliet Township*, (U.S.C.A., 7 Cir.), 425 F. 2d 10 (1970); reversing (U.S.D.C., Ill.), 286 F. Supp. 988 (1968).

gain admission to some other high school in the Houston district. When they took their case to the United States district court, District Judge Woodrow B. Seals first immediately ordered their temporary reinstatement because they had been suspended without any semblance of due process; and then advanced the study of the facts and the law involved in order to afford a prompt decision on the plea for an injunction and a declaratory judgment.

His expedited memorandum opinion was a judgment in favor of the students, declaring the only applicable written regulation of the Houston Board of Education (which merely authorized the principal of a high school to make and enforce "rules necessary and in the best interests of the school") to be unconstitutional and void for vagueness and overbreadth; and granting an injunction preventing the use of this rule in the future, and prohibiting the imposition "of serious disciplinary sanctions, in the absence of precise and narrowly drawn regulations upon students who write, print, distribute or otherwise engage in the publication of newspapers either on or off the school premises during either school hours or non-school hours unless such activities materially and substantially disrupt the normal operations of the school."[17]

The permanent injunction also forbade the suspension or expulsion for a substantial period of time of secondary school students in the Houston school district who are guilty of any misconduct, without compliance with minimal standards of due process: (1) formal written notice of charges and evidence, (2) formal hearing with opportunity to introduce witnesses and other evidence, and (3) decision to be solely on the basis of substantial evidence.

The opinion itself requires approximately 12,000 words. Appended also are some 4,000 words of *Pflashlyte*, and a copy of the judge's "Oral and Informal Findings of Fact and Conclusions of Law" made April 15, 1969, seven months before the date of the court's formal final judgment. Taken together, these documents provide an informative record.

They stimulate the author to make an assertion which he thinks is needed. Morale is not as high as it should be in many high schools and colleges. There is hostility among students and teachers and administrators. Many students are more or less rebellious against "the system."

---

17. *Sullivan* v. *Houston Independent School District*, (U.S.D.C., Tex.), 307 F. Supp. 1328 (1969).

It is neither fair nor correct to blame students, teachers, or administrators for these unhappy facts; and assessing of blame will bring no
cure. Repression is not the answer. It is fortunate that the courts now
seem to be saying that suppression of the constitutional rights of students will no longer be tolerated.

The root of the trouble is that in many high schools and colleges
great crowds of thousands of students are shepherded by only half
enough teachers and counselors, so that opportunity for decent and
humane person-to-person relationships scarcely exists. Huge over-
crowded school buildings are operated somewhat like prisons. Teachers almost unavoidably acquire some of the characteristics of a drill-
sergeant of Marines, and administrators feel compelled to perform the
functions of complainant, judge, jury, and probation officer, to say
nothing of colonel of a regimental combat team.

Twice as many teachers as are now on duty are needed, and better-educated teachers. These could include many trained paraprofes-
sional assistant teachers to help with the debilitating burden of clerical
work as well as some tutoring of slow learners. The same applies to administrators. They should be better-educated, including some knowledge of the constitutional freedoms of American citizens, and there
should be more of them. Thus schools and colleges can fulfill their
highest potentials.

Yet we now hear of a "surplus of teachers" over the next few
years, and a "glut of doctoral degree holders." In the wealthiest nation
on earth, this talk flows from inverted and perverted reasoning which
would lead to the missing of the greatest opportunity of the century.
The facts of the birth-rate prior to about 1960 make it virtually certain
that high school enrollments will continue to grow until about 1978,
and college enrollments until about 1982. We have just come through a
decade of enormous growth. The expansion of numbers will continue
for another decade. What of the improvement of quality? Taxpayers
and private donors have earned praise for good support, but we have
had to improvise in many ways and "muddle through" under the
weight of increasing enrollments. Now, for the first time in many
years, it may be possible to have enough well-educated teachers to
staff the schools and colleges. Shall we think of the enterprise as
though it were permanently frozen in its present mold, and say we
have a "surplus" of teachers? This could become a self-fulfilling

prophecy if it is not scuttled. The great opportunity is coming to put to work twice as many teachers as we now have, and better-educated. There isn't much wrong with schools and colleges that would not be helped by this strategy.

CHAPTER 17

"DUE PROCESS" IN
DISCIPLINARY
PROCEEDINGS

AN INHERENT AND ESSENTIAL PART of the duties of a college or university governing board is to provide for the maintenance of order and decorum on the campus to an extent that will protect the regular operation of the institution from disruption, preserve its property from damage or destruction, and assure that students, teachers, and all other persons having legitimate business there will not be obstructed or threatened. Performance of this obligation is delegated in manifold ways to the president and his administrative staff, to the faculty, and to the students. In a sense, every member of the academic community may be said to share in the responsibility.

Nearly every university or college has among its nonacademic employees a small force of uniformed men (usually armed) now designated euphemistically as a "security service." Sometimes some or all these individuals may be deputized as peace officers or police officers of the local political subdivision in which the institution is located. In any event, in case of serious disorder or violation of criminal law, police forces of the city, county, or state may come upon the campus to restore order and to make arrests if necessary, either with or without the invitation of the college or university authorities.

The campus is not a sanctuary for lawbreakers, regardless of whether they be students or nonstudents. The state's criminal writ runs on the campus exactly as elsewhere. It is not to be confused with the quite separate disciplinary jurisdiction of the university or college.

The State's Criminal Jurisdiction and the College's Disciplinary Power Are Distinct

Universities do not maintain jails. They do not conduct criminal trials, make criminal indictments or convictions, or fine or imprison offenders. They do formulate and administer their own disciplinary rules and inflict appropriate penalities for serious infractions thereof. The severest punishment they can apply is *expulsion,* which is permanent exclusion from the academic community. This is now infrequently used because it may make it very difficult for the offender to continue his education in any other institution, and it is questionable that any disciplinary offense by a college student should forever bar him from further opportunity for formal education.

Hence for practical purposes the severest penalty in the disciplinary lexicon is *suspension* for a substantial period of time. Lesser punishments for lesser infractions run down through suspension for a short period, disciplinary probation, formal censure, reprimand, admonition, and warning.

The "due process" with which we are concerned is the procedure by which students are accused, heard, adjudged, and exonerated or punished for alleged infractions of discipline. These processes are carried on by the university or college itself through its own agencies set up for the purpose. They are not the same, and no one expects them to be the same, as the elaborate adversary procedures required in courts of law, some of which are prescribed in the federal and state bills of rights, and many of which are deeply imbedded in the common law.

For example, the Fifth Amendment guarantees against self-incrimination and double jeopardy are applicable only in criminal law; and the Sixth and Seventh Amendment guarantees of trial by jury have no application to university or college disciplinary cases. (A college or university, being without power to punish for contempt, seems to have no feasible way to compel a witness to testify at all, much less to testify against himself; and no plea of "double jeopardy" can regulate the sequence of separate criminal and disciplinary actions for a single offense, because self-incriminating testimony at a disciplinary proceeding will not be admitted as evidence in a subsequent criminal trial.)

Remembering that the two jurisdictions are quite distinct, and that the "due process" now required in college disciplinary cases is not hedged about with the same formalities as are proceedings in a court of law, yet we may note that there is some resemblance between the two; that each may be said to be derived in some part from the "due process of law" clauses of the Fifth Amendment and the Fourteenth Amendment; and that both are based on a sense of fairness. These considerations justify, in view of the trend of the decisions of the 1960's, the invention of the slogan, "The Constitution comes to the campus."

As we look at the recent decisions specifying some of the essentials of due process in disciplinary cases, it is necessary to keep in mind that we are dealing with only the more serious cases in which the gravest penalties (suspension or expulsion) are likely to be invoked; and not the forest of lesser infractions of varying degrees, in many of which "due process" may consist only of a brief interview with an administrative, faculty, or student officer.

During the second half of the nineteenth century and the first half of the twentieth, the general drift of the decisions in the litigated cases was toward less and less formality in the disciplinary proceedings, and toward the extreme of sanctioning simple summary suspension without any sort of process. One of the better-known steps in this descent was the Illinois case of *Bluett* v. *University of Illinois*, 10 Ill. App. 2d 207, 134 N.E. 2d 635 (1956), wherein the court sustained the expulsion of a medical student for alleged cheating in examinations, without any notification of the cause until a year later, and the accused student was never given opportunity to introduce witnesses in her behalf or present evidence to support her denial of the charge.

Summary Expulsion Will Not Stand

This evoked from Professor Warren A. Seavey of the Harvard Law School an article severely castigating both the university and the appellate court in Illinois: "It is shocking that the officials of a state educational institution, which can function properly only if our freedoms are preserved, should not understand the elementary principles of fair play. It is equally shocking to find that a court supports them in denying to a student the protection given to a pickpocket."[1] These biting words were quoted with approval by United States Circuit Judge Rives in the landmark case of *Dixon* v. *Alabama*, which was definitely "the last straw" and marks the historic turning-point toward closer attention to the constitutional rights of accused students to "procedural due process" in college disciplinary cases.[2]

In that case, under a direct order from the Alabama State Board of Education, the president of Alabama State College at Montgomery had forthwith and summarily expelled certain students named as having taken part in restaurant "sit-ins" in Montgomery and Tuskegee. A federal district court had sustained this action on the old familiar ground, long relied upon by private colleges and perhaps still effective as to them, that a college can reserve the right to dismiss a student at any time without divulging its reason other than its being for the general benefit of the institution, when the reasons actually are "reasonably related to preserving its ideals of scholarship or moral atmosphere."

The Alabama State Board of Education put it this way in a standing rule: "Just as a student may withdraw from a particular college at any time for any personally determined reason, the college may also at any time decline to continue to accept responsibility for the supervision and service to any student with whom the relationship becomes unpleasant and difficult." Distinguishing between private and public institutions, Circuit Judge Rives sharply pointed out that the existence of this published rule could not operate as a waiver of the students' right to notice and hearing of the charges against them, because "only private associations have the right to obtain a waiver of notice and hearing before depriving a member of a valuable right."

Noting that no formal charges were placed against any of these students, and no hearing was granted to any of them prior to their expulsion, he said:

"In the disciplining of college students there are no considera-

---

1. Warren A. Seavey, "Dismissal of Students: 'Due Process.'" 70 *Harvard Law Review* 1406 (June 1957).

2. *Dixon* v. *Alabama State Board of Education*, (U.S.C.A.), 294 F. 2d 150 (1961); reversing (U.S.D.C., Ala.), 186 F. Supp. 945 (1960). *Certiorari* denied, 368 U.S. 930, 82 S.Ct. 368, 7 L.Ed. 2d 193 (1961).

tions of immediate danger to the public, or of peril to the national security, which should prevent the board from exercising at least the fundamental principles of fairness by giving the accused students notice of the charges and an opportunity to be heard in their own defense. Indeed, the example set by the board in failing to do so, if not corrected by the courts, can well break the spirits of the expelled students and of others familiar with the injustice, and do inestimable harm to their education."

Circuit Judge Rives refrained from being too explicit regarding the exact details of the necessary procedure in such cases, believing that these would vary widely according to different circumstances; but he declared that the hearing should embody "at least the rudiments of an adversary proceeding," and in serious cases it certainly should be more than a mere informal interview with a college administrative officer. Although the accused might not always have opportunity to hear all the testimony against him, he should at least have access to the names of the adverse witnesses and to the substance of their testimony, he said.

During the same year the United States Supreme Court declined to review this decision; and another and similar case was decided in accord with it by a United States district court in Tennessee, making 1961 appear to be truly "the year of the turning-point." In the Tennessee case 13 students at the Tennessee Agricultural and Industrial State University (now Tennessee State University) had participated in a "freedom ride" on a bus into the state of Mississippi, and upon their arrival had been arrested and convicted of disorderly conduct by a Mississippi court.

As soon as news of the incident reached Tennessee, and while the 13 students were still in jail in Mississippi, a faculty committee wrote each one a letter placing him "on probation" (in effect, suspending him) until such time as his innocence might be proved to the satisfaction of the committee. This was in pursuance of an order previously received from the State Board of Education instructing the president of Tennessee State "to dismiss promptly any student who shall, in the future, be arrested and convicted on charges involving personal misconduct."

Chief District Judge W. E. Miller wrote the opinion of the court declaring "plaintiffs are entitled to injunctive relief to enforce their rights to procedural due process with respect to any disciplinary action growing out of their Mississippi convictions and any alleged violations under (the above-quoted order of the State Board of Education)."[3] The decision is in full accord with *Dixon* v. *Alabama*, which has become recognized as setting a standard for due process so far as public institutions are concerned.

At Michigan State University in the summer of 1966, Paul M. Schiff was refused readmission as a graduate student in history, presumably for disciplinary as distinguished from academic reasons. He asked the federal district court for a temporary injunction to restrain interference with his attendance. In an opinion by District Judge Noel E. Fox, with Chief District Judge W. Wallace Kent and Senior District Judge Raymond W. Starr sitting *en banc*, the court thought best not to grant injunctive relief, at least until allowing the university a reasonable time in which to adjust the matter fairly. Accordingly the court retained jurisdiction for three months from the date of its first decree.[4]

Judge Fox regarded the matter as highly important, but thought it could be "disposed of without the interference of the United States courts." He said counsel for the university had not properly briefed "the more recent cases having to do with the readmission and expulsion of students from tax-supported educational institutions," specifically directing attention to *Dixon* v. *Alabama* and *Knight* v. *Tennessee*, wherein the modern concept of due process in disciplinary cases is expounded.

The Requisites of Due Process

No court has repudiated the doctrine of *Dixon* v. *Alabama*. It has been followed, in some instances somewhat desultorily, but in others with manifest enthusiasm; and in some recent decisions it has been carried a step or two beyond *Dixon* in detail. Observe first two U.S. District court opinions which have traversed somewhat more comprehensively the requisites of procedural due process. In 1967, students at Central Missouri State College, having been suspended summarily for alleged participation in an unruly demonstration, were ordered rein-

---

3. *Knight* v. *Tennessee State Board of Education*, (U.S.D.C., Tenn.), 300 F. Supp. 174 (1961).

4. *Schiff* v. *Hannah*, (U.S.D.C., Mich.), 282 F. Supp. 381 (1966).

stated by U.S. District Judge Elmo B. Hunter, who set forth the following essentials:[5]

(1) Written charges ten days in advance of scheduled hearing. (2) Student's right to inspect in advance the college's pertinent affidavits or exhibits. (3) Student's right to call witnesses and introduce affidavits or exhibits. (4) Student's right to legal counsel. (5) Right to confrontation and cross-examination of witnesses. (6) Determination by the hearing body solely on evidence in the record. (7) Written findings and disposition. (8) Right of either adversary to make a *verbatim* record at its own expense. (9) Right of the student to appeal to the president of the institution, thence to the governing board. These are probably the most explicit prescriptions extant.[6]

Shortly thereafter the U.S. District Court for the Western District of Missouri took a most unusual step by sitting *en banc* with no case before it, for the purpose of considering and drafting a set of "judicial standards of procedure and substance in review of student discipline in tax-supported institutions of higher learning."

That document included as due process requisites in severe disciplinary cases (1) adequate notice in writing of the charges and the nature of the evidence; (2) a hearing at which the student is given fair opportunity to present his position; and (3) there must be substantial supporting evidence for any disciplinary action taken. The court thought not all the other requisites as listed by Judge Hunter should be rigidly required invariably, but only "in rare exceptional circumstances" where necessary to guarantee the fundamentals of fair play.[7]

Perhaps the most comprehensive list of requisites yet published

---

5. *Esteban* v. *Central Missouri State College*, (U.S.D.C., Mo.), 277 F. Supp. 649 (1967). For other aspects of the same case, see 290 F. Supp. 622 (1968); and (U.S.C.A., 8 Cir.), 415 F. 2d 1077 (1969). *Certiorari* denied, 38 *U.S. Law Week* 3497 (1970).

6. Though perhaps more detailed, they seem not more comprehensive than the holding of a county court in Pennsylvania in 1887, in which the judge said there must be ample notice of the charges against the student, with time to prepare to meet them, and a hearing at which he should have opportunity to hear the evidence against him, confront and cross-examine the hostile witnesses, and call witnesses to introduce testimony in his behalf. *Commonwealth ex rel. Hill* v. *McCauley*, 3 Pa. Co. Ct. 77 (1887). For more than seventy years thereafter, apparently no court reasserted these essentials, prior to the *Dixon, Knight,* and *Esteban* decisions discussed herein.

7. *General Order on Judicial Standards of Procedure and Substance in Review of Student Discipline in Tax supported Institutions of Higher Education,* (U.S.D.C., Mo., *en banc*), 45 Federal Rules Decisions 133 (1968).

was constructed by William W. Van Alstyne, professor of law at Duke University, after studying many sources:[8]

"(a) The student charged with an infraction has been furnished with a written statement of the charge adequately in advance of the hearing to enable him to prepare (e.g., 10 days);

"(b) the student thus charged 'shall be permitted to inspect in advance of such hearing any affidavits or exhibits which the college intends to submit at the hearing';

"(c) the student is 'permitted to have counsel present at the hearing to advise him';

"(d) the student is 'permitted to hear the evidence presented against him, or at least the student should be given the names of the witnesses against him and an oral or written report on the facts to which each witness testifies';

"(e) the student or his attorney may question at the hearing any witness who gives evidence against him;

"(f) those who hear the case 'shall determine the facts of each case solely on the evidence presented at the hearing';

"(g) 'the results and findings of the hearing should be presented in a report open to the student's inspection';

"(h) 'either side may, at its own expense, make a record of the events at the hearing.' "

There is at this writing no exact consensus as to any invariable and comprehensive enumeration of all the requisites. Concerning some of the points on which there does not appear to be complete agreement, it is possible to note some authority and some arguments on both sides.

An Impartial Tribunal

The hearing body of first instance may be a student court or council,[9] or a faculty disciplinary committee, or a committee made up of students, faculty and administration or any two of them, in such proportions as the institutional regulations provide. Some universities have rules establishing a single hearing officer, sometimes a faculty

---

8. William W. Van Alstyne, "The Student as University Resident," in 45 *Denver Law Journal* 582 (Special issue, 1968).

9. *In re Carter*, 262 N.C. 360, 137 S.E. 2d 150 (1964); discussed at pages 20-22 in *The Colleges and the Courts, 1962-1966.* Danville, Ill.: The Interstate Printers & Publishers, Inc., 1967. 326 pp.

member to be appointed by the president for each case *ad hoc*, but more often an experienced and respected lawyer or jurist to hear all cases as they arise. Always there is a channel of appeal to the president, and ultimately to the institutional governing board. Sometimes there is an intermediate reviewing body through which the case is channeled before it reaches the president.

Sometimes it happens that an individual, who is the accuser or prosecutor or a witness adverse to the accused, also sits as a member or chairman of the hearing body. This would not be tolerated in a strictly judicial proceeding, but it is not generally held to be impermissible in this area of informal administrative hearings, though on occasion the courts have declared that when it occurs it justifies especially painstaking scrutiny of the impartiality of the proceedings, as we shall see.

A flagrant departure from the concept of an impartial tribunal occurs when the members of the hearing body communicate with each other and agree on their prospective decision before the hearing begins. Such a case is on record. Richard Perlman, a student at Shasta College, a junior college in California, was first suspended for three days on January 23, 1968, and subsequently expelled on February 21, 1968. The suspension was because he had invited a group of Socialist students to the campus without signing the required forms in the office of the dean of students. Upon the arrival of the invitees the dean of students directed Perlman to ask them to leave, and then to "proceed through channels" with the invitation. Perlman refused, whereupon the dean ordered him to appear at the president's office one hour later.

Perlman did so, and met with the president, the vice president, the dean of students, and the dean of men. He did not deny the dean's story, or ask for any further hearing. Thereupon he was suspended for three days and placed on disciplinary probation to commence at the beginning of the next term, February 13. This meant, among other things, that while on probation he could not collect or in any way handle moneys belonging to the student body or to the college. Within a day or two he violated the terms of his probation (which had been detailed to him in writing); and on February 15 the dean notified him in writing that a special meeting of the board of trustees would be held February 21 "for the purpose of considering a recommendation to suspend or expel you from college."

This notice stated the charges in detail and informed Perlman that he had the right to be represented by counsel, could request that the meeting be open to the public, and could bring witnesses to testify in his behalf. This meeting was held as scheduled, and after the hearing the board unanimously ordered that Perlman be permanently expelled. He immediately asked the Shasta County superior court for an order to strike both his suspension and expulsion from the college records, on the ground of lack of due process. Judge John F. Kean granted the requested relief. Subsequently the Court of Appeal reversed this judgment as to the three-day suspension, but affirmed it as to the permanent expulsion. As to the suspension, although the interview with the four principal college officers was impromptu and on only one hour's notice (unwritten), it met the requirements of due process in view of the facts and the comparative lightness of the penalty.

As to the expulsion, Perlman's allegation that the board of trustees had acted as a biased tribunal and had unanimously agreed in a series of telephone conversations before the day of the hearing to expel him was proved to the satisfaction of the court. Hence the expulsion was of no effect and was ordered stricken.[10]

The opinion was by Justice Bray (assigned), with Presiding Justice Fred R. Pierce and Justice Edwin J. Regan concurring. The *ratio decidendi*: "Due process does not forbid the combination of judging and prosecuting in administrative proceedings. However, it is necessary to review closely the proceedings in order to protect the rights of parties. . . . And if the record shows bias and prejudice upon the part of the administrative body, its decision will not be upheld by the courts."

In at least one instance a federal court held that "The composition of the hearing panel was inadequate under constitutional standards because its chairman, who was also one of its members, participated in the hearing as a witness." This was at Arkansas State University at Jonesboro, where the court also noted that "It is undisputed that the plaintiff was not afforded the opportunity to be confronted by the witnesses and the evidence against him."

Convinced by these and other reasons that due process had not been had, the court issued an injunctive order to reinstate the student

---

10. *Shasta Joint Junior College District* v. *Perlman*, 9 Cal. App. 3d 873, 88 Cal. Rptr. 563 (1970).

and to expunge from his academic record all traces of his suspension, unless and until the university chose to conduct entirely new proceedings in which he might be found guilty.[11]

Assistance of Legal Counsel

The question of whether the accused student has a right to be accompanied at the hearing by his lawyer is one on which unanimity has not been reached. On the one hand, it is said that the Sixth Amendment guarantee of legal counsel applies only to criminal cases. But quite commonly it is thought that the student should be allowed to bring with him to the hearing an adviser or advisers of his own choice, and this could include a lawyer. Generally disciplinary officers oppose having one or more lawyers present, on the ground that this would tend to escalate the proceedings toward the semblance of a court of law, and to destroy the informal "community tribunal" atmosphere of the hearing, turning it into a battle over technicalities not understood by intelligent lay persons, and going astray from the concept of simple fairness which should prevail.

In one of the recent cases in which this question was at issue, U.S. District Judge Sidney L. Christie concluded that *"in the circumstances of this case*, the (Faculty Committee on Student Affairs) did not deny the six aggrieved students due process by refusing their request for counsel."[12]

However, another U.S. District court decided about a year later that, where Southern University in New Orleans had, in hearings involving a group of students accused of disruptive actions, refused to allow their retained counsel to participate in the hearings, that this was a denial of due process, and ordered new hearings held, "in which they will have the right to be represented by their retained counsel, after which the findings of the Discipline Committee will be presented in a report open to the plaintiffs' inspection."[13]

In that case District Judge Comiskey noted that the university had used a senior law student who was within a few months of com-

---

11. *Stewart* v. *Reng*, (U.S.D.C., Ark.), 321 F. Supp. 618 (1970).
12. *Barker* v. *Hardway*, (U.S.D.C., W.Va.), 283 F. Supp. 228 (1968); affirmed without opinion, (U.S.C.A., 4 Cir.), 399 F. 2d 638 (1968). *Certiorari* denied, 394 U.S. 905 (1969).
13. *French* v. *Bashful*, (U.S.D.C., La.), 303 F. Supp. 1333 (1969).

pleting his studies and passing the Louisiana bar examination to conduct its own case in the hearings, thus taking an advantage over the plaintiff students, none of whom had any knowledge or expertise in the law. He also stressed *retained* counsel, expressing his belief that a university should not be subjected to the financial burden of providing *appointed* counsel for plaintiff students in disciplinary cases.

He also said: "Although the right to counsel was not among the rights specifically enumerated by the court in *Dixon*, it can not be denied that the assistance of an attorney in a trial-type proceeding is of considerable value. An attorney is experienced in legal and quasi-legal proceedings. Counsel is best qualified to prepare a defense to the charges, examine the evidence against the defendant, cross-examine witnesses if such a right is permitted, and otherwise to plead the defending student's cause." But also, "In spite of the invaluable assistance to a defendant in a university disciplinary proceeding, it may well be that in many cases the student will not be at such a disadvantage as to require the assistance of counsel."

Two years earlier a United States Court of Appeals had flatly declared that the accused student in an expulsion case is not invariably entitled to representation by counsel at the disciplinary hearing. Circuit Judge Leonard P. Moore of the Second Circuit said: "The requirement of counsel as an ingredient of fairness is a function of all of the other aspects of the hearing. Where the proceeding is noncriminal in nature, where the hearing is investigative and not adversarial and the government does not proceed through counsel, where the individual concerned is mature and educated, where his knowledge of the events should enable him to develop the facts adequately through available sources, and where the other aspects of the hearing taken as a whole are fair, due process does not require representation by counsel."[14]

The pertinency of this decision to universities and colleges is attenuated, however, by the fact that it involved the dismissal of a cadet at the United States Merchant Marine Academy—a federal agency, not a state or municipal institution; and the judge himself had said earlier in his opinion: "Few decisions properly rest so exclusively within the discretion of the appropriate government officials as the selection, training, discipline and dismissal of future officers of the military and

---

14. *Wasson* v. *Trowbridge*, (U.S.C.A., 2 Cir.), 382 F. 2d 807 (1967).

Merchant Marine. . . . And it can not be doubted that because of these factors historically the military has been permitted greater freedom to fashion its disciplinary procedures than the civilian authorities." Nevertheless, he reversed and remanded a District Court decision summarily dismissing the suit on the ground that the complaint did not constitute a deprivation of due process of law; and directed the District Court to hold a hearing on that issue.

Professor Charles Alan Wright takes the view that the right to be represented by counsel should be recognized in "major disciplinary proceedings";[15] and Professor Arthur Sherry believes that at a university disciplinary proceeding the student's "right to counsel, should the matter appear to him to be of sufficient gravity to make legal assistance desirable, should receive ungrudging recognition . . ."[16] The trend of decision will probably move in that direction.

A Private or a Public Hearing

Most educators believe the disciplinary hearing should not be open to the public indiscriminately, at least unless the accused student requests it. At the same time they are unanimous in conceding that in the serious cases the student should be permitted to bring witnesses in his own behalf, and advisers of his own choice, such as his parents, selected fellow-students, or faculty members.

The case against an open public hearing was stated by Chief District Judge Ben C. Dawkins, Jr., in the 1968 decision involving the expulsion of a group of students at Grambling College, Louisiana, wherein the college authorities had conducted a fragmentary and insufficient hearing which the governing board (Louisiana State Board of Education) thought best to disregard and set up its own full hearing de novo. Speaking of this hearing before the State Board of Education, Judge Dawkins said:

"The fact that 'the public' was not allowed to attend the hearings before the State Board in no way tends to establish bias or unfairness in those proceedings. No citation of authority has been submitted, and indeed there is none, which necessitates a public hearing in such

15. Charles Alan Wright, "The Constitution of the Campus," 22 *Vanderbilt Law Review* 1027 (October 1969).

16. Arthur Sherry, "Governance of the University: Rules, Rights, and Responsibilities," 54 *California Law Review* 23 (1966).

matters. Indeed for the benefit of the reputation of the students involved, where they were strongly represented by able counsel, and given the widest possible latitude, it would seem more fitting to allow all charges and defenses to be made before the Board itself, not as a 'Star Chamber' proceeding, but in a genuine effort to protect the students against unwonted and probably inaccurate news media reporting."[17]

Likewise, a federal district court in Puerto Rico, adjudicating a suit brought on behalf of a number of students at the University of Puerto Rico who had been disciplined for alleged participation in several types of campus disorders, held that their constitutional rights had not been prejudiced by the fact that the proceeding in which their case had been heard and determined by the university governing board had not been open to the general public.[18]

Determination Based on Sufficient Evidence

All courts agree that one of their duties is to assure themselves that the determination of the administrative hearing body is adequately supported by the evidence, and does not appear to rest too heavily on rumor, hearsay, pique, or prejudice.

Joseph Scoggin, Jr., and Edward Jefferson, students at Lincoln University, the state institution in Jefferson City, Missouri, were suspended from the university on charges that they "planned and participated in a demonstration which led to destruction of University property on Wednesday, October 18, 1967, at the Student Union Building." The disturbance had occurred in the cafeteria where large numbers of students were present, either eating or waiting to be served. It included the dropping of trays and food, the upturning of tables and chairs and the throwing of dishes and glassware. Property damage was estimated at $1,500.

Telegrams, dispatched to Scoggin and Jefferson at 6:45 p.m. on October 20, directed them to appear before the committee on student personnel services at 10 a.m., October 21 to answer the charge. Both

---

17. *Zanders* v. *Louisiana State Board of Education*, (U.S.D.C., La.), 281 F. Supp. 747 (1968).

18. *Consejo General de Estudiantes de la Universidad de Puerto Rico* v. *University of Puerto Rico*, (U.S.D.C., P.R.), 325 F. Supp. 453 (1971).

appeared during the afternoon of October 21. Neither had an attorney personally present, though Scoggin had conferred with one.

The trouble had been triggered by a recent boost in the charges for room and board. The dean of students, hoping to forestall or minimize any turbulence, had posted a notice advising against any demonstration, but also saying: "But if it becomes apparent that we 'must' demonstrate, it is hoped that we (1) respect the rights of those who may not share in our decided methods, (2) be orderly and peaceful, and (3) respect and care for university property."

Although the committee on student personnel had used three days in its "investigatory phase" before formally charging anyone, and although there was a transcript of its entire proceedings, including the hearing on the charges and the determination to suspend the accused, District Judge John W. Oliver was "left with a firm conviction that the Committee's consideration of the data before it rested on the premise that it was not necessary to establish that the plaintiffs had either (a) planned a demonstration different from that contemplated by the dean's notice, or (b) personally destroyed university property." The proceedings provided *no substantial evidence* that either Scoggin or Jefferson had done either.

Hence, in the judge's view, the committee's determination must be overturned for *lack of sufficient evidence* to support its conclusions. Accordingly he ordered that the suspensions be void; and that the plaintiffs be reinstated as students in good standing, subject to the university's "right to institute a new and proper disciplinary proceeding against the plaintiffs for the alleged violation of any existent regulation of Lincoln University."[19]

Summary Suspension in Emergency, Prior to Hearing

Many federal and state courts have said the requisites of due process must be followed *prior to* a suspension or expulsion. Few would doubt or deny, however, that emergencies may arise wherein it may be in the best interest of the academic community that an accused student be temporarily suspended summarily, pending the holding of a hearing on the matter within the shortest practicable time.

Thus in the case of *Barker* v. *Hardway*, mentioned earlier in this

---

19. *Scoggin* v. *Lincoln University*, (U.S.D.C., Mo.), 291 F. Supp. 161 (1968).

chapter, the college president sought to interview a number of leaders of a violent student demonstration, but could not get them to come to his office. Most of them could not be found in their scheduled classrooms or their places of residence, and the few who were located refused to come for interviews. The president then sent to each a letter of suspension, and notified their parents by telegram. The letters stated the reason for the suspension, stated that the student could have an appeal hearing before the faculty committee on student affairs if he so desired, and contained instructions as to how to request such a hearing.

All of the suspended students requested hearings, which were duly arranged. Four of the students appeared and received hearings, after which the committee recommended that two of these be reinstated and two suspended. Six others appeared, but upon being informed that they would not be permitted to have legal counsel at the hearing, refused to participate in it. Thereafter on two separate occasions the committee offered further opportunities for hearings to these six students, but none accepted. The committee then recommended that these six be suspended. In all cases the college president approved the recommendation of the committee. In the subsequent litigation, U.S. District Judge Sidney L. Christie held that none of the accused students had been deprived of any First or Fourteenth Amendment rights.[20] In the course of his opinion he quoted Mr. Chief Justice Earl Warren, whose opinion in a case involving procedure of the United States Civil Rights Commission had included these words: " 'Due process' is an elusive concept. Its exact boundaries are indefinable, and its content varies according to specific factual contexts." And whether it "requires that a particular right obtain in a specific proceeding depends upon a complexity of factors."[21]

Similarly, in a case arising at the C. W. Post College of Long Island University, it appears that a student was stabbed in a dormitory, whereupon the dean of students immediately investigated the matter, obtaining oral and written statements from the victim and from certain witnesses, after which he dispatched a letter of expulsion to an accused student, also advising him of his rights to appeal to the Student-Faculty Appeal Board. Such a proceeding was set for three months

---

20. *Barker* v. *Hardway*, (U.S.D.C., W.Va.), 283 F. Supp. 228 (1968); affirmed without opinion, (U.S.C.A., 4 Cir.), 399 F. 2d 638 (1968). *Certiorari* denied, 394 U.S. 905 (1969).

21. *Hannah* v. *Larche*, 363 U.S. 420, 80 S.Ct. 1502, 4 L.Ed. 2d 1307 (1960).

later at the request of the accused student, and he and his attorney presented themselves but "declined to defend the substance of the case but objected to the board's procedures."

Later the accused student and his mother sued in the local New York State court (Supreme Court, Nassau County), alleging that he had been expelled without a hearing, contrary to a pertinent New York statute (CPLR Sec. 7801 *et seq.*). Justice Mario Pittoni dismissed the petition, pointing out that the pertinent statute by its own terms can not be used to challenge a determination which is not final or can be adequately reviewed by appeal. Said Justice Pittoni: "Assuming, without deciding, that the petitioner's son should have been interviewed by the Dean of Students before the disciplinary action of May 28, 1969 was taken, it is obvious from the letter of May 28 and from the Student Conduct Handbook that the decision was not final."

Further: "On appeal the petitioner's son was offered full opportunity to present witnesses and to offer his version of his involvement or lack of involvement in the stabbing. The Appeal Board was not required to afford him or his counsel the right to confront or to cross-examine witnesses." He also stressed a sentence in the Appeal Board's report: "The Board does recognize that should the (accused student's) court case end favorably for him he might request and might well be granted another and final hearing here." This illustrates that when a crime is committed on campus, university disciplinary proceedings may proceed quite independently of the criminal proceedings in state courts; and also that in such a case an immediate summary temporary expulsion, *pending* a soon-to-be-arranged hearing before university authorities, violates no civil rights.[22] Noting that the university here was a private institution, Justice Pittoni prefaced his conclusion in its favor by saying "While it may not arbitrarily expel a student." Other decisions touching this point are discussed elsewhere herein, in another chapter.

Three Decisions by U.S. District Judge
James E. Doyle of Wisconsin

A somewhat more stringent view of the requirements of due process in emergency temporary suspension cases was taken by U.S. Dis-

---

22. *Mitchell* v. *Long Island University*, 309 N.Y.S. 2d 538 (1970).

trict Judge James E. Doyle of the Western District, Wisconsin, when he had before him the petition of three students at the University of Wisconsin accused of violent misconduct in disorders occurring on the campus February 27, 1969, and earlier. On March 6, 1969, the Regents of the University of Wisconsin at a meeting heard an oral presentation by the campus police chief describing the disorders and specifically accusing each of the three. Believing there were strong indications that the violence might be repeated, the regents adopted a resolution suspending the three students "immediately" pending a hearing on charges to be brought by the university administration. The administration was directed to bring such charges on or before March 8, and the hearing was ordered to commence on March 19, unless another date were to be set by the board's hearing agent after consultation with counsel for the university and for the accused students.[23]

On March 4 and 5 the vice chancellor for student affairs had notified all of the three students by telephone of the probability of impending charges against them, and invited them to meet him before noon, March 5, or to respond by telephone "to present your side of the case informally before a decision whether or not to bring charges is made." Two of them did meet the vice chancellor on March 5, and the third telephoned him on March 6, after the regents had acted; but apparently none of them made any attempt to explain or defend his conduct on February 27 or earlier.

They proceeded to the U.S. District Court and asked for a judgment declaring their suspensions to be in violation of the due process clause of the Fourteenth Amendment, for injunctive relief, and for damages. Judge Doyle's opinion bore date of March 18. The *ratio decidendi* was: "When appropriate university authority has reasonable cause to believe that danger will be present if a student is permitted to remain on campus pending a decision following a full hearing, an *interim* suspension may be imposed, *but not without a prior preliminary hearing,* unless it can be shown that it is impossible or unreasonably difficult to accord it prior to an *interim* suspension."

Noting that the suspensions in this case were for at least 13 days (March 6-18) and probably more, the judge unequivocally declared

---

23. The board appointed as hearing agent a distinguished former member of the Supreme Court of Wisconsin, to make and report findings of fact and recommendations; and the board resolved to review these findings on the three cases at the earliest possible date.

"A suspension for such a substantial interval imposed as a sanction for misconduct, without prior specification of charges, notice of hearing, or hearing, would violate due process." But the university contended that "Because the continued presence of each of these plaintiffs would endanger persons and property on the campus, he may be suspended, without specification of charges, notice of hearing, or hearing, until the time at which a decision is reached in his case following a hearing."

The judge was able to point to a rule of the regents adopted July 19, 1968 (Section 5 (b) (1) of Chapter V of their *Bylaws*):

"(1) The administration may, in those cases where there is a strong indication that a student's misconduct will be repeated or continued or where the administration believes it necessary to permit the University to carry on its functions, impose immediate suspension with resultant loss of all student rights and privileges, pending hearing before the all-faculty disciplinary committee. The student has a right to immediate hearing on the limited question of whether suspension should remain in effect until the full hearing is completed."

In the present case, however, the regents had exercised their reserved right to deal directly with a disciplinary case (Section 5 (a) of Chapter V of their *Bylaws*) and had denied the plaintiffs a process guaranteed in the same chapter of their own *Bylaws* when disciplinary cases were handled by the administration and faculty. Not to overemphasize this peccadillo, Judge Doyle said "Whether the Regents have honored their own By-laws is not a federal question." But he was deeply impressed unfavorably by the absence of any showing whatever that it was impossible or unreasonably difficult for the regents to provide a preliminary hearing prior to the March 6 *interim* suspension, or after March 6 on whether the *interim* suspension should continue until such time as a decision had been reached following a full hearing.

He declined to define the ingredients of a minimally adequate "preliminary hearing"; but he remarked: "The right of a student in a public university to procedural due process with respect to *interim* suspensions is by its very nature shortlived. But the significance of the right is not diminished by its inherent brevity. It must be vindicated when, as here, the case demands it. I take notice that an extended enforced absence from the university results in irreparable harm to a student."

Accordingly he ordered each of the plaintiffs to be reinstated as of noon March 19, 1969; *provided* "that nothing in this order shall be construed to prevent (the Regents or their agents) from proceeding with the hearing scheduled for March 19, 1969, or from any similar hearing, or from taking appropriate disciplinary action against any of the plaintiffs following any such hearing."[24]

Bearing in mind that this order was dated March 18, it would seem not necessarily to have much practical effect upon the proceedings already under way; but it is more than *pro forma*—it is a lucid enunciation of principle.

In an earlier case, involving the Wisconsin State University at Oshkosh, the conscientious and compassionate Judge Doyle had been equally thoughtful about the danger of inflicting irreparable harm upon students summarily suspended and left to await a foot-dragging arrangement of due process to determine their guilt or innocence. He was keenly aware that suspension for any period longer than a few days can work great inconvenience and expense to a college student, and may indeed spell the ruin of his college career.

November 21, 1968, a shockingly bizarre disturbance occurred. Some 90 persons, mostly black students, entered Dempsey Hall, moved to the second floor and surged into the president's suite, including his secretary's office and his private office, where he was present. They insisted that he sign a list of demands which was slapped on his desk. They jeered and used abusive language and refused to allow him to be heard. They held him prisoner in the office. Some broke into other nearby offices and scattered the contents of filing cabinets, broke windows and art objects, and damaged typewriters. The disturbance began at 8:40 a.m. It was not until 11:45 a.m. that police were present in sufficient numbers to arrest and jail those who refused to leave after warning, on charges of disorderly conduct and unlawful assembly.

The next day President R. E. Guiles sent by registered mail to some 70 persons a notice of immediate suspension, citing pertinent sections of Wisconsin statutes and of the bylaws of the Board of Regents of State Colleges, and informing each recipient that unless he filed within 10 days a written request for a hearing, any right to a hearing

---

24. *Stricklin* v. *Regents of University of Wisconsin*, (U.S.D.C., Wis.), 297 F. Supp. 416 (1969). Dismissed as moot after the students had been given a full hearing in the *interim* and expelled, (U.S.C.A., Wis.), 420 F. 2d 1257 (1970).

would be deemed to have been waived, and his expulsion would there-upon become permanent.

On December 6 (15 days after the suspensions), the board of re-gents informed Judge Doyle, who was that day holding a hearing on a petition by seven of the suspended students, that the board had sus-pended its rules on account of the difficulties involved in conducting hearings for so many accused students, and resolved to employ a hear-ing officer and await his reports before disposing of these cases. A former member of the state supreme court began his duties in that capacity December 9. Also on December 9 Judge Doyle issued his written opinion and order.

He quoted Van Alstyne's list of procedural safeguards,[25] and pointed out that none of them had as yet been made operative in these cases. He doubted that offering a hearing only on request met consti-tutional requirements. His view on that point has since been strongly supported by U.S. District Judge Frank G. Theis in the recent case of *Gardenhire* v. *Chalmers*, (U.S.D.C., Kas.), 326 F. Supp. 1200 (1971), holding that: " 'The right of review,' or a hearing only upon request, does not serve to protect the right of the student to fundamental fair-ness in this type of proceeding. One does not have to be a supplicant for allowance of a constitutional right." Judge Doyle noted that the suspensions had already been in effect nearly three weeks, and that under the scheme of the board of regents substantially more time would likely elapse before hearings were completed. He quoted the *Joint Statement on Rights and Freedoms of Students*,[26] and concluded that the suspended students would be irreparably harmed by any significant extension of their present suspension; and ordered each one reinstated as of 6 p.m. December 11, until the university should accomplish final disposition of the charges against them, with due process; *unless* the university chose to serve notices by registered mail of hearings to be

---

25. Quoted herein in this chapter, in the section "Requisites of Due Process," *supra*.

26. By several national associations in higher education, as published in 53 *AAUP Bulletin* 365 (1967):
"C. *Status of Student Pending Final Action*

"Pending action on the charges, the status of a student should not be altered, or his right to be present on the campus and to attend classes suspended, except for reasons relating to his physical or emotional safety and well-being, or for reasons relating to the safety and well-being of students, faculty, or university property."

held no later than December 16, and to accomplish final disposition by December 20; *or* the university was given the option of filing by December 11 a motion that the reinstatements be deferred for reasons of safety, in which event the motion would be heard by the court on the morning of December 13.

These options were drafted with solicitous care for the rights and interests of the students and of the university. Thus did Judge Doyle pronounce even-handed justice under law in a confused maelstrom.[27]

In a later case, distinguished by an offense such that the continued presence of its perpetrators on the campus would be a clear and present danger to the campus community and to themselves, Judge Doyle countenanced immediate emergency temporary suspensions pending later hearings within a reasonable time.

At Wisconsin State University at Whitewater, a group of about 20 male students invaded the Phi Chi Epsilon fraternity house, some armed with clubs, and physically attacked and beat the occupants, also firing two shots in the melee. President William L. Carter summoned the culprits who were identified to an immediate interview the next day. None denied participation in the fracas, and none offered any explanation. Thereupon President Carter served them with written notice of their immediate temporary suspension, "because your continued presence on this campus poses a clear and present danger to the university community and to yourself." The notice also stated that "a hearing on the merits will be held on January 5, 1970 (twenty days after the offense), and you will be furnished with a formal notice of hearing and statement of charges."

The students immediately sought from Judge Doyle an order cancelling the suspensions until after full hearing and determination of charges. In this set of circumstances, Judge Doyle denied the petition and sustained the emergency temporary suspensions.[28]

Self-Incrimination and Double Jeopardy

In this section let us refer to our own strictures on the sharp distinction between the state's criminal jurisdiction and the university's disciplinary jurisdiction (in the early part of this chapter), as bolster-

---

27. *Vicki Marzette v. McPhee*, (U.S.D.C., Wis.), 294 F. Supp. 562 (1968).
28. *Buck v. Carter*, (U.S.D.C., Wis.), 308 F. Supp. 1246 (1970).

ing the theory that the Fifth Amendment guarantees against self-incrimination and double jeopardy apply only to *criminal* prosecutions. Under this doctrine nothing an accused student says in a disciplinary proceeding will be admitted as evidence against him in a criminal prosecution. It therefore serves no purpose to defer the university's disciplinary action until after the state's criminal prosecution is completed; and the fact that the accused goes through two separate sets of adjudicatory proceedings based on the same offense, and that he may be penalized twice in different manner for that same offense, does not subject him to double jeopardy at all, because he has had only one *criminal trial* and only one criminal penalty, if any. The university disciplinary penalty, if any, is something quite apart.

At least two courts in California, one state and one federal, have espoused this view: the well-known *Goldberg* v. *Regents of University of California*,[29] *supra*, Chapter 13 herein; and a more recent decision in which the sole issue was the plea of suspended students of San Mateo College for an injunction to postpone any college disciplinary hearings on their expulsion until after the completion of their criminal trials resulting from the same allegedly unlawful acts. Their argument was that their testimony at the college hearings might be used against them in the subsequent criminal trials, thus making nugatory the Fifth Amendment safeguard against self-incrimination. Not so, said federal District Judge Stanley A. Weigel. Testimony at a college disciplinary proceeding is properly excluded if offered as evidence against the accused in a subsequent criminal trial arising out of the same set of circumstances.[30]

Similarly, hearing the petition of Columbia University students who found themselves subject to disciplinary action and criminal prosecution at the same time, federal District Judge Marvin E. Frankel of New York pointed out that the district attorney in charge of the prosecutions made an affidavit that he would use neither the testimony nor any of the records of the university disciplinary hearings.[31]

A refreshingly different set of facts and law involved certain midshipmen at the U.S. Merchant Marine Academy who were dismissed

---

29. *Goldberg* v. *Regents of University of California*, (Cal. App.), 57 Cal. Rptr. 463 (1967).

30. *Furutani* v. *Ewigleben*, (U.S.D.C., Cal.), 297 F. Supp. 1163 (1969).

31. *Grossner* v. *Trustees of Columbia University*, (U.S.D.C., N.Y.), 287 F. Supp. 535 (1968). Discussed more fully in the last section of this Chapter herein.

from the academy October 28, 1969, after finding that they had violated regulations by using marijuana on campus. They sought an injunctive order for their readmission. Their main argument was that they had been interrogated in the academy administration building by two federal narcotics agents and a Nassau County detective, with the knowledge and assistance of academy personnel, and that the agents had unequivocally promised them that nothing they said would be used against them; but nevertheless their own admissions there had been made the basis for their dismissal from the academy.

Federal District Judge Jack B. Weinstein issued a preliminary injunction pending a full hearing. Holding that the law enforcement officers were temporary agents of the academy in this instance, he said: "As agents, the questioners were authorized to make promises to the students concerning the use of their statements. They told plaintiffs that if they spoke freely nothing they said would be used against them. Plaintiffs, by speaking freely, accepted this offer, and a contract was made. The academy is bound by this agreement. It can not use as evidence in disciplinary proceedings admissions made by the plaintiffs to the agents."[32]

Recent Change in Stance of Federal Courts

In the *Zanders* case, *supra*, Judge Dawkins wrote an opinion of some 14,000 words, among the longest opinions ever issued by a federal court in this particular field. In general, his outlook seems to be somewhat conservative, as evidenced by his quoting from some of the cogent decisions in cases of as far back as the turn of the present century; yet he recognizes the important changes of recent years. At one point he says:

"While the *public interest* in protection of individual rights and, as far as we are here concerned, student rights in particular, definitely has reached unparalleled heights only in the last few years, jurisprudence concerning the specific requirements for a 'fair hearing' in student disciplinary matters is not new. Neither is it the product of the federal judiciary intervening in affairs traditionally left to administration by the states."[33] And at another point:

32. *Krawez* v. *Stans*, (U.S.D.C., N.Y.), 306 F. Supp. 1230 (1969).
33. *Zanders* v. *Louisiana State Board of Education*, (U.S.D.C., La.), 281 F. Supp. 747 (1968).

"Courts increasingly have found it necessary to enter decrees to fit within the framework of 'fair play.' These orders necessarily encroach upon the well-entrenched, and sometimes severely administered, authority of college and university officials to maintain discipline in their own houses. This judicial entrance into the arena of student disciplinary matters has been a reluctant one, but has come about because of serious, and admittedly complex, considerations which have arisen in the administration of those rules and regulations."

In a footnote Judge Dawkins quotes from two distinguished commentators. First: "There existed for many years a question whether or not the opportunity to obtain a college education was a 'right' or a mere 'privilege,' the latter not being entitled to constitutional protection. However, it is well settled today that, regardless of its classification, this is an interest which is entitled to constitutional protection. Hence it should follow, that where a student's educational opportunities rest in the balance, the proceeding would be classified as adjudicatory even though the student's interest is not categorized as a 'legal right.' "[34]

Also: "The point, then, is this. That the opportunity to maintain one's association with a university is undoubtedly protected by the equal protection clause (of the Fourteenth Amendment)."[35]

Explaining that the constitutional standards of due process must necessarily be somewhat flexible to fit each case, Judge Dawkins said further: "Thus to determine in any given case what procedures due process requires, the court must carefully determine and balance the nature of the private interest affected and of the governmental interest involved, taking account of history and the precise circumstances surrounding the case at hand."

A transaction in mid-1970, between Hunter College of The City University of New York and U.S. District Judge Milton Pollack, uniquely illustrates the transition. On April 27 some students were suspended by Hunter College without notice or hearing for the remainder of the term. The dean of students, Kathryn Hopwood, acted under

---

34. Quoted by Judge Dawkins from Johnson, "The Constitutional Rights of College Students," 42 *Texas Law Review* 344 (1964).

35. Quoted by Judge Dawkins from Van Alstyne, "Student Academic Freedom and the Rule-Making Power of Public Universities: Some Constitutional Considerations," 2 *Legal Transactions Quarterly* 1 (1965).

Paragraph 18.6 of Article 18 of the Bylaws of the Board of Higher Education:

"A dean, in case of violation of college regulations, breach of the peace or damage to property by a student may . . . suspend a student for a period of time not exceeding one term. . . ." It turned out that the whole of this article had been superseded by a new Article 15 two weeks prior to the suspension. There was no provision similar to the old Paragraph 18.6, and the new Article 15 guaranteed a certain level of due process. The dean acted under the old rule because the hearing procedures under the new rule had not yet been set up.

Events were then swift. The suspended students asked Judge Pollack for a constitutionally mandated hearing. Hunter College agreed to conduct the hearing. Its student-faculty hearing panel recommended reinstatement of all the plaintiffs before any hearing was held, and they were reinstated. Hunter College then asked for dismissal of the case because it had become moot. Judge Pollack granted this motion, and his judgment was affirmed by the U.S. Court of Appeals for the Second Circuit, *per curiam*, by Circuit Judges J. Joseph Smith and Paul R. Hays, and Senior District Judge Richard H. Levet.

"Once the students were reinstated, there was no justiciable controversy before the court. There was no likelihood shown that the old bylaw claimed to be unconstitutional would be enforced against them. 'Federal judicial power is to be exercised to strike down legislation, whether state or federal, only at the instance of one who is himself immediately harmed, or immediately threatened with harm, by the challenged action,' A hypothetical threat is not enough."[36]

Cases in Alabama, Virginia, and South Carolina

Fifty students at Alabama State College at Montgomery were indefinitely suspended or expelled for participation in prolonged disorders in and around the college dining hall from March 29 to April 8, 1969, which resulted in the closing of the college from April 7 to April 21.

About 80 students had been served with "form letter" statements of charges. Hearings were held April 23. Counsel for the students objected that the charges were too vague, and requested more specificity.

---

36. *Demby v. Wexler*, (U.S.C.A., N.Y.), 436 F. 2d 570 (1970).

This request was denied, whereupon the 50 students, on advice of counsel, dramatically refused to participate in the hearings, and walked out.

The *Ad Hoc* Faculty-Student Committee went ahead with the hearings, heard the evidence against each student charged, made specific findings with respect to each charge, and made recommendations to President Levi Watkins concerning the disposition of each case. Seven students were expelled, 43 indefinitely suspended, 21 found not guilty, and 3 cases otherwise disposed of. All were given opportunity to have their cases reviewed by President Watkins; and at least eight thus had their indefinite suspensions reduced to special probation.

Almost all had received notice of at least one specific charge of some definite offense connected with the dining-hall disorders; but three had been charged only with open-ended wordings such as "violation of a rule of Alabama State." These three were ordered reinstated (pending new charges and new hearings at the option of the college) by Chief District Judge Frank M. Johnson, Jr. He denied any injunctive order as to all others suspended or expelled; instead, he issued an injunction restraining them from remaining on the campus, intimidating other students and faculty members in an effort to force a boycott, or damaging college property.[37]

Judge Johnson was nettled by the fact that activities of that type had continued while the case was pending before him; and also critical of the walkouts from the college hearings. He pointed out that such walkouts constitute a waiver of due process; that the correct course for counsel when the hearing body refuses a request is to have an objection noted in anticipation of an appeal to higher authority; not to walk out.

Whether termination of student aids or opportunities for practice teaching requires a hearing, he said, was a question of first impression; and he did not decide it, because it was already moot for the students suspended and expelled, and premature for those who were reinstated.

At Virginia State College at Petersburg eight students were suspended after a student court had recommended suspension, but an appellate panel appointed by the administration had reversed that deter-

---

37. *Scott* v. *Alabama State Board of Education*, (U.S.D.C., Ala.), 300 F. Supp. 163 (1969).

mination. Then, without notice to the accused students and without their knowledge, a special meeting of the governing board (board of visitors) was convened and voted the suspension. At the student court hearing no counsel was allowed, no examination of witnesses, and no objections to evidence. The review by the appellate panel was solely on the record of that hearing. The accused students were given no transcript of the appellate panel's proceedings or of the extraordinary meeting of the board of visitors, and did not learn of the panel's conclusion until six days after it was arrived at. The federal district court decided due process had not been afforded, and issued a temporary restraining order to restore the students to good standing, including the right to enroll in the forthcoming summer session, and to retain their current student aids such as loans and part-time employment.[38]

A crowd of students at the University of South Carolina occupied a campus building known as Russell House on the afternoon of May 7, 1970, and refused to leave. University officers told them they would be suspended, and police officers told them they would be arrested. Ultimately about 40 were arrested, removed from the building, and charged with trespass in criminal court.

The university afforded the accused students a disciplinary committee hearing May 11; and the board of trustees conducted a *de novo* hearing August 25, with the result that some were permanently suspended. One of these stood on his alleged constitutional rights and asked U.S. District Judge Robert W. Hemphill to arrange for a trial before a special three-judge federal court. This request was denied, and the petitioner then asked for an order requiring the university to readmit him. Much of the argument concerned due process; but it appeared that no First Amendment or Fifth Amendment or Fourteenth Amendment rights had been violated.

An unusual item, verging on triviality, was the petitioner's contention that other students equally guilty had been given lighter penalties than he. To this the court gave no countenance; and rendered summary judgment for the university.[39]

---

38. *Baugh* v. *Quarles*, (U.S.D.C., Va.), Civ. Action No. 385-70-R (July 31, 1970).

39. *Bistrick* v. *University of South Carolina*, (U.S.D.C., S.C.), 324 F. Supp. 942 (1971); after denying motion for three-judge federal court in 319 F. Supp. 193 (1970).

Exhaustion of Administrative Remedies

A student in the curriculum leading to the B.S. in Education degree at the Salem State College in Massachusetts, having been arrested by local city police in March 1969, was tried and found guilty of possessing marijuana with intent to sell. On January 27, 1970, he was notified by the college committee on selective admission to teacher education to appear for a hearing before it January 30. The hearing was held, and February 2 he was advised that the committee had decided not to allow him to continue courses toward a degree in education. Without further recourse to the president of the college or to the board of trustees of state colleges, he sought injunctive relief from the U.S. District Court under Civil Rights legislation. District Judge Andrew A. Caffrey dismissed the petition, holding that the plaintiff must first exhaust his state administrative remedies before coming into federal court.[40]

There are several U.S. Supreme Court decisions indicating that in specific cases a plaintiff standing on federal civil rights may go directly to a federal district court; but these decisions, said Judge Caffrey, are in cases where the administrative remedy is inadequate, or certainly or probably futile, or illusory, as for instance it sometimes is when race prejudice is involved.

The selection of persons to be educated as teachers in its schools is eminently a matter of interest and concern to the state, in which a federal court should not take jurisdiction, even on federal civil rights grounds, until state administrative remedies have been exhausted, in this view which had been enunciated by the First Circuit Court of Appeals in a 1969 decision.

The doctrine of abstention was also adhered to in the more recent case of *Woodruff* v. *West Virginia Board of Regents*, (U.S.D.C., W. Va.), 328 F. Supp. 1023 (1971), by a special three-judge federal court which declined to declare that the Student Code adopted by that board in 1970 was *prima facie* unconstitutional, when it appeared that there were no allegations of actual or imminent damage, or of immediate or threatened harassment or irreparable harm to the plaintiffs, whose complaints could be said to be conjectural.

---

40. *Armsden* v. *Cataldo*, (U.S.D.C., Mass.), 315 F. Supp. 129 (1970).

Municipal Universities and Other Local
Public Colleges Are State Agents

"Acting under color of state law" are all colleges controlled and supported (even in part) by local subdivisions of the state, such as cities, counties, or community college districts. This brings them within the meaning of the parts of the Constitution and federal civil rights legislation appertaining to restraints on state action.

Thus, when the University of Louisville, a municipal university partly state-supported and largely sustained by fees and gifts, with only small percentages of its operating income from the city and county, was sued by students alleging that they had been permanently expelled without due process, and the federal district court dismissed their suit, this summary judgment was reversed and remanded by the Sixth Circuit Court of Appeals.

The complaint of expulsion without due process made a cause of action against the municipal university, and must be heard in federal court, said Circuit Judge Wade A. McCree, Jr., joined by Chief Circuit Judge Harry Phillips and Circuit Judge Anthony J. Celebrezze.[41]

The Constitutional Restraints on Governments
Do Not Apply to Private Colleges

Students at Howard University in Washington, D.C. were disciplined for disrupting a speech on the campus by General Lewis B. Hershey, the director of selective service, in 1967. Although the students were excluded from the university without due process, they got no relief because Howard University, although largely supported by annual appropriations by Congress, is a private university with all the prerogatives of a private nonprofit corporation, and as such its actions are not "governmental actions" within the purview of the civil rights amendments and statutes.

Hence its archaic clause in its catalog is taken literally, with no requirement of notice or hearing or other trappings of due process: "The University reserves the right, and the student concedes to the University the right, to deny admission to and to require the withdrawal of any student at any time for any reason deemed sufficient to the Uni-

---

41. *Brown* v. *Strickler*, (U.S.C.A., Ky.), 422 F. 2d 1000 (1970).

versity." Along with this U.S. District Judge Alexander Holtzoff delivered some philosophy:

"It would be a dangerous doctrine to permit the Government to interpose any degree of control over an institution of higher learning, merely because it extends financial assistance to it. . . . In recent years, numerous universities, colleges and technical schools have received Governmental aid of various kinds. . . . Surely it should not be held that any institution by entering into a contract with the United States and receiving funds for that purpose, has placed its head in a noose and subjected itself to some degree of control by the federal Government. Such a result would be intolerable, because it would tend to hinder and control the progress of higher learning and scientific research. Higher education can flourish only in an atmosphere of freedom, untrammeled by Governmental influence in any degree."[42]

Nine plaintiffs (including five students) involved in the sensational disturbances at Columbia University in 1968 sought an injunction *pendente lite* to restrain the university from proceeding against them punitively, on the theory that their acts of protest (including sit-in occupation of four university buildings and the president's office uninterruptedly for a week until they were forcibly removed) were merely an exercise of their right to petition government for redress of grievances, fully protected by the First Amendment.

Federal District Judge Marvin E. Frankel denied the petition chiefly on the ground that Columbia University is a private institution, not a state university, and the fact that it receives large sums from the federal government for research and other services does not bring it within the prohibitions of the First, Fifth, and Fourteenth Amendments relating to due process. Nearly half of the university's operating income for the two years 1966 and 1967 came from public funds; and it was also argued that its function of education is a public function which should bring it within the orbit of "state action." Not so, said Judge Frankel, and he went on to find no merit in other contentions, including the claim that university disciplinary proceedings should be halted and held in abeyance until the criminal actions pending against the accused were finally adjudicated, to avoid the asserted evils of self-incrimination and double jeopardy.

The court footnoted an affidavit by the district attorney in charge

---

42. *Greene* v. *Howard University*, (U.S.D.C., D.C.), 271 F. Supp. 609 (1967).

of the criminal prosecutions: "The prosecution will not offer in evidence on the People's case against any student of Columbia University, any statement, declaration or testimony made by such student in his own behalf in connection with or during the course of the disciplinary proceedings of Columbia University. Further, it has been decided that the prosecution will not utilize the records of the said disciplinary proceedings as a source for discovery of other evidence against students accused of criminal offenses." No court, thought Judge Frankel, would permit an attorney to deviate from his representation of this kind.[43]

Alfred University is a private institution operating a liberal arts college, a nursing school, and a graduate school; but also administering the New York State College of Ceramics, adjacent to its campus, under contract with the state. Seven students who had attempted to disrupt an ROTC ceremony on the football field were disciplined by Alfred University. Four were students in the liberal arts college, and could obtain no civil rights relief because there was no "state action"; hence the federal courts lacked jurisdiction.

The State College of Ceramics is state-supported and is a component of the multi-campus State University of New York. As to the three Ceramics students, the action disciplining them was "state action"; but the Second Circuit Court of Appeals held that the rules on which the action was based and the procedures by which it was determined satisfied the requirements of due process, leaving no cause for complaint. This was the gist of the decision by Circuit Judge Henry J. Friendly, joined by Circuit Judges Harold R. Medina and J. Joseph Smith, affirming with one modification the judgment of District Judge John T. Curtin.[44]

Two years later, after the state of New York had enacted a law requiring all colleges to formulate rules for the maintenance of public order on campuses, including a program for the enforcement thereof, and to file a copy of such code with the Board of Regents of the University of the State of New York and the Commissioner of Education (Section 6450, *Education Law*), a different view of "state action" in private college discipline cases became possible, as indictated in a 1970 decision of the Second Circuit Court of Appeals.

---

43. *Grossner* v. *Trustees of Columbia University*, (U.S.D.C., N.Y.), 287 F. Supp. 535 (1968).
44. *Powe* v. *Miles*, (U.S.C.A., N.Y.), 407 F. 2d 73 (1969).

Twenty-four students at Wagner College, well-known Lutheran church-connected college on Staten Island, were summarily expelled for staging a prolonged confrontation in the office of the dean of the college. There was no violence, no personal injuries, no damage to college property. The U.S. District Court dismissed their petition for an order of reinstatement and held it had no jurisdiction because the constitutional restraints on state action do not apply to private colleges. This judgment was reversed by the Court of Appeals, and remanded with instruction to explore the issue further.

Circuit Judge Irving R. Kaufman mentioned, among other factors: "A reasonable and widespread belief among college administrators that Section 6450 required them to adopt a particular stance toward campus demonstrators would seem to justify a conclusion that the state intended for them to pursue that course of action. And this intent, if present, would provide a basis for a finding of state action."[45]

Thus the unnecessary, redundant and repressive state statute of 1969 may eventually have the probably wholly unintended effect of bringing all private colleges in New York under the same constitutional requirements as to due process in disciplinary cases as now apply to state and other public colleges and universities.

The Tenth Circuit Court of Appeals, dealing solely with the issue of whether a disputed disciplinary action of the University of Denver constituted "action under color of state law," decided that question in the negative and therefore affirmed a judgment of District Judge Olin Hatfield Chilson adverse to the students. The University of Denver is a private institution, receiving no state appropriations. The Colorado Constitution prohibits appropriations to any educational activity "not under the absolute control of the state." (Article V, Section 34.)

The university's property is exempt from state taxation, as is generally true of nonprofit colleges in all states; but unlike most others, the exemption derives from an early charter by special legislative act which extends the exemption to cover income-producing property not directly used for educational purposes. This does not change the matter, in the view of Chief Circuit Judge Alfred P. Murrah, joined by Circuit Judges Delmas C. Hill and Oliver Seth. The tax exemption amounts to only about $210,000 a year, and there is no

---

45. *Barbara Coleman* v. *Wagner College*, (U.S.C.A., N.Y.), 429 F. 2d 1120 (1970).

likelihood that the state will try to control its expenditure; hence no "state action."[46]

Somewhat similarly, six students suspended by Puerto Rico Junior College, who alleged that their constitutional rights to due process had been invaded by "state action," were told by the federal district court that the institution is private, and its character is not changed by its receipt of some federal funds for plant development and some small appropriations by the Commonwealth of Puerto Rico for scholarships. The funds thus received were insubstantial as compared to the institution's total income. "The evidence taken as a whole does not establish, even remotely, . . . that Puerto Rico Junior College . . . is acting under color of state or federal authority. . . ."[47]

Non-renewal of the contracts of six non-tenured faculty members triggered turbulence among students at Voorhees College at Denmark, South Carolina, which escalated into a boycott of classes with intimidation and harassment of some students by others, and ultimately caused the temporary closing of the college in February 1970. In early March 163 students were given notice by registered mail to their home addresses that they were charged with certain violations of the college regulations, and that they would be heard before the college disciplinary committee. The promised hearings were held at Columbia, March 9 through 13. Eighty-five students appeared, and 78 failed to appear. Of those appearing, 31 admitted the acts charged, 20 others were found guilty as charged, and 19 guilty of only part of the charges, and 15 not guilty. Penalties ranged from probation to permanent expulsion.

When suit was brought under the familiar Title 42, *U.S. Code*, Section 1983, District Judge Charles E. Simons, Jr., noted, that although the disciplinary procedure had been in accord with due process, the point was outranked because Voorhees College is private and no "state action" was involved; hence the section is not applicable, nor does the receipt of some federal funds by the college make any difference, because the section is aimed at *state* action, not federal.[48]

---

46. *Browns* v. *Mitchell*, (U.S.C.A., Colo.), 409 F. 2d 593 (1969).
47. *Torres* v. *Puerto Rico Junior College*, (U.S.D.C., P.R.), 298 F. Supp. 458 (1969).
48. *Counts* v. *Voorhees College*, (U.S.D.C., S.C.), 312 F. Supp. 598 (1970).

CHAPTER 18

HOW SPECIFIC MUST
DISCIPLINARY
RULES BE?

ONE OF THE EARLY REACTIONS of a student accused of a serious infraction of university or college discipline is likely to be, "What particular rule am I charged with violating? Surely unless you point to a specific rule and show explicitly that I acted contrary to it, you can't discipline me!"

From the simplest viewpoint, it is obvious there can be two very extreme views of this matter: (1) there may be a college regulation that only commands the students to comport themselves with the dignity and decorum befitting a college student; but such a broad rule is vulnerable to the assertion that it is susceptible of arbitrary interpretation, including possible abridgement of the accused person's constitutional rights; and (2) college committees and governing boards may sweat for months on end to draft long codes of explicit regulations of student conduct, but they can never cover every possible contingency; besides, although penal statutes in the criminal law must be specific, and are unconstitutional and void if too vague, the disciplinary rules of a college are not criminal statutes, and ought not to be held to the same standards of specificity.

The federal courts are not fully in agreement as to the proper placement of cases between these two extremes.

The View of the United States Court of Appeals, Seventh Circuit

When certain students at the University of Wisconsin at Madison determined to prevent the customary interviewing of prospective employees by representatives of the Dow Chemical Corporation on the campus, and with that purpose congregated in the first floor of the Commerce Building, physically obstructed the halls and doorways, intentionally denied the students who had come for interviews their opportunity to have them, also disrupted classes in the building, and refused to leave the building when ordered to do so by the university police chief, they were subsequently suspended by the university on charges of (1) misconduct, and (2) violation of Chapter 11.02 of the University Regulations, which specified:

"*Scope of Student Freedom.* Students have the right, accorded to all persons by the Constitution, to freedom of speech, peaceable assembly, petition and association. Students and student organizations may examine and discuss all questions of interest to them, and express opinions publicly as well as privately. They may support causes by lawful means which do not disrupt the operations of the University, or organizations accorded the use of University facilities."

In the United States district court, District Judge James E. Doyle concluded that in the circumstances, neither of the two bases was sufficiently explicit. He said: "A standard of 'misconduct' without more, may not serve as the sole foundation for the imposition of the sanction of expulsion, or the sanction of suspension for any significant time, throughout the entire range of student life in the university."

As to the Chapter 11.02 rule, he said: "When the standards of vagueness and overbreadth are applied to Chapter 11.02, I am obliged to find it invalid. Neither the element of intention, nor that of proximity of cause and effect, nor that of substantiality, for example, is dealt with by its language. Nor does it contain even the most general description of the kinds of conduct which might be considered disruptive of the operations of the university, or does it undertake to draw any distinctions whatever as among the various categories of university 'operations.'" He granted a permanent injunction against further use or enforcement of Chapter 11.02; but refrained from giving injunction relief against the standard of "misconduct," in order to allow a reasonable time within which the university could recast its regulations in that area.

Earlier in his opinion he had laid down with clarity a digest of his reasoning: "The question here concerns the relationship, in today's world, between the university board, faculty, and administrators as the governors, and students as the governed. Although there is considerable ferment in the universities on this very relationship, I see no constitutional bar to an arrangement by which the state vests in a board of regents and the faculty the power to govern a university and to discipline its students; nor do I see any constitutional bar to a prompt and severe disciplinary response to violence and rioting and other constitutionally unprotected conduct. The more precise question concerns the manner in which this power to govern and to discipline is exercised. It concerns whether the manner of its exercise is wholly immune to the application of the standards of vagueness and overbreadth. Even more precisely, it concerns whether the courts may—and if they may, whether they should—measure the sufficiency of university rules and regulations against these constitutional standards."

And elsewhere: "In this area, when the potential for the imposition of serious sanctions is present, the standards of vagueness and overbreadth are unquestionably applicable; whether with a stringency equal to that operable in the criminal law it is not necessary to decide."[1]

This decision was affirmed by the United States Court of Appeals by Circuit Judges Roger J. Kiley, Luther M. Swygert, and Walter J. Cummings, in an opinion written by Judge Cummings, who said:

"Pursuant to appropriate rule or regulation, the University has the power to maintain order by suspension or expulsion of disruptive students. Requiring that such sanctions be administered in accord with pre-existing rules does not place an unwarranted burden upon university administrations. We do not require University codes of conduct to satisfy the same rigorous standards as criminal statutes. We only hold that expulsion and prolonged suspension may not be imposed on students by a university simply on the basis of allegations of 'misconduct'

---

1. *Soglin* v. *Kauffman*, (U.S.D.C., Wis.), 295 F. Supp. 978 (1968). Affirmed in (U.S.C.A., 7 Cir.), 418 F. 2d 163 (1969).

without reference to any pre-existing rule which supplies an adequate guide. The possibility of the sweeping application of the standard of 'misconduct' to protected activities does not comport with the guarantees of the First and Fourteenth Amendments. The desired end must be more narrowly achieved."

Judge Cummings noted that he was aware of an earlier federal district court decision in Colorado in which the offenses charged against a group of students at the University of Colorado were practically the same as those in the case before him. There, Chief District Judge Alfred A. Arraj had denied the students' motion for an injunction against the university and dismissed the complaint. The accused students had been given well-conducted hearings before the university discipline committee, and had appealed first to a subcommittee of the administrative council and thence to the board of regents, where their cases had been re-heard. At all stages these bodies for hearing and review had voted unanimously for declaring these students guilty as charged, and for imposition of the three levels of penalties (forms of suspension) determined for different individuals according to the gravity of their offenses.

The immediate point for the present purpose is that they were charged with violating a rule of the regents which read: "Hazing in all forms is prohibited in this University. Students who thus interfere with the personal liberty of a fellow-student are rendered liable to immediate discipline. This rule is extended to cover class conflicts, injury to property on the campus or elsewhere and interference in any manner with the public or private rights of citizens."

This was the rule on which the subcommittee of the administrative council had based its decision; and Judge Arraj had concluded: "We are persuaded that the 'hazing' rule is not on its face a prior restraint on the right of freedom of speech and the right to assemble. The language is clear; it authorizes discipline for 'any interference with the public or private rights of citizens.' "[2]

Without expressing any opinion regarding that decision, Judge Cummings in Wisconsin observed that he was aware of it. His judgment in the University of Wisconsin case currently stands as law in the Seventh Circuit, but it is not in entire harmony with an opinion of the Court of Appeals in the Eighth Circuit, written by Circuit Judge

---

2. *Buttny* v. *Smiley*, (U.S.D.C., Colo.), 281 F. Supp. 280 (1968).

Harry A. Blackmun, in one of his last decisions in that capacity prior to taking his seat as an Associate Justice of the Supreme Court.

A Different Position in the Eighth Circuit

A case arose at Central Missouri State College, where two students, Alfredo Esteban and Steve Roberds, and others, were suspended for alleged participation in campus disturbances on two successive days in the Spring of 1967, and (Esteban) for addressing vulgar and profane language to the resident assistant in their dormitory and to other disciplinary officers.

When the case first came before United States District Judge Elmo B. Hunter, he gave primary attention to the complaint that the students had been suspended without the type of notice and hearing required by due process under the Fourteenth Amendment, and ordered that they be given a new hearing by the college within one month after this decision. (The due process aspect of the case is treated in more detail at another point herein, under "Due Process in Disciplinary Cases.")[3] The new hearing was held as ordered and the suspensions were reaffirmed. Thereafter Esteban and Roberds brought a second action in federal district court, the emphasis in this new complaint being on the alleged invalidity of the college rules under which the suspension had been made. The most specific of these rules was:

"Participation in mass gatherings which might be considered as unruly or unlawful will subject a student to possible immediate dismissal from the College. Only a few students intentionally get involved in mob misconduct, but many so-called 'spectators' get drawn into a fracas and by their very presence contribute to the dimensions of the problems. It should be understood that the College considers no student to be immune from due process of law enforcement when he is in violation as an individual or as a member of a crowd."

On the issue of generality versus specificity, Judge Hunter took a strong position for the former:

"Judicial notice is taken that outstanding educational authorities in the field of higher education believe that detailed codes of prohibited student conduct are provocative and should not be employed in higher education. (Citing p. 378 of Brady and Snoxell, *Student Personnel*

---

3. *Esteban* v. *Central Missouri State College*, (U.S.D.C., Mo.), 277 F. Supp. 649 (1967).

Work in Higher Education, 1961.) For this reason, general affirmative statements of what is expected of a student may be preferable . . . Standards so established may apply to student behavior on and off the campus when relevant to any lawful mission, process, or function of the institution."

He concluded, "A federal court should not intervene to reverse or enjoin disciplinary actions relevant to a lawful mission of an educational institution unless there appears one of the following:

"(1) A deprival of due process, that is, fundamental concepts of fair play;

"(2) Invidious discrimination, for example, on account of race or religion;

"(3) Denial of federal rights, constitutional or statutory, protected in the academic community;

"(4) Clearly unreasonable, arbitrary or capricious action."

Thus he dismissed the suit.[4]

A year later this judgment was affirmed by a majority of the United States Court of Appeals, Eighth Circuit, with the opinion written by Circuit Judge Harry A. Blackmun, joined by Circuit Judge Pat Mehaffy, but with Circuit Judge Donald P. Lay filing a cogent dissent.

After noting that District Judge Doyle, in the University of Wisconsin case cited earlier herein, had expressed disagreement with District Judge Hunter's observations regarding vagueness or specificity in college rules, Circuit Judge Blackmun wrote:

"To the extent that, in this area, Judge Doyle is in disagreement with Judge Hunter, we must respectfully disagree with Judge Doyle."

And, "We see little basically or constitutionally wrong with flexibility and reasonable breadth, rather than meticulous specificity, in college regulations relating to conduct . . .

"We do not hold that any college regulation, however loosely framed, is necessarily valid. We do not hold that a school has the authority to require a student to discard any constitutional right when he matriculates . . . We do hold . . . that a college may expect its students to adhere to generally accepted standards of conduct; that, as to these flexibility and elbow room are to be preferred over specificity . . ."

---

4. *Esteban* v. *Central Missouri State College,* (U.S.D.C., Mo.), 290 F. Supp. 622 (1968).

The majority of the court perceived no denial of any constitutional rights of Esteban or of Roberds.

June 11, 1970, the Supreme Court declined to review this case. Mr. Justice William O. Douglas dissented, favoring review; and Mr. Justice Harry A. Blackmun took no part.[5]

Circuit Judge Lay's dissent was based, first on his strong objection to District Judge Hunter's *reviewing the evidence to appraise its substantiality* rather than confining himself to the taking of evidence in a trial *de novo*:

"Public education is within the control of state and local officials and should remain there. We are in agreement that principles of federalism do not justify federal court intervention in the daily operation of school systems and the resolution of problems which are remote from federal rights. These principles should make clear that federal courts do not possess the competence in the field of public education to moralize, lecture or otherwise *review* the evidence resulting in discipline of students by school officials. This is not the purpose of the Civil Rights Act. To hold that it is, truly arrogates to federal courts that which is a function of the states themselves. And conversely, but of greater significance, *a federal Judge should not yield his jurisdiction or competency to protect fundamental liberties of individual citizens to a school administrator.*"

In short, he maintains that federal courts do not have power of *general review* of administrative decisions of state agencies (as they do in the case of federal administrative agencies); but only to adjudicate *de novo* cases in which abridgement of federal constitutional rights is alleged.

The more immediately germane part of Circuit Judge Lay's dissent from Judge Blackmun's opinion is as follows in his own words: "Dr. Lovinger (President of the College) clearly had the authority to warn students that their participation in an unruly demonstration would subject them to disciplinary action. His observation and warning (as phrased in the rule previously quoted) that students as spectators are often drawn into unruly demonstrations and that when they so participate they would be disciplined is beyond doubt a proper one. How-

---

5. *Esteban* v. *Central Missouri State College*, (U.S.C.A., 8 Cir.), 415 F. 2d 1077 (1968); affirming 290 F. Supp. 622 (1968). *Certiorari* denied, 38 *U.S. Law Week* 3497 (1970).

ever, to suggest by regulation that anyone present at any demonstration which might become unruly may be punished, smacks of 'prior restraint' and cannot be condoned.

"A university or college cannot constitutionally place a ban on all student demonstrations simply because they *may* incite some students to unlawful acts.

"Mere presence at a demonstration is not and cannot be the basis for university regulations which attempt by 'prior restraint' to prevent demonstration itself. Nor can it be the basis for state exclusion from educational opportunity." Judge Lay had concluded that Esteban's offenses were beyond the pale of constitutional protection; but that Roberds actually had done nothing other than to stand as a spectator at the riotous scenes (as indeed the findings of President Lovinger indicated), and therefore should be granted relief from the penalty for alleged participation.

What Judge Lay was concerned about was apparently that the college rule was so vague as to be likely to support a deprivation of civil rights—and that it actually swept so broadly as to constitute on its face a "governmental encroachment on the exercise of free speech and free assembly incompatible with the Constitution of the United States."[6]

The decision in this case was dated August 28, 1969, and rehearing was denied October 3, 1969. The decision in the University of Wisconsin case (Soglin) by the Seventh Circuit Court of Appeals was dated October 24, 1969.[7] Early in 1970 the Supreme Court, as previously noted, declined to review it, with Mr. Justice William O. Douglas dissenting. Mr. Justice Harry A. Blackmun took no part.

At this writing, the law regarding the precise point of clash between the First and Fourteenth Amendments on the one hand, and vagueness or overbreadth in college rules on the other, must be said to be somewhat different in the Seventh Circuit (Wisconsin, Illinois, and Indiana) from what it is in the Eighth Circuit (Minnesota, Iowa, Nebraska, Missouri, Arkansas, and the two Dakotas). Unless and until a case in point reaches the Supreme Court, other federal courts have opportunity to choose between the reasoning of Judge Blackmun

---

6. Dissenting opinion of Circuit Judge Donald P. Lay in *Esteban* v. *Central Missouri State College*, (U.S.C.A., 8 Cir.), 415 F. 2d 1077 (1969).

7. Footnote 1, *supra*.

(from whose opinion Judge Lay dissented), and that of the Seventh Circuit Court of Appeals as expressed by Judge Cummings for his unanimous court. At the federal district court level, the judgment of Judge Doyle in Wisconsin is matched against that of Judge Hunter in Missouri. There seems to be a gray area, not sharply limned in black-and-white, awaiting clarification.

In Another Circuit

A more recent decision by a United States district court in the Second Circuit, involving the rights of a high school student in Connecticut, held a school rule invalid because unconstitutionally vague. The words of the rule:

"Students are to be neatly dressed and groomed, maintaining standards of modesty and good taste conducive to an educational atmosphere. It is expected that clothing and grooming not be of an extreme style and fashion." A 15-year-old boy who grew a full beard was first told that this did not conform to the school dress code, and was advised to shave. Upon his refusal, he was suspended. District Judge T. Emmet Clarie held that "The high school dress code relied upon . . . is unduly vague, uncertain and ambiguous. Public school rules and regulations which are intended to limit the personalized freedom of privacy and self-expression in one's personal appearance, implemented by such drastic enforcement procedures, . . . are required to be stated with sufficient clarity and specificity that students will be adequately informed as to what conduct will invite administrative discipline. . . . The school grooming code in this case is unconstitutionally vague and unenforceable. . . . It leaves to the arbitrary whim of the school principal, what in fact constitutes extreme fashion or style . . . and permits his own subjective opinion to be the sole measure of censorship."

Not wishing to be misunderstood as inclined to interfere in the management of schools, the court continued: "It is expressly stated that the school board does have the authority to adopt formally a standard of personal grooming for high school pupils. However, such a code must clearly define the standards and it should be reasonably designed to avoid the disruption of the classroom atmosphere and decorum, prevent disturbances among students, avoid the distraction of other pupils or interference with the educational process of the school."[8]

There is a spate of other recent decisions of federal and state courts regarding haircutting and skirt lengths, more often than not placing these matters within the category of constitutionally protected personal liberties unless constituting a "clear and present danger" to the orderly processes of the school. See Chapter 8 herein, "Various Facets of Student Life," specifically the final section thereof, "Dress and Grooming Regulations: the Battle of the Beards."

The central topic of this present chapter, namely, the alleged unconstitutionality of university or college rules on account of vagueness or overbreadth (lack of specificity) appears at various other points in this volume, such as within Chapters 13, 14, and 17. Most of these cases can be readily located by consulting the alphabetical index under such rubrics as "vagueness," "overbreadth," and "specificity."

---

8. *Crossen* v. *Fatsi*, (U.S.D.C., Conn.), 309 F. Supp. 114 (1970).

CHAPTER 19

STATE STATUTES AS APPLIED
TO CAMPUS DISRUPTIONS

THERE IS A SHARP DISTINCTION between disciplinary rules of a university and criminal statutes of a state. The latter are unconstitutional if unduly vague or overbroad; the former must also be reasonably explicit,[1] but usually are not held to as high a standard of specificity as the criminal statutes.

Wisconsin Statute on Disorderly Conduct

Some of the students involved in the disturbance at the University of Wisconsin at Madison in *Soglin* v. *Kauffman*[2] were arrested by city police and charged and convicted of disorderly conduct under a Wisconsin statute:

"Whoever does any of the following may be fined not more than $100 or imprisoned not more than 30 days: (1) In a public or private place, engages in violent, abusive, indecent, profane, boisterous, un-

---

1. For the current lack of unanimity of judicial opinion on this point, see Chapter 18, "How Specific Must Disciplinary Rules Be?"
2. The campus incident is described herein under another rubric, as set out in Footnote 1.

reasonably loud, or otherwise disorderly conduct under circumstances in which such conduct tends to cause or provoke a disturbance."

To prevent prosecution, the plaintiffs began an action in Wisconsin courts, and also a suit in the federal district court, in both cases asking that the statute be declared unconstitutional and invalid for overbreadth, and that its enforcement in this case be enjoined. While the suit in state courts was pending, the United States district court entered a temporary restraining order, after which a special three-judge federal court was convened because of the constitutional question involved. This court was headed by Circuit Judge Thomas E. Fairchild, sitting with District Judges James E. Doyle and Myron L. Gordon. Three opinions were written—the judgment of the court by Judge Gordon, with Judge Fairchild concurring specially, and Judge Doyle writing 6,000 words of dissent. The judgment was against the plaintiffs, on the holding that the statute was not unconstitutionally overbroad.[3]

This judgment was later affirmed in a *per curiam* opinion of the United States Supreme Court, with Mr. Justice William O. Douglas writing a 2,500-word dissent, saying the Court should note probable jurisdiction, vacate the judgment, and remand the case for a preliminary hearing "on the issue of the use of a disorderly conduct statute to punish people for expression of their unpopular views."

Justice Douglas quoted the federal statute (Civil Rights Act, 42 United States Code, section 1983) under which the suit was brought:

"Every person who, under color of any statute, ordinance, regulation, custom, or usage, of any State or Territory, subjects, or causes to be subjected, any citizen of the United States or other person within the jurisdiction thereof to the deprivation of any rights, privileges, or immunities secured by the Constitution and laws, shall be liable to the party injured in an action at law, suit in equity, or other proper proceeding for redress."

He thought "Where there are allegations of bad faith, harassment, and discrimination, critical evidence on the matter can only be drawn out upon cross-examination of the officials involved."

When the suit in state courts involving the same offenses and the same adversary parties reached the supreme court of Wisconsin, Justice

---

3. *Zwicker* v. *Boll*, (U.S.D.C., Wis.), 270 F. Supp. 131 (1967); affirmed in 391 U.S. 353, 88 S.Ct. 1666, 20 L.Ed. 2d 642 (1968).

Connor T. Hansen wrote for the majority, with Justices Horace W. Wilkie and Nathan S. Heffernan joining in a dissent based entirely on their conclusion from the evidence that the conduct of Robert K. Zwicker had been so moderate as not to fall within the meaning of the statute, and that the conviction as to him alone should be reversed, but affirmed as to the other accused students. The judgment of the court was that the statute was neither unconstitutionally vague nor over-broad, and the conviction of all the defendants was affirmed.[4] The Supreme Court of the United States dismissed an appeal.

A Texas Penal Statute

"Every person who, at a time and place and under circumstances reasonably calculated to produce a clear and present and immediate threat or danger to the physical well-being, property or life of another, knowingly and willfully commits an act, or urges another to commit an act, so calculated and tending to produce injury or damage . . . shall be guilty of a misdemeanor . . .," runs a criminal statute of Texas.[5]

When Eugene Locke and Dwight Allen, students at the University of Houston and officers of a civil rights organization on the campus (Afro-Americans for Black Liberation), were charged with violation of this statute in a Texas court, they asked the federal district court to enjoin their prosecution on the ground that the statute was (1) unconstitional as applied to them, being used by their accusers in bad faith to suppress their First Amendment rights, and (2) unconstitutional on its face for vagueness and impermissible overbreadth.

The facts were that the A.A.B.L. had presented a list of 10 demands to the university administration on February 7, 1969, including the hiring of more black administrators and faculty members, and the establishment of a comprehensive department of Afro-American studies. President Philip G. Hoffman had thereupon appointed a special task force to consider the demands. During the ensuing five weeks the A.A.B.L. at various times organized rallies on the campus, and conferred both publicly and privately with university officials. There was no violence, no damage to persons or property, and no administrative interference or disciplinary action.

4. *State of Wisconsin* v. *Zwicker*, 41 Wis. 2d 497, 164 N.W. 2d 512 (1969). Appeal dismissed, 396 U.S. 26 (1969).
5. *Texas Penal Code*, Art. 466 a, section 1.

On the morning of March 17 Locke was subjected to a physical attack by three unidentified persons in a wooded part of the campus. Allen organized a rally which was held at 1:00 p.m. that day, and addressed by both Locke and Allen, protesting the lack of police protection for black students. When this rally terminated, the crowd reassembled at the office of the traffic and security department. There the idea of seizing the university center building developed. It was alleged that several members of the crowd of perhaps 1,000 persons were heard to express that idea, including Allen; and it was deposed that when the university police chief appealed to Locke "not to let those people go over there and tear that building up; you are the one who could stop them, if you would," Locke made no favorable response or effort. The crowd dispersed and reassembled inside the university center, where windows were broken and furniture damaged in the lounge and the university bookstore. This was the basis of the statutory charge in the state court.

In response to the federal suit of Locke and Allen, a special three-judge court was convened, composed of Circuit Judge Homer Thornberry and District Judges Woodrow B. Seals and Joe McDonald Ingraham. Judge Ingraham wrote the opinion of the court, deciding that injunctive relief from the pending criminal proceedings in the state court could not be granted, because Locke and Allen had "failed to show that the statute was unconstitutionally applied to them."

The declaratory judgement asked for was also refused. Judge Ingraham concluded that "Article 466 a of the Texas Penal Code does not embrace within its sweep, protected rights, nor can it be interpreted as doing so." Therefore he declared the statute constitutional on its face.[6]

Common-Law Breach of the Peace in Kentucky

A 1969 decision of the highest state court in Kentucky affirmed the conviction of four students at the University of Kentucky—Kristina Lewis, Dan S. O'Leary, William Murrell, and Rodger A. Woock—for breach of the peace, their offenses being that they, with other students, protested the holding of employer interviews by the Defense Intelligence Agency, by occupying and blocking the narrow hall

---

6. *Locke* v. *Vance*, (U.S.D.C., Tex.), 307 F. Supp. 439 (1969).

leading to the interview rooms, and refusing to leave when requested by the associate dean of students, necessitating their arrest and physical removal by the campus police. They were not accused of any violence, either physical or vocal. They contended that the Kentucky breach of the peace statute[7] was invalid under both the federal and state constitutions for vagueness.

The Kentucky Court of Appeals, in an opinion by Associate Justice John S. Palmore, declared that breach of the peace is a common-law crime, for which the punishment is prescribed by statute; and "as in the instance of murder and other common-law crimes, it may be committed in new ways if they fall within the interdict of the old principles."

This does not mean, however, that because of the breadth of the definition, "unlawful and proper conduct may constitute a breach of the peace just because it provokes violence or disorder." Under Kentucky precedent, the lawful exercise of a constitutional right (such as the right of assembly) can not be a breach of the peace. "We therefore do not feel that the law against breach of peace, as it has been construed in Kentucky, is so vague or overly broad in scope as to pose any threat to the rights of free speech and assembly guaranteed by the First and Fourteenth Amendments to the Constitution of the United States."[8]

The appeal in this case was dismissed by the United States Supreme Court November 17, 1969.

Thus Wisconsin's statute prohibiting disorderly conduct, Kentucky's statute against breach of the peace, and an analogous penal statute of Texas have each withstood attack in federal courts for alleged unconstitutionality on the ground of vagueness or overbreadth, in cases brought by students being prosecuted in state courts for disruptive offenses on campus within the purview of these criminal statutes.

A Wisconsin senate resolution adopted to authorize probing into a campus disruption as an exercise of the investigative power of the legislative body also withstood the same type of attack, though admittedly it is understandable that a federal court would be hesitant to intrude in the investigative sphere of a state legislative body—at least

---

7. *Kentucky Revised Statutes*, sec. 437.010.

8. *O'Leary* v. *Commonwealth of Kentucky*, (Ky.), 441 S.W. 2d 150 (1969). Appeal dismissed, U.S. Supreme Court Docket No. 526 (November 17, 1969); 396 U.S. 40 (1969).

to intrude prematurely—though this is an area in which infringement of civil rights is prominently possible. See Chapter 11, "Confidentiality of Student Records."

The fact that not one of the statutes herein mentioned thus far was held unconstitutional for vagueness or overbreadth could probably be correctly interpreted as indicating that new statutes to deal with criminal offenses deriving from student rebellion are not needed. The rash of bills recently introduced in the national and state legislatures, most of which were fortunately not enacted, seem to have been largely redundant and unnecessary. Some, especially those directed at university governing boards and presidents, and ordering them to "expel automatically and permanently any student who, etc." were patently unconstitutional on their face. They were also a humiliating and indeed galling type of uninformed, emotional, and prejudiced invasion of the sphere of discretion which belongs to the heads of academic institutions.

Michigan "Trespass-after-warning" Statute

At a "career carnival" in the student union building at Michigan State University, a small group of students cluttered the area around the Marine Corps recruiting booth with their presence and their placards, posters, and literature against the Vietnam War. There was no blocking, no obstructing, no violence. In the afternoon, a university administrator directed these students to remove their signs and materials from the building. Having ignored this order, they were arrested and convicted in Ingham County circuit court of violating both the state statute against trespass-after-warning and Section 16.01 of Michigan State University's ordinances, which forbids "obstructing free and normal use of a university building."

The convictions were reversed. Said Judge T. G. Cavanaugh of the court of appeals: "The conviction for trespass can not stand. The claimed objectionable conduct was neither an unlawful entry into the building nor an unlawful presence there. . . . The gist of the order given in this case was that they remove their signs and materials from the building, . . ." but that they were personally welcome.[9]

As to the university ordinance, conviction could not stand because

---

9. *People of Michigan* v. *Harrison*, 13 Mich. App. 54, 163, N.W. 2d 699 (1968).

there was no obstructing, though the presence of the demonstrators added a little to the congestion at that part of the crowded carnival.

It is to be observed that the practice at Michigan State University of making alleged violation of a university rule the subject of a criminal charge in court seems unique. University rules (variously called ordinances, regulations, or bylaws) regarding student conduct are elsewhere generally enforced through the university's disciplinary machinery, the severest penalty being expulsion. Violations of state statutes or municipal ordinances are enforced by criminal prosecutions. The concept of the university as a civil subdivision of the state, capable of enacting criminal ordinances enforceable in the state courts, seems a confused one.

Vagrancy Statute of Washington State

A nonstudent who insisted on selling copies of an underground newspaper, *Spokane Natural,* on the campus of Spokane Community College, in violation of its rules, was arrested and convicted under *Revised Statutes of Washington,* Section 9.87.010 (the vagrancy statute):

"Every—

"(7) Lewd, disorderly or dissolute person; or

"(13) Persons, except person enrolled as a student in or parent or guardian of such students, or person employed by such school or institution, who without a lawful purpose therefor wilfully loiters about the buildings or grounds of any public or private school or institution of higher learning or the public premises adjacent thereto—

"Is a vagrant. . . ."

The conviction under (7) was reversed, and the conviction under (13) in this case was affirmed by the Washington supreme court, in an opinion by Chief Justice Orris L. Hamilton.[10]

Two Maryland Statutes

Article 27, *Maryland Annotated Code,* has been the subject of one U.S. Supreme Court decision and one U.S. Court of Appeals judgment in 1970 and 1971. Section 123 prohibits "acting in a disorderly manner to the disturbance of the public peace, upon any public

---

10. *State* v. *Maloney,* (Wash.), 481 P. 2d 1 (1971).

street . . . in any city. . . ." Convicted under this section were young men who peacefully picketed in front of an army recruiting station in downtown Baltimore. In the afternoon they entered the station and staged a sit-in, refusing to leave at the 5 p.m. closing hour, and were arrested. There was irreconcilably conflicting testimony as to whether they were carried out to the patrol wagon or violently thrown out to the sidewalk.

Not only were the facts difficult to discern, but the record of the proceedings in the Maryland court were, in the opinion of Mr. Justice William J. Brennan, characterized by imprecision in the charges and in the basis of the verdict and the conviction. So far as the record showed, he said, the result may have been based on any one of several grounds, some of which were patently unconstitutional. Accordingly the U.S. Supreme Court reversed the Maryland conviction.[11]

Section 577B of the same *Code* provides that: "The highest governing body or official of the University of Maryland, any of the state colleges, any community college or public school may deny access to the buildings or grounds of the institution to persons who are not *bona fide,* currently registered students, staff, or faculty at the institution, and who have no lawful business to pursue at the institution, or who are acting in a manner disruptive or disturbing to the normal educational functions of the institution."

Acting under this statute, President Wilson H. Elkins of the University of Maryland, at a time when the College Park campus had suffered protracted disorders and had recently been occupied by the Maryland National Guard, notified in writing an individual nonstudent who was known to have been a frequent visitor and speaker at student rallies on the campus, to stay off the campus on pain of arrest.

This order was contested. The plaintiff asked a federal court to declare the statute unconstitutional. The litigation was adjudicated by a special three-judge district court in an opinion by District Judge Frank A. Kauffman, sitting with Circuit Judge Simon E. Sobeloff and District Judge R. Dorsey Watkins. The court held that the statute is not unconstitutionally vague or overbroad. Further, it is constitutional when read in conjunction with Article 41, Section 251 (Administrative Code) which requires a hearing on contested administrative decisions.

---

11. *Bachellar* v. *Maryland,* 397 U.S. 564 (1970); reversing 3 Md. App. 626, 240 A. 2d 623 (1970).

The implication is that the president's order to a non-member of the academic community to stay off the campus is unconstitutional unless accompanied by a hearing on the issue. (Both sides in this controversy had argued that the Administrative Code was not intended to apply to the university, but to no avail.)

President Elkins' order to the plaintiff had been withdrawn in November 1970. Being satisfied that in the future the university would afford an administrative hearing to any person to whom a notice is sent under Section 577B, the court held 577B constitutional and denied relief.[12]

Tennessee Campus Trespass Law Is an Unconstitutional Prior Restraint on First Amendment Freedoms

On petition of students at the University of Tennessee, a special three-judge federal court composed of Chief Circuit Judge Harry Phillips, Chief District Judge Frank W. Wilson, and District Judge Robert L. Taylor (opinion by Judge Taylor) ruled on the constitutionality of several Tennessee statutes in 1970. In most instances the court withheld judgment until adjudications by state courts could be made; but retained jurisdiction. In the one instance, most pertinent here, the court declared unconstitutional Section 39-1215:

"Any person who enters the campus, buildings, or facilities of a junior college, state university, or public school and is committing, or commits, any act which interferes with the normal, orderly, peaceful, or efficient conduct of the activities of such campus or facility. . . ." may be ordered to leave, and, if he does not go shall be guilty of trespass, and upon conviction be punished as for a misdemeanor as provided in Section 39-105.

Said Judge Taylor: "The entire statute is vague and overbroad." He cited the decisions in *Cox* v. *Louisiana* and *Edwards* v. *South Carolina* (discussed herein in Chapter 13, "Freedom of Speech and Assembly"), and remarked: "Little imagination is required to conceive of acts interfering or tending to interfere . . . which fall within the protection of the First Amendment. An obvious danger is that the administrator's hostility to the acts committed will influence his decision."[13]

---

12. *Dunkel* v. *Elkins*, (U.S.D.C., Md.), 325 F. Supp. 1235 (1971).
13. *Baxter* v. *Ellington*, (U.S.D.C., Tenn.), 318 F. Supp. 1079 (1970).

Arizona Flag Desecration Statute
Is Held Unconstitutional

Sharon Crosson participated in a public burning of a United States flag on the campus of the University of Arizona May 6, 1970. Concurrently with the burning she made remarks of a derogatory nature directed at the flag and the foreign policy of the United States with respect to the Southeast Asia military involvement. She was about to be prosecuted under the Arizona statute which declares that "a person who publicly mutilates, defaces, defiles, tramples upon, or by hand or act casts contempt upon a flag is guilty of a misdemeanor. . . ."

The state postponed the trial and awaited the outcome of an action in federal court to have the statute declared unconstitutional. A special three-judge court (Circuit Judge Walter Ely, Chief District Judge James A. Walsh, and District Judge Walter Early Craig) held the entire statute unconstitutionally overbroad; but expressly "leaving to the legislature the enactment of a statute which properly protects the state's interest in preventing breaches of the peace"; and noted: "This does not mean that a public flag burner can not be prosecuted under traditional breach of the peace statutes where, for example, the words accompanying the burning raise the entire act to the status of provocation."

Apparently public flag-burning is no more than symbolic speech, protected by the First Amendment, unless the act itself or its immediate accompaniments causes violence or creates a clear and present danger thereof. The federal court did not issue an injunction against the state prosecution, but "anticipated that the state will discontinue prosecution in light of our opinion."[14]

---

14. *Sharon Crosson v. Rose Silver*, (U.S.D.C., Ariz.), 319 F. Supp. 1084 (1970).

CHAPTER 20

EXECUTIVE, JUDICIAL, AND
GRAND JURY OVERKILL

REPRESSIVE ACTION to suppress nonviolent student demonstrations of protest, and in some instances violence or threatened violence on the campus came sometimes from state governors who acted hastily, often without consulting or even communicating with the university president. Governors in California, Mississippi and Ohio ordered detachments of the National Guard or of state police to enter a campus armed with rifles or other small arms carrying live ammunition; and, notably in Ohio and Mississippi, this resulted in the killing of some students and the wounding of others.

Such occurrences produce a polarization of opinion. Some persons, upon learning that a volley from National Guard rifles had killed four students and wounded nine others at Kent State University in Ohio, passionately declared that more should have been killed; and similar reactions were heard to the killing of two students at Jackson State College in Mississippi, where state police fired indiscriminately into a girls' dormitory.

On the other hand, those of different views see these killings as murders which were unjustified and which could and should have been avoided; and the verdict of history will probably be that these tragedies mark a stained page in the annals of the American Commonwealth.

There is no question that the civil and military authorities are lawfully empowered to suppress insurrection anywhere in their jurisdiction, including university and college campuses; but they are not authorized to use unnecessary force or undue brutality, or any lethal force except when necessary to prevent imminent destruction of life or great bodily harm.

The Tragedy at Kent State University

After considerable disorders by students and nonstudents, in the town of Kent, Ohio, and on the campus of Kent State University during April and early May 1970, including the burning of the ROTC building, Governor James A. Rhodes of Ohio responded to requests from local civil authorities (not the university authorities) and ordered a detachment of the Ohio National Guard to the scene.

It seems that near noon on May 4 a platoon of the guard was maneuvering about on the campus in some sort of effort to prevent an expected gathering of students. While many students moved away as the platoon approached, others loosely followed it, some hostile, some merely curious, some no more than passers-by, and none visibly armed, though a few of the more hostile probably carried sticks or stones. Suddenly, allegedly under a panicky impression that they were "surrounded" and that their lives were in danger, a number of the guardsmen whirled about, took the kneeling position for firing, and fired a volley into the assembly behind them.

Although at least one officer of the rank of brigadier general was present or nearby, it may never be known whether an order to fire was given and who gave it, or whether the firing was wholly the result of spontaneous panic. The four students killed included two male and two female; the nine wounded included one paralyzed from a bullet in the spine. The spirit of the occasion was caught for posterity in a fortuitous photograph of a girl, on her knees, with arm upraised and face utterly distraught as she averted her eyes from the prostrate body, a few feet away, of a male student who had been shot down.

The United States Department of Justice, in a published summary of the reports of the Federal Bureau of Investigation, comments that "We have some reason to believe that the claim by the National Guard that their lives were endangered by the students was fabricated subse-

quent to the event."[1] Some of the guardsmen maintained that immediately preceding the volley, a sniper shot was directed at them from
some concealed source; but no shred of proof was found to support
this. The *Scranton Report on Campus Unrest* found no evidence that
any of the guardsmen who shot the students were in danger of any
serious physical harm at the time. (This report included many photographs of the scene.)

Probably one of the most important central facts is that no one
would have been killed if the recommendations of the *Kerner Commission on Civil Disorders*, and the guidelines of the Department of
the Army on the control of civil disturbances, had been followed. Various non-lethal weapons are available. Police or partly-trained troops
should not be sent against unarmed civilians while carrying high-pow-
ered military rifles loaded with live ammunition. This error lies at the
door of the Ohio National Guard authorities, and ultimate responsibility with Governor Rhodes, who was at the time completing his second term and engaged in the late stages of an unsuccessful campaign
for nomination for U.S. Senator.

Some of the actions taken (many not yet terminated at this
writing) are recounted here in chronological order.

May 4, 1970. The local prosecuting attorney of Portage County
filed a petition for injunction asking that Kent State University be
ordered closed until the court should be satisfied that it could be
reopened safely; that no person, not even an administrative officer, be
permitted on the campus except with express permission of the National Guard. Dormitory residents would be given a little time to make
necessary arrangements to leave. The petition was summarily granted
by the Portage County Common Pleas Court on May 7; and the order
dissolved, June 13.[2]

June 10. In the United States District Court, Northern District
of Ohio, Eastern Division, Arthur Krause, as administrator of the
estate of his daughter, Allison Krause, one of the four students killed,
filed an action against Governor Rhodes of Ohio and the top officers
of the Ohio National Guard, asking compensatory damages of $1 mil-
lion and punitive damages of $5 million under 42 U.S. Code Section

1. I. F. Stone, *The Killings at Kent State: How Murder Went Unpunished.*
New York: Random House (Vintage Paper), 1971. 158 pp.
2. *State of Ohio* v. *Robert White, President*, No. 39346, Common Pleas Court
of Portage County (1970).

1983. He alleged that the defendants had insufficient cause to send armed troops to the campus, that they knew the troops were not properly trained in the correct and reasonable use of loaded weapons in the presence of civilians, and that the presence of improperly trained troops so armed on the campus created imminent risk of injury and death. The subsequent actions, allegedly wilfully and maliciously in disregard of the lives and safety of the students, deprived them of their rights to equal protection of the laws and of due process.[3]

September 5. The mother of Sandra Scheuer, one of the two girl students killed by National Guard rifle fire on May 4, sued the governor, the adjutant general, and other officers and enlisted men of the Ohio National Guard for $1 million actual damages under 42 U.S.C. Section 1983, alleging that the defendants wilfully and wantonly gave orders and took actions substantially increasing the risk of violence, and caused the carrying of loaded weapons when their use was unjustified, which resulted in the reckless shooting death of Sandra Scheuer. This is similar to the suit filed by Arthur Krause on June 10, and in the same court.[4]

October 14. The student body president and other students at Kent State University filed in federal district court a class action asking an injunction to restrain the governor and the adjutant general of Ohio from prematurely using the National Guard to displace civilian forces in campus disorders; from allowing summary beatings and non-arrest detentions of students by guardsmen on campus; from breaking up peaceable assemblies; from sending in troops improperly trained in disorder-control techniques; and from permitting the use of lethal weapons loaded with live ammunition. The petition also asks that the court decree that National Guard troops used in such circumstances be provided with non-lethal weapons and be instructed that deadly force may not be used unless deadly force is used or threatened against them.

It also requests a declaration that Section 2923.55, *Ohio Revised Code* ("the Riot Act") is unconstitutional as a denial of due process because it stipulates that members of the organized militia shall be guiltless for killing or injuring a rioter as a consequence of the use of such force as is necessary to suppress a riot after an order to desist and

3. *Krause* v. *Rhodes*, No. C70-544, U.S.D.C., Northern District of Ohio, Eastern Division (Filed June 10, 1970).

4. *Scheuer* v. *Rhodes*, No. C70-859, U.S.D.C., Northern District of Ohio, Eastern Division, filed September 5, 1970.

disperse has been communicated pursuant to Section 2923.51 of the *Revised Code*.[5]

October 16. The report of the special state grand jury, which had been ordered by Governor Rhodes shortly after the May 4 tragedy, was made public. It exonerated all members of the Ohio National Guard, and was highly critical of the conduct of administrators, faculty members, and students at the university. It returned indictments against 25 persons, mostly students, but including 3 members of the faculty. Common Pleas Judges Edwin W. Jones and Albert Caris issued orders prohibiting discussion or criticism of the report by witnesses or others involved in the grand jury's deliberations, and forbidding any protest or demonstration in or around the Portage County courthouse.

Also October 16. Students indicted by the special state grand jury, joined by some members of the faculty and campus pastors, filed a suit in federal district court, against the Ohio attorney general and members of the grand jury, asking temporary and permanent injunctive relief to restrain prosecutions under the Ohio riot law; the institution of prosecutions arising out of events which were the subject of the grand jury report; and prosecution of the indicted plaintiffs in this case. The complaint averred that the grand jury report was flatly contradictory of the conclusions both of F.B.I. investigators and of the President's Commission on Campus Unrest, and that it was made in bad faith and designed to intimidate the plaintiffs and other members of the university community in the exercise of their rights to discuss and dissent from national policies, and to impose upon the plaintiffs and the community at large the views of the defendants. Moreover, the complaint said, the Ohio statute on riots is vague, overbroad, and chills free expression.[6]

October 25. Seabury H. Ford, one of the state prosecutors, and Glen Frank, a professor of geology, pleaded guilty of contempt of court for having given interviews to a Knight Newspapers writer in violation of the October 16 order of the Common Pleas court. They were released on $500 bond because Judge Jones deferred sentencing pending the outcome of the suits filed following the release of the grand

5. *Morgan* v. *Rhodes*, No. C70-961, U.S.D.C., Northern District of Ohio, Eastern Division. Filed October 14, 1970.

6. *Hammond* v. *Brown, Attorney General*, No. C70-998, U.S.D.C., Northern District of Ohio, Eastern Division, filed October 16, 1970.

jury report. The *Akron Beacon-Journal* quoted Seabury H. Ford as saying the Ohio National Guard "should have shot all" troublemakers at Kent State, but he denied it, saying he had been misquoted. The same newspaper described Glen Frank as speaking out "in contempt of the naive and stupid conclusions of the special grand jury, specifically as to the reasons for the May 1-4 disturbance."

November 3. Upon petition by the American Civil Liberties Union of Ohio, U.S. District Judge Ben C. Green nullified the Portage County Common Pleas order of silence, saying a court can not silence witnesses or prevent criticism of a grand jury. Concerning the sweeping order against all demonstrations in or at the courthouse, he declared a total and unselective ban on such conduct is an infringement of the constitutionally guaranteed right of free speech. He said, "In exercising the right of reasonable regulation, public officials may not wield an ax when a scalpel is required."[7]

Pending before that court at this writing are at least four suits: two for damages against the former governor and his guard commanders, and two for injunctive and declaratory relief to restrain premature or destructive use of National Guard troops and to forbid prosecutions under an allegedly unconstitutional state riot law, and specifically prosecutions of persons indicted by the special state grand jury at Kent State University.

It is unlikely that much of consequence will come of the suits for damages against former Governor Rhodes and his official associates, on account of the general rule that public officers are not personally liable for mistakes of judgment, no matter how horrible their results. Possibly the only recourse of the parents of the slain and injured students for indemnity for the wrongful deaths and injuries may be in a petition to the Ohio legislature to specially appropriate funds for that purpose. Whether this would be successful, no one can tell.

Additional Chronology

January 28, 1971. U.S. District Judge William K. Thomas decided that the investigative report of the special grand jury (but not the indictments returned by the same jury) was unlawful and beyond the powers of the grand jury and would prejudice the right to a fair trial

---

7. *King* v. *Jones*, (U.S.D.C., Ohio), 319 F. Supp. 653 (1970).

of the indicted persons; and ordered the report (except a few introductory pages) expunged from the records of the Portage County court, and all extant copies destroyed. The court did not grant the petition for an injunction against the prosecution of the persons indicted.[8]

July 23, 1971. U.S. District Judge James C. Connell dismissed, on the ground of the sovereign immunity of the state of Ohio, a suit for $4 million damages for wrongful death filed by Louis Schroeder of Lorain, Ohio, father of William Schroeder, one of the four students killed at Kent State University May 4, 1970.

July 24, 1971. The Sixth Circuit U.S. Court of Appeals agreed to review the suit by three student leaders at Kent State University asking that a part of the Ohio riot statute, which holds militiamen guiltless for "killing, maiming, or injuring" while engaged in suppressing a riot, be declared unconstitutional and invalid.

Also July 24. It was reported in the press that a letter signed by 20 members of Congress, addressed to the Attorney General of the United States, asking for a federal grand jury investigation of the shootings at Kent State because important questions remained unanswered, had as yet elicited no reply.

At the same time it was reported that Peter Davies, a New York insurance broker and close friend of the parents of one of the slain students, had released a report to an agency of the United Methodist Church, in which it was asserted that some of the guardsmen had agreed in advance to fire on the students on signal, when a certain sergeant drew his pistol and faced the students.

August 13, 1971. Attorney General John N. Mitchell announced that there would be no federal grand jury investigation of the fatal shootings at Kent on May 4, 1970; but he expressed agreement with the words of the report of the President's Commission on Campus Unrest, that the rifle fire was "unnecessary, unwarranted, and inexcusable."

December 7, 1971. After trials of five of the persons indicted by the special state grand jury on October 16, 1970, the Portage County common pleas court dropped the prosecution of the remaining twenty indicted persons for lack of evidence. This closed the Ohio special grand jury aspect of the matter; but some of the suits by parents of the slain students, and by others challenging the constitutionality of certain Ohio statutes, continued pending in federal courts.

---

8. *Hammond* v. *Brown*, (U.S.D.C., Ohio), 323 F. Supp. 326 (1971).

Use of Agents Provocateurs *and Entrapment*
on College and University Campuses

The peculiar career of one Thomas Tongyai (known among students in upstate New York as Tommy the Traveler, who was said to move from campus to campus and infiltrate disruptive groups, instructing and inciting them in unlawful acts, and eventually assisting in their arrest as an undercover law enforcement officer) led to near-violence on one occasion on the campus of Hobart College.

When a police car arrived with uniformed officers and also with the well-known Tongyai inside, evidently bent on making arrests, the vehicle was tightly surrounded and immobilized by a crowd of angry students, and the danger of violence seemed so imminent that the college authorities and the district attorney thought it advisable to make then and there an announcement that no criminal charges would be prosecuted against certain students previously arrested, and that an arrest warrant then in the hands of the sheriff would not be executed.

Thereafter an Ontario County grand jury indicted the Hobart College corporation for "coercion in the first degree" in violation of the *New York Penal Code*, Sections 20.20, 135.60, and 135.65. There was no steam in the state's side of this controversy, and on February 8, 1971, the trial judge entered a directed verdict of innocent on the ground that the state had failed to produce sufficient evidence.[9]

It is known that Tongyai's activities had been carried on at several upstate colleges. Apparently he was in the employ of the respective county sheriffs. Nothing is known of the extent, if any, to which he was directed or paid from the state capital, or by any federal agency. It is also known that tactics of entrapment have been employed at other campuses in other states by various agencies of law enforcement —practices that are generally both unlawful and contemptible.

Use of Injunctions Against Students

In some instances, during the height of the campus disruption fever, it was found that groups of students engaged in unlawful sit-ins

---

9. *New York State* v. *Colleges of the Seneca, also known as Hobart and William Smith Colleges,* Ontario County supreme court, Indictment No. 70-5, dropped by directed verdict February 8, 1971.

would ignore warnings of suspension from the college, and sit tight in the face of police warnings of arrest on criminal charges, but meekly walk out after an injunctive order of the local court forbidding the sit-in was read to them, and it was explained that violation of a lawful injunction makes one subject to summary fine and imprisonment for contempt of court. (One who commits an act of contempt not in the immediate presence of the court must be given a hearing, but is not entitled to a trial by jury.)

The use of injunctions in labor disputes has a long history, which includes some instances of unsavory excess. However, the process is not wholly without meritorious uses, as was indicated by Chief Justice Bernard H. Levinson of the Hawaii supreme court in sustaining the propriety of an injunction against students who were occupying the office of the Chancellor of the East-West Center, on the Manoa campus of the University of Hawaii:

"In this situation the use of the injunctive process was not a futile exercise; it enabled the parties to enjoy the benefits of a form of anticipatory litigation, to gain for them an immediate entry to the judicial process.

"For the defendants, the value of a judicial proceeding, as against immediate arrest by the police, is that it provides the most effective means of informing those who wish to stay within the bounds of legally protected expression exactly where that elusive line lies.

"In addition, it provides an immediate opportunity for the parties to resolve their differences peacefully, in accordance with a judicial determination of the question of right and wrong."[10]

At Washington University in St. Louis, in violation of a restraining order of the local court, some students and nonstudents engaged in breaking windows, setting fire to an ROTC building, and interfering with firemen, police, and security guards by throwing rocks and firecrackers. Seven persons were given separate sentences for criminal contempt and civil contempt. The St. Louis Court of Appeals, in a *per curiam* decision, held that where criminal contempt exists, it embraces civil contempt, and therefore the separate sentences for civil contempt must be vacated. Also, three of the seven persons under sentence were ordered discharged at once, because the evidence did not show that they had actual knowledge of the restraining order. Im-

---

10. *Kleinjans* v. *Lombardi*, (Hawaii), 478 P. 2d 320 (1970).

prisonment of the other four, for periods varying from three months to six months, with fines of $150 to $500, was lawful.[11]

Judicial Orders to Keep the University or College in Operation

One type of overreaction, akin to that of the parent who demanded a *pro rata* refund of tuition fees for each day on which regularly scheduled classes did not operate (See *Paynter* v. *New York University*, herein in Chapter 5, "Tuition Fees and Other Charges," section on "The Contract to Pay Fees"), took the form of petitions for court orders to keep the college or university in operation with all classes exactly as scheduled at the beginning of the semester.

(As is well known, many institutions were temporarily closed for brief periods, and many others chose to deviate somewhat from their traditional practices with respect to class schedules, class attendance, examination schedules, and methods of grading. Usually the students were given some options regarding the changes, so that those who preferred to follow the conventional paths could do so.)

Queens College of The City University of New York was closed May 6 and 7, 1970. May 10 the board of higher education enacted a resolution:

"It is the duty of The City University to remain open. . . .

"Faculties have the responsibility to meet with and teach their students in order to pursue the academic missions of their colleges.

"Colleges may adjust their programs of courses, attendance, examinations, and grading as in their judgment may seem necessary and appropriate.

"Letter grades will be given to students who request them. . . ."

Three disgruntled students at Queens College asked Justice Mario J. Cariello of the Queens County supreme court for an order commanding Queens College to afford them opportunity to complete the exactly specified courses of instruction which they had begun at the beginning of the semester. They alleged that for a few recent days the faculty had discontinued some of the courses of study and either suggested that the students attend the emergency seminars being held, or conducted the seminars in place of the regular curriculum.

---

11. *Mechanic* v. *Gruensfelder*, (Mo. App.), 461 S.W. 2d 298 (1970).

Wisely sensing his own unfamiliarity with the problems of administering a large urban college, Justice Cariello declared that the resolution of the board of higher education must be complied with, and granted the order; but *limited its effect to the three plaintiffs in this case.*[12]

Thus the order would have very small impact toward invading the wide sphere of discretion which the board of higher education had properly left open to the colleges composing The City University.

Fortunately, most courts, state and federal, at all echelons, are aware of and respectful of the fact that any college or university, private or public, small or large, must, in the nature of things, be to a reasonable extent a "self-governing academic community," with much autonomy in the management of its own complex and detailed internal affairs, both academic and fiscal.

---

12. *De Vito* v. *McMurray*, Queens County supreme court, 311 N.Y.S. 2d 617 (1970).

CHAPTER 21

SELECTIVE SERVICE IN
THE ARMED FORCES

THE POLICY of deferments for college students gives rise to interactions between the colleges and the selective service system, intimately affecting the near-future careers of many students and others of their age-mates. It also is at the root of simmering disputes. Deferment for college students is said by many to be unjust because young men of the middle and upper economic classes attend college in much larger proportions than those of lower family income, including many blacks, Chicanos, and Indians. Put bluntly, the poor become cannon-fodder, while the well-to-do are given safe havens.

Thus it is sometimes grumpily argued that the colleges are full of draft-dodgers, many of whom would not be there were it not for selective service, and few of whom have much real interest in or capacity for higher education. This view is greatly exaggerated. One item of partial evidence against it is the fact that in recent years the numbers of female students above high school have been increasing slightly more rapidly than those of males.

It has also been said that selective service contaminates college life by intolerably intensifying the competitive preoccupation with high marks among students at the expense of thoughtful and meditative learning. For the immediate purpose, it is the grades that count, and not the learning. Thus much student effort and ingenuity are thought to be expended in outflanking the professors and outwitting the bureaucracy and cynically "beating the system."

This tendency has always been present. It was probably escalated during the short period when selective service made deferments contingent on the achievement of a certain academic class standing or the passing of a standardized examination. It may have been less accentuated after the requirement became only to "pursue satisfactorily a full-time course of instruction." Of the meritocratic standards, the brilliant historian, Walter P. Metzger, has written: "If one concedes that such legal classifications would have been harmful to the institutions they refer to, one can not doubt that in academic, no less than in conjugal, parental and economic circumstances, freedom and vitality are threatened when virtue is not in its own but the state's reward."[1]

This present chapter, coming at the end of a book that has grown larger than anticipated, is no more than an abbreviated sketch of some of the pertinent litigation, affording only partial impressions of the flavor of the umbrageous rain-forest of selective service laws, regulations, and litigation.

Induction Not to Be Used as a Punishment or a Threat

One *cause célèbre* was the invalidation of the famous "Hershey directive" of October 1967, by the United States Court of Appeals for the District of Columbia, with the opinion of the court delivered by Chief Circuit Judge David L. Bazelon. The thrust of the directive, addressed to all elements of the selective service system by its national director, was to threaten war protesters with loss of their draft deferments and in some cases with immediate induction into the armed forces as delinquents:

"Demonstrations, when they become illegal, have produced and will produce much evidence that relates to the basis for classification and, in some instances, even to violation of the Act and Regulations. Any material of this nature received in National Headquarters or any

---

1. Walter P. Metzger, at pp. 61-62 in *Neutrality or Partisanship: A Dilemma of Academic Institutions*. New York: Carnegie Foundation for the Advancement of Teaching (Bulletin No. 34, 1971). 82 pp.

other segment of the System should be sent to the state directors for forwarding to appropriate local boards for their consideration.

"A local board, upon receipt of this information, may reopen the classification of the registrant, classify him anew, and if evidence of violation of the Act and Regulations is established . . . also . . . declare the registrant to be a delinquent and . . . process him accordingly. This should include all registrants with remaining liability up to 35 years of age."

Judge Bazelon characterized the communication with some apparent impatience: "Whatever it is in law, it purports to be an authoritative declaration of policy issued for the guidance of the System's line officers. Neither they nor the average would-be protester whose destinies they control are likely to suspect that, for all its official pretensions, it is really only a reflective letter from an interested citizen, and that its exhortation to 'expedite responsive classification' is nothing but the personal prayer of a venerable patriarch."

Concluding: "We hold that the deferment policy announced in the Hershey directive is unauthorized and contrary to the law . . . a registrant's protest activities are not to be considered in determining his selective service classification."[2]

Questioning the Constitutionality of Student Deferments

Reaching the First Circuit Court of Appeals in 1967 was a suit in which a young man, convicted of refusal to submit to physical examination and induction, attacked the constitutionality of the selective service regulations governing temporary deferment of college students, alleging that (1) they were unconstitutionally vague, lacking fixed standards binding upon local selective service boards, and (2) they were arbitrary and unreasonable, giving preference to those economically and socially advantaged enough to attend college, without reference to their contributions to the national health, safety, or interest.

His conviction in U.S. District Court before District Judge Frank J. Murray was affirmed by the First Circuit (Chief Circuit Judge Bailey Aldrich and Circuit Judges Edward M. McEntee and Frank M.

---

2. *National Student Association v. Hershey*, 134 App. D.C. 56, 412 F. 2d 1103 (1969).

Coffin), in an opinion by Judge Coffin, who noted that "The issue of constitutionality not having been raised before the trial court, we do not feel constrained to pass upon it." The judge made some remarks, however, regarding the plaintiff's pleas.

"His present argument is simply that his chances of escaping induction would have been enhanced had a greater number of college students enlarged the available pool of manpower. . . . We think that an individual must show a closer nexus between private interest and public good before he may assert an alleged defect in a public law or regulation as a defense to an alleged infringement of his rights."

At other points: "There is no justification for the argument about the selective service system's failure to operate according to the same standards of precision required of a criminal statute. This 'obscures the difference between a branch of law imposing minimum standards for society's safety and one which seeks optimum adjustment of resources to needs for society's strength.'

"We read the Universal Military Training and Service Act as defining the national interest as something to be advanced not only by encouraging students in rocket engineering, but also in the social sciences and the humanities."[3]

In the next year certain draft registrants, not complaining about their own classification or status, challenged the constitutionality of student deferments, focusing their attack on the provision that courts should have no jurisdiction in grievance cases until the complainants had either been inducted or formally charged with refusing induction. There is, of course, some substance in the contention that many damaging uncertainties and stresses may be suffered prior to induction. A special three-judge federal court (Circuit Judge Paul R. Hays and District Judges Edward E. McLean and David N. Edelstein), in an opinion by Judge Hays, joined by Judge McLean, concluded that no justiciable controversy was presented, and the court had no jurisdiction.

Judge Hays: "Courts, commentators, and Congress agree that any incidental inconvenience to plaintiffs is outweighed by the value of keeping the Selective Service System from becoming entangled in litigation which may prove unnecessary."[4]

---

3. *Talmanson* v. *United States*, (U.S.C.A., Mass.), 386 F. 2d 811 (1967).

4. *Boyd* v. *Clark*, (U.S.D.C., N.Y.), 287 F. Supp. 561 (1968). Affirmed, *per curiam*, 393 U.S. 316, 89 S.Ct. 553, 21 L.Ed. 2d 511 (1969).

Deferment of Undergraduates

Daniel L. Brandt, a third-year student at the University of Southern California, was classified as II-S (student deferment), to extend until October 1968. The Selective Service Act provided three grounds on which a II-S classification might be discontinued: (1) completion of the requirements for a baccalaureate degree, (2) failure to pursue satisfactorily a full-time course of instruction, and (3) attainment of age 24; whichever occurred first.

Brandt had, upon receiving his latest notice of classification, returned it in its original envelope, marked "Refused—Daniel L. Brandt." Later the board was informed from official sources that Brandt had relinquished his registration and classification cards, and expressed support and sympathy for an individual who had been indicted for violation of the selective service laws. The board wrote him a warning letter saying it was considering his reclassification; and on June 6, 1968, it reclassified him I-A and ordered him to report for physical examination June 12. He did not report.

After another warning letter, the board declared him delinquent December 20, and ordered him to report for induction January 7, 1969. At that time he was continuing as an undergraduate student in good standing. He failed to report and was convicted of that offense before U.S. District Judge A. Andrew Hauk; but this was reversed by the Ninth Circuit Court of Appeals in a *per curiam* opinion by Circuit Judges Stanley N. Barnes and Shirley M. Hufstedler, and District Judge Fred M. Taylor. Brandt was entitled to the II-S classification of which he was unlawfully deprived. His I-A reclassification was without basis in fact or law.[5]

Timothy J. Breen, a resident of Connecticut and an undergraduate at the Berkeley School of Music in Boston, was classified II-S. In mid-November 1967 he gave his draft card to a clergyman in Boston to protest involvement of the United States in Vietnam. On January 9, 1968, his local draft board notified him that he had been declared delinquent and reclassified I-A for delinquency. (A basic regulation requires that the registrant have his card in his possession at all times). He sought declaratory relief, an injunction against induction, and $20,000 damages. His complaint was dismissed by Chief District Judge

---

5. *United States* v. *Brandt*, (U.S.C.A., Cal.), 435 F. 2d 324 (1970); reversing (U.S.D.C., Cal.).

William H. Timbers. In the Second Circuit Court of Appeals the judgment was affirmed, in the opinion by Circuit Judge Henry J. Friendly, joined by Circuit Judge Leonard P. Moore; with Circuit Judge Wilfred Feinberg prophetically dissenting.[6]

The judgment of this court was reversed by the U.S. Supreme Court, holding that:

1. Section 1 (b) (3) of the Act did not bar pre-induction judicial review of the delinquency classification which deprived Breen of a deferment to which he was entitled under the Act.

2. In the context of the case there is no meaningful distinction between "exemption" and "deferment"; a registrant with either classification can not be inducted; and

3. Congress did not authorize induction by local boards as a penalty for violations of administrative regulations.

The opinion of the high court was by Mr. Justice Hugo L. Black. Justices John M. Harlan, William J. Brennan, and Potter Stewart wrote separate concurrences, the latter being joined in his opinion by the Chief Justice.

As to the difference between "exemption" and "deferment," which had led the inferior federal courts into a morass in this case, observe the *Oesterreich* case (*infra* in this chapter), which they had undertaken to follow, but in this attempt had not been entirely successful.

"Satisfactorily Pursuing a Full-time Course of Instruction"

Burley Coleman entered Morgan State College in Baltimore as a freshman in September 1966, and was classified II-S. His local draft board in North Carolina reclassified him I-A November 13, 1968, and he was inducted into the Army June 6, 1969. The Fourth Circuit Court of Appeals ordered him snatched from the Commanding General at Fort Bragg with a writ of *habeas corpus*.

The registrar at Morgan State had explained: "Approximately one-half of the first-year class is required to pursue a minimum full-time credit load. This means that instead of the usual two semesters required for the completion of the first college year, three semesters are

6. *Breen* v. *Local Board No. 16*, (U.S.D.C., Conn.), 284 F. Supp. 739, (1968); affirmed in (U.S.C.A., Conn.), 406 F. 2d 636 (1969); reversed in 396 U.S. 460, 90 S.Ct. 661, 24 L.Ed. 2d 653 (1970).

required. After two semesters, if the student is permitted to remain in school, his scholastic performance has given every indication that he will be able to complete all requirements within the normal four-year period."

The registrar also certified that Coleman's scholastic performance had been satisfactory. Circuit Judge J. Braxton Craven, Jr., sitting with Circuit Judges Herbert S. Boreman and Albert V. Bryan, held that the certification by the college should be accepted; and the fact that Coleman was seven hours short of the normal accumulation, through no fault of his own, should not deprive him of his status as a satisfactory full-time student. There was no basis in fact for his reclassification.[7]

Stephen Keith Canepa flunked out as a freshman at Monterey Peninsula College in California during the academic year 1965-66. After a year out in the cold world, with some added maturity, he re-entered in September 1967, and thereafter his grades were consistently in the "B" range. The registrar certified on November 26, 1967, and again on September 30, 1968, that he was a successful full-time student.

Nevertheless his local draft board ordered him to report for induction April 19, 1969. He reported, but refused induction. He was charged with refusal to submit to induction, and tried in federal district court.

U.S. District Judge Robert F. Peckham rendered a judgment of acquittal. The Selective Service Act of July 1, 1967, which clarified student deferment policy, was intended to be only prospective in application, he said. Therefore a student's record after that date was what counted.[8]

Graduate and Graduate-Professional Students

Rolf J. Kolden of Minnesota was a graduate student, aspirant to a degree of Doctor of Philosophy at Harvard University. He was classified II-S until after he turned in his draft card to an officer of the government October 16, 1967, at a meeting protesting the Vietnam War. Thereafter he was reclassified and about to be inducted. He asked District Judge Miles W. Lord for a temporary injunction, which was

---

7. *Coleman* v. *Tolson*, (U.S.C.A., N.C.), 435 F. 2d 1062 (1970).
8. *United States* v. *Canepa*, (U.S.D.C, Cal.), 319 F. Supp. 1319 (1970).

denied. The U.S. Court of Appeals affirmed the denial, with instruction to dismiss the action.

"Where, as here, a registrant is deprived of a deferment that had been granted as a matter of administrative grace in the first instance, the courts can review the classification only in a criminal case or a *habeas corpus* proceeding." The opinion was by Circuit Judge M. C. Matthes, sitting with Circuit Judges Floyd R. Gibson and Myron H. Bright.

This meant that Kolden could not be heard in court until after he had either been inducted or charged with the crime of refusing induction. The decision of the Second Circuit in the *Breen* case (*supra* in this chapter) was cited before it had been reversed by the U.S. Supreme Court; and Judge Matthes expressly stated that the decision had been postponed until after the U.S. Supreme Court had decided the *Oesterreich* case (*infra* in this chapter). The final judgment in *Breen*, however, makes it appear that the interpretation placed upon *Oesterreich* by the Circuit and District courts in this type of case was not considered correct.[9]

Michael L. Rosenfield was a second-year law student in the academic year 1967-68. He had had undergraduate and post graduate deferments for four consecutive years. June 20, 1968, he was reclassified I-A; August 14, again I-A after appeal; ordered to report for induction November 20. The state director postponed his induction until the end of the semester, January 31, 1969; and he was ordered to report for induction February 20, 1969.

District Judge Gerald J. Weber denied an injunction for lack of jurisdiction. He said the only authority for Rosenfield's deferment in 1967-68 was Executive Order 11360, of July 4, 1967: "Any registrant enrolled in his first year of postgraduate study in a graduate school or a professional school on October 1, 1967 . . . may be placed in Class II-S . . . and shall be deferred for one academic year only. . . ." There was no statutory mandate for the deferment of a second-year law student.[10]

A suit reached the Sixth Circuit Court of Appeals in 1971, challenging the prevailing rules defining eligibility for "fatherhood" defer-

---

9. *Kolden* v. *Local Board No. 4*, (U.S.C.A., Minn.), 406 F. 2d 631 (1969).
10. *Rosenfield* v. *Selective Service System*, (U.S.D.C., Pa.), 298 F. Supp. 276 (1969).

ments, focused specifically on the regulation which preconditioned fatherhood deferments upon not having requested and received a graduate student deferment in an earlier year. The court said this was not without statutory authorization, because the law gave the President discretion to make rules for eligibility for both graduate student and fatherhood deferments; both were matters of "executive grace"; and the rule was not subject to pre-induction judicial review. Circuit Judge Paul C. Weick thought it was a reasonable rule to discourage "pyramiding" of deferments so as to become the equivalent of exemptions. Sitting with Judge Weick were Circuit Judges Wade H. McCree, Jr., and Henry L. Brooks.[11]

James J. Oesterreich, a theological student, was classified IV-D under the section of the Selective Service Act which exempted "students preparing for the ministry" in qualified schools. He returned his registration certificate (draft card) "for the sole purpose of expressing dissent from the participation of the United States in the war in Vietnam." His local board declared him delinquent and changed his classification to I-A. His case reached the Supreme Court of the United States in 1968. The decision was terse: "There is no legislative authority to deny an unequivocal statutory exemption to a registrant who has qualified for one, because of conduct or activities unrelated to the merits of granting or continuing the exemption, and delinquency proceedings can not be used for that purpose."[12]

The majority opinion was by Mr. Justice William O. Douglas. Mr. Justice John M. Harlan concurred in the result. Justices William J. Brennan and Byron R. White joined in a dissent entered by Mr. Justice Potter Stewart. This decision of 1968 apparently was somewhat "over-interpreted" by some of the lower federal courts during the ensuing two years, to mean that *only* registrants entitled to mandatory statutory *exemptions* could be heard in court prior to induction; and this led to an exaggerated refinement of distinctions between *exemptions* by statute and *deferments* on the authority of executive orders or administrative regulations, when confronted with the interface between administrative action and freedom of expression as protected in the First Amendment. This confusion was clarified by the United

---

11. *Gregory* v. *Tarr*, (U.S.C.A., Mich.), 436 F. 2d 513 (1971).
12. *Oesterreich* v. *Local Board No. 11, Cheyenne, Wyoming*, 393 U.S. 233, 89 S.Ct. 414, 21 L.Ed. 2d 402 (1968); reversing (U.S.C.A., Wyo.), 390 F. 2d 100 (1968).

States Supreme Court in the *Breen* case, decided in 1970 (*supra*, in this chapter).

Chronological treatment of the cases in this chapter has been foregone in favor of what is thought to be a better topical sequence. At best the chapter is no more than a series of brief abstracts of some of the opinions of the courts, necessarily omitting much, and always beset by the hazard of missing or misconstruing the essence. Readers who want more than a light impressionistic flavor of the field are advised to peruse the official reports in full, including newer decisions as they appear. This advice also applies to the whole of this volume. The copy went to press soon after the enactment of the new Selective Service Act in midsummer 1971, and before any judicial decisions or even any administrative regulations pertaining to it had been published. Comprehensive new regulations, embodying many changes, were published in the *Federal Register* for November 3, 1971 (pages 21072-21083).

BIBLIOGRAPHY

BOOKS AND PAMPHLETS

1. American Association of State Colleges and Universities. *Student Freedoms and Responsibilities.* Washington, D.C.: AASCU, 1970.
2. American Association of University Professors and nine other national associations. *Joint Statement on Rights and Freedoms of Students.* Washington, D.C.: American Association of University Professors, 1967, with later revisions.
3. American Bar Association. *Report of the Commission on Campus Government and Student Dissent.* Chicago: American Bar Foundation, 1970. 36 pp.
4. American Civil Liberties Union. *Academic Freedom and Civil Liberties of Students in Colleges and Universities.* New York: American Civil Liberties Union, April 1970. 47 pp.
5. Benton, Fred G., Jr. *Legal Aspects of Parietal Rules.* Washington, D.C.: American Association of State Colleges and Universities. Tenth Annual Meeting, November 17, 1970. 52 pp.
6. Brubacher, John S. *The Courts and Higher Education.* San Francisco: Jossey-Bass, Inc., Publishers, 1971. 150 pp.
7. Fischer, Thomas C. *Due Process in the Student-Institutional Relationship.* Washington, D.C.: American Association of State Colleges and Universities, January 1970. 37 pp.
8. Gaddy, Dale. *Student Activism and the Junior College Administrator: Judicial Guidelines.* Los Angeles: University of California at Los

Angeles, Clearinghouse for Junior College Information, December 1968. 47 pp.

9. Holmes, Grace W. *Law and Discipline on Campus.* Ann Arbor: University of Michigan, Institute of Continuing Legal Education, 1971. 381 pp.

10. Holmes, Grace W. *Student Protest and the Law.* Ann Arbor: University of Michigan, Institute of Continuing Legal Education, October 1969. 403 pp.

11. Mills, Joseph L. *Legal Rights of College Students and Administrators: A Handbook.* Washington, D.C. 20001: Lerner Law Book Publishing Co., Inc., 509 E. Street, N.W., 1971. 177 pp.

12. National Association of College and University Attorneys. *The College Counsel.* Evanston, Illinois: NACUA, 1970. 290 pp. (Report to the American Council on Education on the use of injunctions against campus disorders and transcript of Proceedings of the Tenth Annual Conference.)

13. Nussbaum, Michael. *Student Legal Rights: What They Are and How to Protect Them.* New York: Harper and Row, Publishers, 1970. 160 pp.

14. Phay, Robert E. (editor). *Trustees' Responsibility for the Campus in Crisis.* Chapel Hill: University of North Carolina, Institute of Government, 1970. 71 pp.

15. Phay, Robert E., and Jasper L. Cummings. *Student Suspensions and Expulsions.* Chapel Hill: University of North Carolina, Institute of Government, 1970. 50 pp.

16. President's Commission on Campus Unrest. *The Report of the President's Commission on Campus Unrest.* Washington, D.C.: U.S. Government Printing Office, 1970. 537 pp.

17. Sims, O. Suthern, Jr. *New Directions in Campus Law Enforcement, A Handbook for Administrators.* Athens: University of Georgia, Center for Continuing Education, 1970. 79 pp.

18. Young, D. Parker. *The Legal Aspects of Student Dissent and Discipline in Higher Education.* Athens: University of Georgia, Institute of Higher Education, 1970. 65 pp. (Updating and revision of earlier version, *Briefs of Selected Court Cases Affecting Student Dissent and Discipline in Higher Education.*)

ARTICLES

General

19. Beaney, William M. "Students, Higher Education, and the Law." *Denver Law Journal* 45:512 (1968).
20. Caldwell, Wallace F. "The Changing Legal Relationships Between Students and Universities." *College and University* 45:245 (Spring 1970).
21. Furay, Sally M. "Legal Relationship Between the Student and the Private College or University." *San Diego Law Review* 7:244 (1970).
22. Hentoff, Nat. "Why Students Want Their Constitutional Rights Now." *Saturday Review,* May 22, 1971, p. 60.
23. "Judicial Intervention in Expulsions or Suspensions by Private Universities." *Willamette Law Journal* 5:277 (1969).
24. Kurland, Philip B. "Equal Educational Opportunity: The Limits of Constitutional Jurisprudence Undefined." *University of Chicago Law Review* 35:583 (1968).
25. O'Neil, Robert M. "Private Universities and Public Law." *Buffalo Law Review* 19:155 (1970).
26. "The Scope of University Discipline." *Brooklyn Law Review* 35:486 (1969).
27. "Students and the University: Group Interaction and the Law." *Kentucky Law Journal* 59:407 (1970-71).
28. Van Alstyne, William W. "A Suggested Seminar in Student Rights." *Journal of Legal Education* 21:547 (1969).
29. Wright, Charles Alan. "The Constitution on the Campus." *Vanderbilt Law Review* XXII, No. 5 (October 1969), pp. 1027-1088.
30. Yegge, Robert B. "Constitutional Dimensions of Student Protest." *Higher Education: The Law and Individual Responsibilities,* University of Georgia, 1971. 51 pp.

Nonresident Tuition Fees

31. Clarke, Charles H. "Validity of Discriminatory Nonresident Tuition Charges in Public Higher Education Under the Interstate Privileges and Immunities Clause." *Nebraska Law Review* 50:31 (Fall 1970).
32. Hollenbach, Joan M. "The Equal Protection Clause and Durational Residency Requirements for Tuition Purposes at State Universities." *Journal of Public Law* 139 (1970).

33. Masters, Deborah F. "Nonresident Tuition Charged by State Universities in Review." *University of Missouri at Kansas City Law Review* 38:341 (1970).

Racial Desegregation

34. "The Affirmative Duty to Integrate in Higher Education." *Yale Law Journal* 79:666 (1970).
35. Douglas, William O. "Some Dicta on Discrimination." *Loyola University of Los Angeles Law Review* 3:207 (1970).

Protected Freedoms and Due Process

36. Beaney, W. M., and J. C. S. Cox. "Fairness in University Disciplinary Proceedings." *Case Western Reserve Law Review* 22:390 (April 1971).
37. Berkman, Richard L. "Students in Court: Free Speech and the Functions of Schooling in America." *Harvard Education Review* 40:567 (November 1970).
38. Caruso, L. R. "Privacy of Students and Confidentiality of Student Records." *Case Western Reserve Law Review* 22:379 (April 1971).
39. Chambers, M. M. "Legal Rights of College and University Students." *NOLPE School Law Journal* 1:81 (Fall 1970).
40. "College Searches and Seizures: Privacy and Due Process Problems on Campus." *Georgia Law Review* 3:426 (1969).
41. "The Constitutionality of a Requirement to Give Notice Before Marching." *University of Pennsylvania Law Review* 118:270 (1969).
42. DeJarmon, LeMarquis. "Students' Right to Privacy—Residence and Records." *Higher Education: The Law and Individual Responsibilities,* University of Georgia, 1971. 51 pp.
43. Denno, Theodore F. "Mary Beth Tinker Takes the Constitution to School." *Fordham Law Review* 38:35 (1969).
44. Killian, J. D. "Law, the Counselor, and Student Records." *Personnel and Guidance Journal* 48:423 (February 1970).
45. Phay, Robert E. "Higher Education and Due Process of Law." *Popular Government* 37:9 (April 1971).
46. "Public Universities and Due Process of Law: Students' Protection Against Unreasonable Search and Seizure." *Kansas Law Review* 17:512-29 (1969).

47. "Reasonable Rules, Reasonably Enforced—Guidelines for University Disciplinary Proceedings." *Minnesota Law Review* 53:301 (1968).

48. Rivers, William L., and Leonard Sellers. "Student Newspapers in Transition." *Research Currents* (ERIC) in *College and University Bulletin* 24:3-6 (December 15, 1971).

49. Shaman, J. M. "College Admission Policies Based on Sex and the Equal Protection Clause." *Buffalo Law Review* 20:609 (Spring 1971).

50. "Student Due Process in the Private University: The State Action Doctrine." *Syracuse Law Review* 20:911 (1969).

51. "Student Voting Rights in University Communities." *Harvard Civil Rights Law Review* 6:397 (March 1971).

52. Trager, R. "Freedom of the Press in College and High School." *Albany Law Review* 35:161 (1971).

State Actions Against Campus Disruptions

53. "Campus Confrontation: Resolution by Injunction." *Columbia Journal of Law and Social Problems* 6:1 (January 1970).

54. "Effect of House Bill No. 1219 on Controlling Campus Disorders." *Ohio State Law Journal* 32:198 (1971).

55. Fishbein, Estelle A. "The University's Right of Control over Student Publications." *The College Counsel* V:65-78 (1970).

56. Gordon, Milton J. "Student Disciplinary Hearing Procedures from the Institutional Standpoint." *The College Counsel* V:90-107 (1970).

57. Gray, Fred D. "Analysis of State and Federal Laws Relating to Student Unrest." *The College Counsel* V:118-133 (1970).

58. Herman, Joseph. "Injunctive Control of Disruptive Student Demonstrations." *Virginia Law Review* 56:215 (Spring 1970).

59. Kalaidjian, Edward C. "The Injunctive Process in Student Uprisings." *The College Counsel* V:43-65 (1970).

60. Mardian, Robert C. "Student Unrest—Role of the Federal Government." *The College Counsel* V:108-117 (1970).

61. O'Neil, Robert M. "Judicial Overkill." *Change: The Magazine of Higher Education* 2:39-42 (September-October 1970).

62. "The Power of a Governor to Proclaim Martial Law and Use State Military Forces to Suppress Campus Demonstrations." *Kentucky Law Journal* 59:547 (1970-71).

63. Rosenthal. "Injunctive Relief Against Campus Disorders." *University of Pennsylvania Law Review* 118:746 (April 1970).

64. Wells, Arthur, Jr. "Student Disciplinary Hearing Procedures from the Student's Viewpoint." *The College Counsel* V:90-107 (1970).

65. Wilson, James B. "Suits by Students, Taxpayers, and Others Against Institutions, Arising Out of Disruptions in Educational Processes." *The College Counsel* V:134-158 (1970).

TABLE OF CASES

UNITED STATES SUPREME COURT

UNITED STATES SUPREME COURT

(Declining to review, or dismissing appeal)

INFERIOR FEDERAL COURTS
AND STATE COURTS

(Cases in federal courts are entered under the name of the state in which they originated. They are preceded by the letters "US.")

INDEX